DUET

DUET

An Artful History of Music

Eleanor Chan

DUCKWORTH

First published in the United Kingdom by Duckworth in 2025

Duckworth, an imprint of Duckworth Books Ltd
1 Golden Court, Richmond, TW9 1EU, United Kingdom
www.duckworthbooks.co.uk

Copyright © Eleanor Chan, 2025

All rights reserved. No part of this publication may be reproduced, stored in a retrieval system, or transmitted, in any form or by any means electronic, mechanical, photocopying, recording or otherwise, without the prior permission of the publisher.

The right of Eleanor Chan to be identified as the Author of this Work has been asserted by her in accordance with the Copyright, Designs and Patents Act 1988.

A catalogue record for this book is available from the British Library

Design and typesetting by Danny Lyle

Printed and bound in Great Britain by CPI Books

The authorised representative in the EEA is Easy Access System Europe, Mustamäe tee 50, 10621 Tallinn, Estonia.

Hardback ISBN: 9780715655719
eISBN: 9780715655726

This is a love letter to St Catharine's College Chapel Choir.

You are my downsitting and mine uprising, and my thought afar off. You infuriate me, and fill me with joy. Somewhere, in an alternate universe, I am still dancing to Cascada with you all in a ramshackle, threadbare room, and I always will be.

    Bedrudgingly,
        effusively:
            this is for all of you.

CONTENTS

List of Illustrations	ix
Prelude	xvii
Chapter 1: Curtain Up	1
Chapter 2: Feather on the Breath of God	44
Chapter 3: The Hand of Guido	86
Chapter 4: Sheet Music Scrolled Across the Inside of My Lungs	127
Chapter 5: One Sweet Liquorice Stick	173
Chapter 6: Watching Paint Sing	209
Cadenza	251
Notes	259
Selected Bibliography	279
Index	293

List of Illustrations

Plate section

Edgar Degas, *Dancers, Pink and Green*, oil on canvas, c. 1890. Metropolitan Museum of Art, New York, 29.100.42. Public Domain.
Jan Vermeer, *Girl Interrupted at her Music*, 1658–59. Frick Collection, New York. Public Domain.
Eleanor Chan, *If*, liquid acrylic and ink on canvas, 2023.
Cave paintings of bison at Marsoulas, c. 16,000 BCE. Wikimedia. Public Domain.
Alexander on the way to conquer India, in Ferdowsi's *Shahnameh*, c. 1411. Metropolitan Museum of Art, New York, Accession No. 13.228.19. Public Domain.
Edgar Degas, *Fan Mount image of ballet dancers from the wings*, watercolour and metallic paint on silk, 1879. Metropolitan Museum of Art, New York. Public Domain.
Natalia Goncharova, 'Cherub' costume design for *La Liturgie*, 1915.
Fanny Hensel Mendelssohn, 'Praeludium and Choral' from *Das Jahr*, 1841. Public Domain.
Aram Gulezyan's 'ancient Egyptian' colour music notation, second or third decade of the twentieth century. Edinburgh: Blackie House Library and Museum.
Alexander Wallace Rimington's diagram of how to map colour frequencies onto sound frequencies to produce a colour octave. From *Colour-Music: The Art of Mobile Colour*, 1912. Public Domain.
George Field's correspondence of colour and octave, from *Chromatics, or, the Analogy, Harmony and Philosophy of Colour*, 1817. Courtesy of the Smithsonian Library. Public Domain.

Megan Watts-Hughes, *Sound Impression of Voice Flowers*, pigment on glass, undated, c. 1885–1904. Cyfarthfa Castle Museum and Art Gallery. Photo © Heather Matthew.
John Piper, *Dungeness*, 1938. Private Collection. Photo: Matthew Hollow. © The Piper Estate/DACS.
Louise Bourgeois, *La Chanson*, 2009. Photo: Peter Butler © The Easton Foundation/VAGA at ARS, NY and DACS, London.
Tin-glazed delftware violin, 1705–10. Rijksmuseum, Amsterdam. Public Domain.
Porcelain flute, seventeenth century, from Jingdezhen, Jiangxi province, China. Asian Civilisations Museum, Singapore. Accession No. 2002-00078.
Taylor Swift playing her candyfloss pink *Lover* guitar during the Eras Tour, 2024. Photo: Paolo Villaneuva. Wikimedia. Public Domain.
Detail from Anna Casparsson, *Sagor (Stories: Little Claus and Big Claus, the Story of Little Rose and the Little Mermaid)*, 1947. Moderna Museet, Stockholm. Photograph author's own.
Aubrey Williams, *Shostakovich Symphony No. 6*, oil on canvas, 1981. © Courtesy of Arts for Health Milton Keynes/DACS.

Prelude

Page xxii: May Ray, *Le Violon d'Ingres*, gelatin silver print photograph, 1924. J. Paul Getty Museum, Los Angeles.

Chapter 1

Page 6: Conch shell horn from Marsoulas cave, c. 16,000 BCE. Wikimedia. Public Domain.
Page 11: Sufi mystics or Dervishes dance as part of the *sama*, Folio from a Divan of Hafiz (c. 1325–90), opaque watercolour and gold on paper. Metropolitan Museum of Art, New York. Public Domain.

List of Illustrations

Page 12: Manohar and Muhammad Husain Kashmiri, *The Youth of Rum is Entertained in a Garden by a Fairy and her Maidens*, from a *Khamsa* of Amir Khusrau Dihlavi, 1597–8. Metropolitan Museum of Art, New York. Public Domain.
Page 16: John Wastell, fan vaulting of the ceiling of King's College Chapel, Cambridge, 1512–1515. Wikimedia. Public Domain.
Page 18: The underside of the fan vaulting at King's College Chapel, Cambridge. Photo author's own.
Page 19: Graffiti above the fan vaulting at King's College Chapel, Cambridge. Photo author's own.
Page 26: Interior of the Teatro Amazonas. Wikimedia. Public Domain.
Page 27: Ceiling of the Teatro Amazonas. Wikimedia. Public Domain.
Page 32: Natalia Goncharova's costume for the eponymous golden chicken in *Le Coq D'Or*. Wikimedia. Public Domain.
Page 35: Ensemble of jellyfish, fish, squid and seaweed dancers for *Sadko*, 1916. New York Public Library.
Page 39: The edge of the stage at the Minack Theatre, complete with Rowena Cade's designs carved into the concrete. Wikimedia. Public Domain.

Chapter 2

Page 45: Master of the Countess of Warwick, *Four Children Making Music*, c. 1565.
Page 54: Tablet with Temple Hymn in cuneiform, c. 1800–1600 BCE. Walters Art Museum, Accession No. 48.1802. CC0 Public Domain.
Page 55: The Seikilos epitaph, first/second century CE. Wikimedia. Public Domain.
Page 60: Hildegard von Bingen's music notation in the *Dendermonde Codex*. KU Leuven. Public Domain.

Page 62: Hildegard's illustration of heavenly music, from the *Scivias*. Wikimedia. Public Domain.
Page 66: Instructions for hand positions for playing the qin, from the *Taiyu Yiyin*, 1413. Wikimedia. Public Domain.
Page 67: Madam Zhong's 'Heartfelt Words on Going Through Bitterness', from *Sizhaitang Qinpu*, 1620. Wikimedia. Public Domain.
Page 70: Illuminated Gospels from the Amhara region of Ethiopia, late fourteenth/early fifteenth century. Metropolitan Museum of Art, New York. Public Domain.
Page 71: The nativity scene, from Illuminated Gospels from the Amhara region of Ethiopia, late fourteenth/early fifteenth century. Metropolitan Museum of Art, New York. Public Domain.
Page 80: Khaz notation in an Armenian hymnal, 1679. Wikimedia. Public Domain.
Page 81: Christine Sun Kim, *When My Voice Can't Shut Up*, 2015.
Page 82: Christine Sun Kim, *Waiting in a Line at a Grocery Store*, 2017.

Chapter 3

Page 88: Guido's hand. Wikimedia. Public Domain.
Page 91: Guido showing Bishop Tedald his scale. Wikimedia. Public Domain.
Page 93: Robert Fludd's 'temple of music', showing the musical scales, 1619. Wellcome Images. Public Domain.
Page 97: Zhu Zaiyu's calculation of pitch pipes and their relationship to measure, 1584. Courtesy of Harvard University Library. Public Domain.
Page 99: Zhu's proposed thirteen-string qin, to create equally-tempered music. Courtesy of Harvard University Library. Public Domain.
Page 106: Septimus Piesse's 'The Gamut of Odours – Bass, or F-Clef', from *The Art of Perfumery*, 1862. Photograph author's own.

List of Illustrations

Page 107: Septimus Piesse's 'The Gamut of Odours – Treble, or G-Clef', from *The Art of Perfumery*, 1862. Photograph author's own.
Page 108: Septimus Piesse's 'Bouquet of Chords', from *The Art of Perfumery* (1862). Public Domain.
Page 122: Megan Watts Hughes' voice flower representation of the note A, from *The Eidophone Voice Figures: Natural and Geometrical Forms Produced by Vibrations of the Human Voice*, 1904. Public Domain.
Page 123: Megan Watts Hughes' 'Seaweed' or 'Landscape' forms. Wikimedia. Public Domain.

Chapter 4

Page 131: Gentile di Fabriano, *Coronation of the Virgin*, tempera and gold leaf on panel, 1420. Getty Museum, Parma. Public Domain.
Page 132: Yōshū (Hashimoto) Chikanobu, *Concert of European Music*, 1889. Metropolitan Museum of Art, New York. Public Domain.
Page 133: Katagawa Shigenobu, *Geisha Turning a Samisen/ Flower Matching Contest No. 4*, 1835. Los Angeles County Museum of Art. Public Domain.
Page 141: Esther Inglis's embroidered cover for her *Argumenta psalmorum David's dedicacion*, 1608. Folger Shakespeare Library.
Page 143: Esther Inglis's self-portrait with a music book, ink on paper, 1601. New York Public Library. Public Domain.
Page 144: Musical Graffiti in a 'To The Reader', copying the full music. Photograph author's own.
Page 145: Musical Graffiti in a 'To The Reader', copying the staves. Photograph author's own.
Page 146: An improvised 'To The Reader' music-reading guide in *The Whole Booke of Psalmes*. Photograph author's own.
Page 148: Close-up of the Eglantine Table with an intarsia copy of Thomas Tallis's 'O Lord in Thee Is All My Trust', c. 1567. Wikimedia. Public Domain.

Page 154: Musical wall painting, 1560s. Thame, Oxfordshire: Thame Museum. Photograph author's own.
Page 161: Sheet Music Notation dress by The Emperor's Old Clothes, 2024. Cecily Blondel.
Page 170: Moritz von Schwind, 'Die Katzensymphonie', 1869. Staatliche Kunsthalle Karlsruhe. CC0 Public Domain.

Chapter 5

Page 176: Flute carved from the wing bone of a griffon vulture, Peiligang Culture, Wuyang, Henan province, China. Photo: Gary Lee Todd. Wikimedia. Public Domain.
Page 179: Korean Goryeo celadon flute, stoneware ornamented with gilding, flying cranes, meringue clouds and miniature chrysanthemum blossoms, early thirteenth century. Metropolitan Museum of Art, New York. Public Domain.
Page 180: *Xiao*/flute, jade with red silk tassel, eighteenth/nineteenth century. Metropolitan Museum of Art, New York. Public Domain.
Page 181: Persian *ney* used for remembrance ceremonies, incised bone, ninth century CE. Metropolitan Museum of Art, New York. Public Domain.
Page 183: Pueblo petroglyph of Kokopelli, c. 1300 CE. Mortendad Cave, New Mexico. Wikimedia. Public Domain.
Page 184: Porcelain and gilt copper flute, possibly made by the Meissen factory, c. 1760. Metropolitan Museum of Art, New York. Public Domain.
Page 187: Anonymous, bird of prophecy idiophone, bronze and iron, sixteenth to nineteenth century. Metropolitan Museum of Art, New York. Public Domain.
Page 189: Anonymous, an egogo or double bell, ivory, early sixteenth century, Benin kingdom. Brooklyn Museum, New York. Accession No. 58.160. Public Domain.

List of Illustrations

Page 193: The Royal Privy Garden of the Topkapi Palace, where Dallam's blackbird organ stood, from the Hunername, 1584. Wikimedia. Public Domain.
Page 197: Porcelain delftware mandolin (1800–1825). Antwerp: Museum Vleeshuis.
Page 201: Section of Cathy Berberian's *Stripsody*, 1966. Courtesy of Edition Peters.

Chapter 6

Page 213: Levina Teerlinc, *An Elizabethan Maundy*, 1560s. Wikimedia. Public Domain.
Page 218: Anna Casparsson, detail of *Life Saga from Blue Fairy Tales by Laboulaye*, 1930. Moderna Museet, Stockholm. Photograph author's own.
Page 219: Anna Casparsson, detail of *Life Saga from Blue Fairy Tales by Laboulaye*, 1930. Moderna Museet, Stockholm. Photograph author's own.
Page 226: Barbara Hepworth at work on *Contrapuntal Forms* in her garden. Barbara Hepworth © Bowness.
Page 228: Barbara Hepworth, *Forms in Movement (Galliard)*, copper, 1956. Barbara Hepworth © Bowness.
Page 230: Barbara Hepworth, *Apollo*, 1951. Barbara Hepworth © Bowness.
Page 238: Tōkō Shinoda, *Interval*, 1999. © Courtesy of Gifu Collection of Modern Arts/DACS.
Page 240: Tōkō Shinoda, *Cadenza*, 1998. © Courtesy of Gifu Collection of Modern Arts/DACS.
Page 245: A reimagination of the goddess variously known as Oshún, Oxum and Ochún. Wikimedia. Public Domain.
Page 247: Ancient shrine to Oshún, in the Òṣun-Osogbo Grove, Nigeria. Wikimedia. Public Domain.

Cadenza

Page 252: Eleanor Chan, *Fields of Gold*, 2017.

Prelude
Noisy Pictures and Music for the Eyes

An enormous, coiling twist of gold erupts over my head, scales glinting, claws out, its jaws open in a majestic roar. The year is 1997 or 1998.

I am about seven years old, and I am in the Music Room at Brighton Pavilion.

I am about to play in my first professional concert.

Of all the eccentric, extravagant and downright absurd places I have performed over the past twenty-five years, this is the one that stays with me. Many years after I hung up my descant recorder and moved on to instruments new, this scene haunts me, indelibly scrawled across my brain under the title 'THIS is the stage'. For as long as I live, I suspect my experience of performing music will be shot through with the memory of this elaborately gilded phantasmagoria of a room: the way it smelled; the lusciously garish thickness of the carpet under my jelly shoes; the sound interacting with the gold cornicing, domes and minarets plastered on every surface.

At the same time, this first public performance is also inflected with a sense of intimacy. The Music Room is a relatively small space. You can see more or less every face in the audience; and so you have to make your own stage, in a sense. You erect your own fourth wall, and perform the magic trick inside your head that smudges facial features and transforms faces that you know into just *a* face, or even an abstract shape: 'audience', for the space of the music. I will never be able to detach the act of making music from the visual experience that first accompanied it, all those years ago.

Music is, first and foremost, a thing we listen to – isn't it? But music has never just been an aural medium. Its visual aspects – the enjoyment we gain from *watching* a performance in a beautiful space like the Music Room, the cues we get from fellow musicians and their visible gestures as we perform, and the way it is written down – have been vital to the way that music has gained meaning and been disseminated throughout the centuries.

Alluring musical performances do not begin or end with a musician swaying with the swell of the music; indeed, they can happen without any visual stimulation, which you can experience simply by shutting your eyes, or listening to your favourite piece of music over a streaming service or the radio. The desire to *see* music, though, is important. We want to plot sound into visual shapes, a schema, into palpable form: to pin down this forever-fleeting art form into something more concrete. We have always *seen* music, even as it has infused our ears. Indeed, as deaf and hearing-impaired music lovers have known for centuries, there are multiple ways to experience music that have nothing to do with our ears.[1] But throughout history, this crucial visual aspect of music has rarely been given its due. Those moments where it is acknowledged are fleeting and evocative, like the theatre director Peter Brook's passing observation that 'a musician is dealing with a fabric that is as near as a man can get to an expression of the invisible. His score *notes* this invisibility.'[2]*

Duet explores what happens in the liminal space offered by that 'as near as'. It's a story of music from pre-history to the present day that delves right to the heart of our selves: these curious mammals who for thousands of years have sought to create and then capture

---

*   My italics.

music. In its pages, I'll lead you through all the ways that the visual has been crucial to music, from the familiar to the unexpected. From performance spaces to written music and the very tools we have used to organise and visualise musical scales, seeing has always played a part in the way we experience music. When we foreground these objects, ideas and spaces we gain a view of music from a different angle which, in turn, presents us with the opportunity to interrogate how we think about music as a whole, and focus on the aspects that have slipped through the cracks of our conceptual understanding.

Cognitive neuroscientists now think that our capacity for music evolved alongside our capacity for language.[3] Music helped us to communicate; in other words, it was integral to our early efforts to build community, and to emphasise our togetherness as human beings. The entanglement of seen and heard at the heart of music reaches right back to these origins, and the ways that we interacted as early humans. By subtly retuning our eyes and ears, we can reignite our understanding of this ancient practice and recognise that music is not just a plaything or a recreation, but a crucial part of what makes us human.

The visual manifestations of music are things that everyone can spot, once you know what to look for. To show its workings, I need you to join in a little experiment with me. Take a moment to enjoy your music; put on your favourite song. As you listen to it, look around. Let your imagination wander. What are you playing it on? Why did you choose that specific sound system, speaker, record player, instrument? What does the music make you think about? You'll find that, like me, you have plenty of memories of music that are profoundly visible and visual. Images are more than simply what is left after the music has stopped playing. Throughout millennia, human beings have created music-making cultures such that our eyes can accompany, accentuate, commemorate and sometimes contradict what our ears tell us, as we listen to music.

Once you get past the slightly jarring experience of trying to switch your focus from ears to eyes, it's likely you'll discover that you do, in fact, have a pretty clear image of music. Not only is this fascinating in itself; it's also fascinating that although almost everyone will have a visual sense of music in mind, very few of these senses will be exactly the same.

My own image of music has accompanied me for decades, like a talisman. Art and music were everywhere in my childhood, though their connection was always tacit, never explained. There wasn't much money when I was small, but the adults around us found a way: second-hand books from car boot sales, free concerts, free exhibitions, cassette tapes of performances taped from the radio, anything, everything, a hodgepodge cornucopia of whatever was going. When I was a tiny baby, my godmother, an artist, started to send postcards of her favourite artworks. I have them still, in an old, decoupage-style cigar box. Some of them are furry-soft at the corners and riffled from where I have taken them out and shuffled them like a deck of tarot, telling fortunes with sheaves of Alberto Giacometti, J.M.W. Turner, Leonora Carrington, whole moods and lives through paint and ink and line. The backs are covered with her looping handwriting, speaking to me from a world that I can barely remember, from when I could neither speak nor read nor write. Every now and then I look through what she's making now, and it strikes me that I am still looking at the world through her eyes.

Over time, I began to add to this collection myself. The first I remember including was Man Ray's surrealist fever dream *Le Violon d'Ingres* (1924). I found it in the shop at the Musée National d'Art Moderne in the Pompidou Centre in Paris, and it instantly captivated me. My family was in France to visit our cousins; normally, they spent the summer term in England because their schools broke up for the holidays earlier than ours, and my aunt and uncle were keen for them to grow up fully bilingual. This time, my parents had painstakingly saved up and we made the pilgrimage to see the classic sights. For them, this meant the Louvre and the Pompidou alongside the Eiffel Tower, the Arc de Triomphe, the Champs-Elysées and so on. I suspect art featured more heavily in the original itinerary, but when you have four children aged between three and ten, you have to take your kicks where you can. Alongside my Man Ray, I selected a poster advertising the 1896 tour of performers from the impresario Rodolphe Salis's cabaret club Le Chat Noir from a *bouquiniste* on the Left Bank. My ten-year-old brain failed to note the musical theme of my treasured souvenirs. These sound like ridiculously precocious choices to me now, but, in all honesty, I remember simply liking the way they looked.*

The *Violon d'Ingres* haunted me for many, many years. I dutifully tacked it up on my pinboard at university at the beginning of every term, through each and every house move. Lynda Nead's and Kenneth Clark's works on the nude eventually crossed my desk, and I came to realise how problematic the image was.[4] Where were her arms? Was there ever a more complete transformation of person into object, no matter how tongue-in-cheek it was? But, sheepishly, I still quietly loved this surreal photograph.

It was a long time before I discovered that the woman on whose back those f-holes** had been painted was Alice Ernestine Prin, alias Kiki de Montparnasse. Prin was an artist in her own right, *and* a singer. Under her pseudonym Kiki, she exhibited a solo show of her own paintings in 1927 that was received with great acclaim. In the 1930s she owned the Montparnasse cabaret club Chez Kiki, where she performed music-hall-style sets, wearing black stockings and garters. She left Chez Kiki only to escape the occupation of Paris when the Nazis invaded the city in June 1940.[5]

---

* Not all my tastes were quite so discerning. At the time I was also fond of beach plastic: shards of old toys in bright lollipop colours that had been eroded to soft edges by the sea, sand and shingle, making Polly Pocket or Barbie's Dreamhouse look as though they had survived some sort of apocalypse.

** The holes that allow the violin to have resonance.

Duet

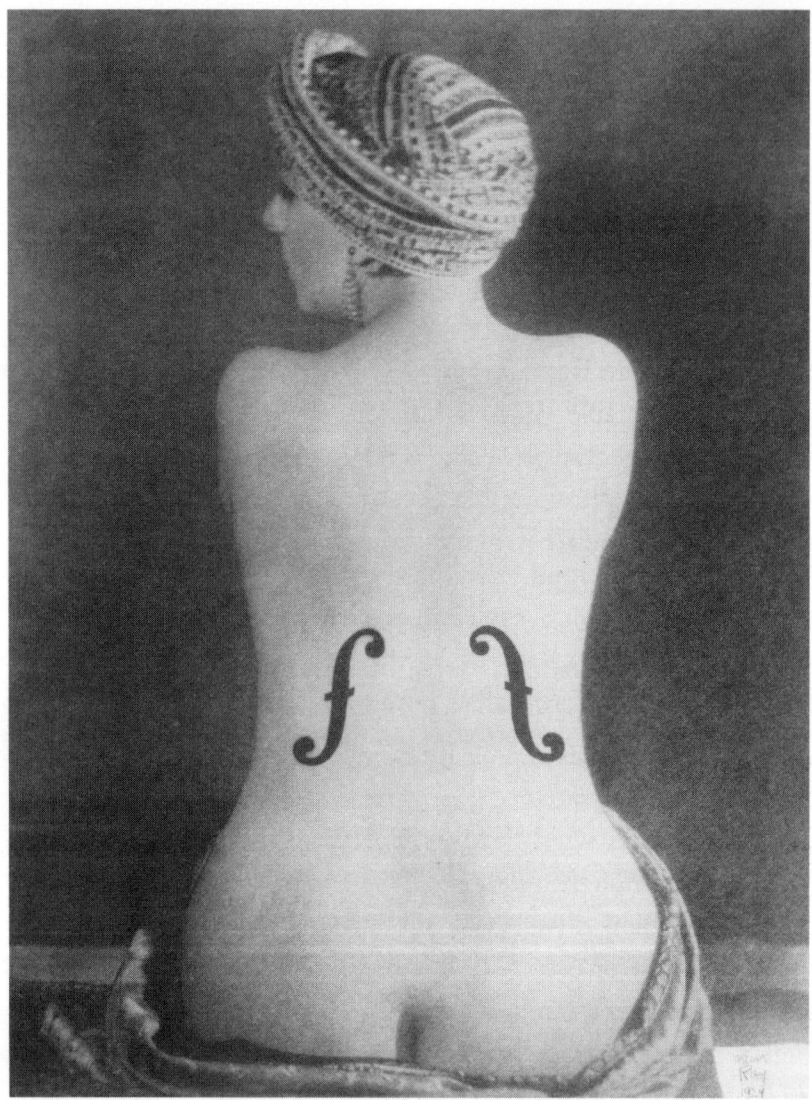

Man Ray, *Le Violon d'Ingres*, 1924.

There are multiple, shifting layers to *Le Violon d'Ingres*. Yes, there is a certain unsettling – we might even argue violent – manipulation of a body here, made more troubling by the fact that Prin was Man Ray's lover (and ten years his junior). Their turbulent relationship raged through eight years of furious artistic production, and it is not too hard to imagine the impact of its relentless drama in Prin's apparently lopped arms that force her torso into the shape of a violin. But this image is also a direct response to another, older painting: *The Valpinçon Bather* (1808) by Jean-Auguste-Dominique Ingres.[6] Man Ray's image isn't simply a statement out of the blue: it is a mocking comment on the tradition of the nude, and on what Ingres did with it. The apparent dismemberment and distortion can be read as a comment on centuries of objectification and voyeurism, rather than that of Man Ray himself.

It is undeniable that the choice of the violin as object is strikingly reverential. It is the kind of object that is cherished. Ancient Greek thinking posited that humans had their own music that interlaced with that of the cosmos itself. *Le Violon d'Ingres* says something rather beautiful about the human body and its capacity: Man Ray transforms Prin into the holder of a deep musical harmony. The turban-like hat, inscribed with geometrical floral patterns that seem to pull our eyes down to those painted f-holes and back again, led by the long drops of her earrings that frustrate our eyes, part elaborate, decorated tuning pegs, part simply what they are. She thrums with resonance.

This is a thoughtful image, even down to the very level of the title. 'Violon d'Ingres' is a French idiom meaning 'private passion', hobby or even side-hustle. The phrase came into usage after the painter's famous love of violin-playing: music wasn't Ingres' main vocation, but it was his favourite pastime when he wasn't painting. Both phrase and image are emblematic of the way that music, although so often relegated to a supporting role – 'my *other* hobby' – has been crucial to the way that artists have seen the world. Throughout history, the theme of music has enabled human beings to refine their ways of seeing, and to challenge the limits of their vision. Music is the lens through which we have brought things into, and out of, focus.

Seven years after my first concert, I am at Glyndebourne Opera House, nestled deep in the lush, rolling folds of the South Downs. A man has come to my state comprehensive school, looking for fifteen children: ten for the production and five as understudies. My rendition of 'Consider Yourself' from the musical *Oliver!* has put me into the coveted ten. Now, front stage right, opening night.

It's a contemporary-dress season of *La bohème*, so I'm decked in the highest of fashion: Y2K low-slung cargo trousers, midriff-skimming tee and rainbow crochet poncho. In this finery, for the next twenty bars or so it is my role to sprawl on the floor at the front of the stage, belligerently blowing the 'smoke' (flour) from my fake cigarette at the audience in my best impression of a *ragazza* or Artful-Dodger-esque 'street urchin'. Briefly, as I stare insolently out at the audience, with nothing but the orchestra pit between us, I am struck by the oddity of the situation: the warm bluish-white haze of stage lighting prevents me from seeing a single face in the audience. I am a visualisation of the music, but those for whom I am performing are completely invisible. The experience is jarring in a way my teenage brain can't quite, for now, put its finger on.

The next night, I pay closer attention to this strangely visible invisibility. Because the choreography requires us to erupt onto stage right at the beginning of Act II, and there is only the briefest of pauses between that and the end of the previous act, we must be in place beforehand. The final moments of Act I are the quietest in the whole of *La bohème*, so we creep. Mimì and Rodolfo, the star-crossed lovers, are singing to each other, astounded by the 'sublime sweetness that already trembles in their souls'.* Hand in hand, they wander off stage right, still singing. In the wings, the orchestra silent, nothing but their two voices crooning *'amor, amor, amor!'* to each other (love, love, *love*). My mind is quietly blown. The dynamic of who is and isn't seen is suddenly reversed:

---

* *'Fremon già nell'anima le dolcezze estreme'* in the original.

Prelude: Noisy Pictures and Music for the Eyes

Mimì and Rodolfo are entirely invisible to the audience – but not to me, waiting in the wings. They are bathed in the spectral blue backstage light that will continue to obsess me for the next twenty years, reminding me not of nightclub bathrooms with drug consumption issues, but of the sorcery of music. They do not angle themselves to ensure they are more audible. They face each other, gazing into each other's eyes, enraptured: a visual performance simply for their own benefit, and for the gaggle of *ragazzi* opposite them. It is a moment of pure enchantment.

Something happens, I realised, between the eyes and the ears when we experience music. Something tantalises the brain, sparking and fizzing the reflexes of our visual sense when we listen, regardless of whether we can literally see anything. How far we tune into or out of this 'seeing' is a matter of personal taste in any given situation. But, regardless, there it is. That is why it is so jarring to be able to see Mimì and Rodolfo, bathed in softly glowing blue, in that moment. They can see each other, and we can see them, but they are invisible to the audience: a part of the performance that was designed *not* to be seen, paradoxically making the visibility of the rest of the music all the more blatant to my ingenuous teenage eyes.

I chalk it up as a lesson to fuel what I am now sure is going to be my profession, and to which I am going to dedicate my life. To be a musician is to walk this tightrope and continually negotiate the balance between the visibility of what we hear, and the acoustics of what we see.

You might not have had the opportunity to experience this for yourself, but many artists have helpfully found themselves drawn to the phenomenon and talked their way into the wings to depict what they see. The painters Edgar Degas and Laura Knight are perfect examples. Of the two, Degas' works are perhaps more familiar, with their froths of tutus and the *sfumato* of fluffy brush strokes capturing ballet dancers in motion – themselves visualisations of music.[7] Degas frequently depicts the shadowy figure of a spectator waiting in the wings, observing the other performers, seeing what our brains tell us shouldn't be seen. In his *Dancers, Pink and Green* (1890), which can be seen in the plate section, the figure bisects the composition down the right-hand side, a sinister top-hatted shadow in shocking contrast to the glowing turquoise of the dancers' costumes.

But we're not asked to identify with this slab of black. Instead, the figure closest to us is a dancer to the far right of the painting. She leans into the other side of the wing against which the shadowy figure rests, her left hand just out of his sightline. She is behind him, perhaps just waiting, perhaps listening, perhaps watching him. We are part of this grouping: seeing the seers. Her fellow dancers fix their hair and their costumes, and stretch; beyond them, on the stage, a figure in palest pink stands against the painted backdrop. This figure is unseen by the others; none of the turquoise dancers, nor the top-hatted observer, look towards the stage. Instead, the unseen dancers, like Mimì and Rodolfo, are the cynosure of visibility.

𝄞

Generally speaking I am an introverted person, although persistent ideas about East Asian femininity and silence can skew people's impressions. Against the odds, those very early exposures to public performance excised something from my brain: I will sing for you or play for you and I do not care (indeed, I am not even necessarily aware) whether you are watching, or whether you aren't. Theoretically this would have helped me thrive in a conservatoire environment, but as it happens, I never got to find out.

The toll of performing three shows a week with Glyndebourne during the first term of the first year of my GCSEs, paying very little attention to my vocal health, left me with callus-like growths on my vocal cords, known as nodules. Nodules are, without exaggeration, a singer's worst nightmare. When they arrive, they can last anywhere between six months and an entire lifetime. They can be alleviated by 'steaming', inhaling moist, warm water vapour for short, daily bursts, but really the best thing to do is to rest. I didn't realise they were anything more serious than a sore throat until huge chasmic gaps in my range appeared during that year's run of Christmas concerts. I sang again, piecemeal, after a few months, but really my voice didn't return to its former self for an entire decade. 'I've lost my voice,' I'd say to anyone and everyone. Their response was usually a politely veiled expression that clearly said, 'What voice?' or 'It's been four (five, seven) years, just let go...'

It is hard to calculate the magnitude of this loss. When you are young, you don't necessarily realise the ramifications of something being taken from you: it can feel so temporary, so unserious in the face of your burning ambition. You also don't realise its benefits. It was almost certainly in that decade of voicelessness that the seeds for this book were sown; that my subconscious mind began to feed on all the crumbs of a shattered youthful plan for how a life was going to pan out, and to fit them together into new, kaleidoscopic combinations. Mine is just one story among thousands, probably millions, of children who find an early passion and who, as they grow, find it drifting out of reach because their body or their brain or even just money, parents and guardians, or schooling won't allow it.

Walk down the street and you won't struggle to find people who once dreamed of playing children in the musicals *Billy Elliot*, *Oliver!* or *Matilda*, or in operas like *La bohème*. I met a couple of my fellow child performers at university. One had played a boy in *The Magic Flute* that same season at Glyndebourne, and I used to leave him notes in his costume shoes. He became a surgeon; it never bothered him that music didn't end up being his career. The ether is full of these little balloons, inflated with the helium of hope and ardour, tugged loose from so many hands. I know now that I am lucky it happened before I had thrown too much of my life into it. Other friends and acquaintances went through the same process in their late teens or twenties, or even thirties. The world is less forgiving to those trying to start afresh and rebuild their lives and careers the further you get from those odd, diminishing years of youth. What is seen as finding your way at the age of twenty-two is a red flag at thirty-two: why couldn't you just get it right the first time and realise you haven't got 'what it takes'?

So, you won't see my name splashed across posters or billboards to advertise concerts. You won't see me onstage singing the solo parts. I am not a superstar performer. But over those sprawling years as the bearer of a broken voice, I realised that my definition of what made a musician was far, *far* too narrow. In those wilderness years, I still sang with my broken, unruly voice. Bewilderingly, people still enjoyed those performances and the distinctive frazzled texture of my voice. Music lingered at the corners of my consciousness, infusing everything I experienced: my musician's brain still simmering in the way that I approached the phrasings and rhythms of words I encountered in my literature degree, in the way I looked at paintings as I transitioned from studying literature to studying art history, in how I listened and how I moved through the world.

What is it about music that makes us so rigid in our definitions, so unimaginative about its scope? There are musicians all around us. Our friends in amateur choirs and orchestras and bands, our self-effacing neighbours who joke about the dog singing along to their guitar practice, buskers on the street: all make up our musical experience. The big-name virtuosic performers aren't the only ones feeding our concept of music. Indeed, some of the most powerful contributions to the way we understand music are those that do not even offer audible music at all.

I learnt this lesson most viscerally as my research career began, with the art of the Dutch Golden Age. In this period of art, which was intensely obsessed with ways of knowing and the limits of the human senses, musical instruments so often take centre stage: broken, slung across still lifes with the curling skins of half-peeled lemons, glowing glasses of wine, dirty sheaves of paper.[8] Looking at them made every cell of my musical body crackle.

Musical references – either sheet music or instruments – appear in twelve out of thirty-six of Vermeer's surviving attributed paintings.[9] *Girl Interrupted at her Music* (see plate section) is my favourite. The girl, in a vermilion jacket, is seated at the far right of the painting. She glances up, perhaps disdainful, perhaps shocked or guilty, the expression on her face not yet settled. Her tutor leans over her, emphatically clutching the sheet of paper in her hands as though attempting, quietly but firmly, to remove it. But look closer. Is this a music lesson? Is that music on that sheet of paper? No, it's blank. The music book and the cittern* lie abandoned on the table at the far left of the painting, beside a somewhat incriminating blue and white porcelain ewer and glass of wine. The figure of Cupid, murky in the frame on the wall at the centre of the image, suggests something shady. Vermeer has made Cupid deliberately obscure, goading us to lean in further and look harder. This isn't a music lesson, the abandoned musical paraphernalia declares, but a secret romantic tryst.

Music is integral to Vermeer's visual storytelling. Arguably his love of depicting music is inevitable: Vermeer was working during the Dutch Golden Age, and these developments and fascinations (with geography, with mathematics, with physics) are the theme of many of his paintings, too.[10] As a theme, music plays into the same allure: the paradoxical limits and limitlessness of our eyes, when faced with all that we cannot see.

These paintings show us music as a way of knowing, and of seeing. Vermeer and his colleagues recognised how it could enhance understanding, how it acted like a lens that could bring

---

* A kind of guitar.

aspects of the world into sharper focus. This is a lesson that we could do with learning today: things are not as they first appear, or rarely just one thing at a time. Our perceptual edges – the hazy space where vision and hearing blur together – can reveal those difficulties, and make us look, and listen, again.

Vermeer and his fellow painters from the Dutch Golden Age can show us the value of music as a device for puzzling out the limits of perception. The visual elements of music can have other uses, too, including one that has become integral to my musical practice.

𝄞

A decade after my vocal nodules appeared, I am sitting in my kitchen in the ramshackle flat my partner and I rent from our college in Cambridge, a stone's throw from the Botanic Garden. A score is open on the table: English composer Judith Bingham's twelve-part 'The Spirit of Truth'. She wrote this incredible, mysterious piece of music as a fantasia on a theme of the sixteenth-century composer Thomas Tallis's evergreen little piece, 'If Ye Love Me'. It is, without exaggeration, a masterpiece: an entanglement of parts that manages to be both densely textured and diaphanously gossamer-fine.

My voice has returned, and I am now a choral singer. There is no denying it – of all forms and styles of classical music, choral singing could be the nerdiest of all. But it is the *Dungeons & Dragons*, Seth Cohen-style of nerdiness: ironic, self-aware. It is also where some of the most cutting-edge classical music can be found. 'Cutting-edge classical music' might sound oxymoronic, but composers are writing new choral music all the time, pushing the boundaries of what can be done with the human voice, and stretching the very limits of what can count as music. I sing in my college chapel choir, and so am part of a writhing, cut-throat organism in a constant battle for excellence. Under the shadow

Prelude: Noisy Pictures and Music for the Eyes

of King's College and their Christmas Eve broadcasting set-up, competition to get into most of these choirs is fierce. Almost all of them are audition-only; they carve twelve hours a week out of your already gruelling schedule, and more like twenty if a recording is coming up. Each choir fights to have its own particular renown: to have a distinctive niche. Ours, for now, is this new music.

Nevertheless, I am painfully aware that I'm very much not who the English choral system was designed for. Arundel was the closest cathedral to where I grew up, and it did not take girl choristers until the advent of Elizabeth Stratford as Director of Music the year I turned thirteen. The nearest Anglican cathedral, Chichester, only started taking girl choristers for the academic year beginning September 2022.

Moreover, being mixed race has always placed me outside the logic of the lyrics of English choral music and what it aspired towards. The hopeful, hopeless, much-co-opted, much-maligned hymn 'Jerusalem' is merely one of many examples: 'And did those feet in ancient time/Walk upon England's mountains green'. A surprising number of people see race as an either/or rather than a both/and, so to them I am either 'basically Chinese' (which, to anyone even remotely aware of the East Asian beauty quest for double eyelids, is laughable) or 'basically white' (again, risible considering the volume of 'Where are you *really* from?'/'Do you "go back"?'/'How did your English get so good?' questions I've had over the years). It turns out you cannot have the 'voice of an angel' when you are a little bit Chinese – instead, your voice is 'surprising' or 'doesn't fit your face', both things that people have said to compliment me on my singing. This is not to mention the pervasive belief that people of my ethnicity are somehow biologically programmed to be good at music, paradoxically twinned with the idea that I must have a tiger mother lingering somewhere in the background, making me practise every waking hour. But you'd be hard pressed to find a genre of music that isn't infected with this interlacing of expectations, stereotypes and boxes that constantly need dismantling.

Nonetheless, there's something beautiful about the fragile, problematic, precious nature of choral music. In an English context, it developed out of a fear that music would become redundant after the Reformation, when Henry VIII broke from Rome.[11] English choral composers invented a purely 'native' musical tradition to ensure that music was seen as of national importance and continued to be an integral part of the Anglican church service. It has always been a heady concoction of nostalgia for something that never was, laced with a striving towards something it cannot reach.

It is also, somewhat oddly, named for something both musical and visual. 'Choir', meaning group of singers, comes from the Greek *khoros* via Latin *chorus* and the Old French *quer*. It's also the *quire*, the particular section of a church where the choir traditionally sat, between the altar and the congregation. And it's a physical part of a book manuscript, through which you might read music: a gathering of pages. There's a further layer of music and visual entanglement: the ancient Greek word *khoros* actually meant dance, a physical dancing place, and a group of performers (singers or dancers). Orchestra has the same etymological root, ὀρχέομαι or *orkhéomai*, to dance.

This might sound bizarre to you if you've never indulged in a bit of a choral singing. To me, though, this history has always rung poignantly true. Navigating this genre of music as a performer feels like intricate choreography – like a dance with steps that you are marking out with muscles deep inside your body, in your core and your posture and your lungs.

People often think that singing is easy. Almost anyone can do it, so surely to sing for an hour or two isn't too much of an effort? Have a go, and you'll see that parts of your body soon start to ache – a scratchiness in your throat, something almost muscular in the back of your throat as your vocal cords start to complain, a spasming in your diaphragm.[12] You aren't just born with a good voice. You can have the bare bones, but you need to work it and develop it. Singing is a physical workout that takes years of developing technique to hone and needs to be carefully warmed up, just like any athletic activity. And this is not even taking into account what your brain has to do while you are singing choral music repertoire: paying minute attention to the other parts – shifts in timing, shifts into flatness or sharpness – to the sheet music and to the conductor themselves. All this, to make a sound that is light and airy and 'angelic'. Behind that celestial sound is grit, grind and a heavy dose of carb-loading before a concert because you are going to burn a whole lot of energy.

'The Spirit of Truth' has landed on my kitchen table because we'll be recording it in a month's time, for an album of choral works by contemporary female composers. Each of the twelve voice parts is relatively, deceptively simple: a floaty, ululating series of intersecting fourths. It's the intersection of parts – where they interlock, where each one passes a melodic skein to another, where they switch places or braid together in the texture – that is tricky. A minutely observed choreography is required. The interplay is there, when I follow the sheet music and hear the voices jump across parts and back again, to fill where the part fell out of the range of the singer allocated it.

Listening to it now, I remember how, even in recording, we would glance at each other as we did so, handing the line on. When you are particularly far apart (either due to the architectural space, or to the acoustic demanded by what you are recording), you watch each other's lips instead, as they form the words, because it helps you to navigate that split-second delay before your ears receive their voice. The intimacy is profound. You do this even if you aren't especially enamoured of that person at that point – because the music asks it of you, and in that moment you *are* the music. Your breath is my breath, your heartbeat is my heartbeat. And it hurts.

At the end there is the relief, the release, of falling into Tallis like the shimmering, turquoise cool of the sea on a hot day. Those last four bars of the Bingham, as she stacks up that opening chord, send shivers down my spine…

If.

If ye love me, keep my commandments.

Something more than the sound itself is needed for me to master it, to internalise its harmonics and capture its musicality. I glance through my part, once, twice, sing it through. Then I reach for a paintbrush and paper. Still humming the notes under my breath, I start to paint what I hear/see: the colours, the dense texture, the stacks of chords, that shimmer of the original piece as it glints through. A chunky blackish turquoise line begins to take shape, bleeding through the translucent white.

It worked, and I learnt my part. But I was never quite satisfied with what I produced. Even nine years later I occasionally find myself picking up the score, putting it on the speaker, and trying to pin down its wispy, smoggy solidity with my paintbrush, ever striving, ever falling short.

𝄞

I want to change the way we think about music. Each of these moments I've shared reveals that there is something more to music than meets the ear. What they suggest is nothing that your brain doesn't already know and that I feel sure you understand deep down in your bones: the traces of these practices have always been there in the way that human beings approach music, because for as long as we have made music we have *seen* it. Part of music's magic is the very illusion that it is invisible.

Somewhere along the way we've lost the subtlety of thought that allows us to understand music as entertainment but also as crucial to our wellbeing as humans. Recreation feeds our brains, and allows us to be, among other things, more effective.[13]

There appears to be a causal link between music and neuroplasticity – that is, our brain's ability to form and reorganise synaptic connections, thus shaping and improving our cognitive function – although scientists still disagree about quite how this works.[14] Music could literally make us more intelligent. It's been long established that providing children with music education enhances their ability to learn other vital subjects like literacy and numeracy;[15] nonetheless, music education is in decline across the West. In the UK, for example, fewer and fewer children are choosing to study music at GCSE and A-level.[16] In the US, a similar decline is reported: in 2021, a staggering number of children, almost 3.8 million, were unable to access any kind of music education in schools.

Common narratives would have you believe that this is because fusty old education tactics using the fusty old structures of the classical 'canon' are failing to seduce new musicians, and the mounting expense and lack of subsidy for practical music lessons cannot be helping matters – how can you love playing the cello when you've never even had the chance to hold one? Along with the decline in music education, we have fallen into bad habits in how we ascribe value to music: we've started to simply accept the idea that jobs in music are not things you do for money but for 'the love of it'. This is a fallacy, and essentially nothing but a sanitised version of the idea that music is only for people who can afford it.

But music is an integral part of all of us, knitted deep into the twists of our DNA. The history of music is, in a very real sense, the history of humanity. We evolved around music, our capacity for language and communication governing how we were shaped as human beings.

Crucially, the communicative power of music has always extended beyond what is spoken, what is audible. Music is a language that has always been visual – as musical notes, as images of music-making, but also in some unexpected, artful ways that can expand our understanding of what music is, in its very essence.

So, this is a history of music, told artfully. An artful, art-full history of music offers access to untold moments, and a new way of imagining what music can and should be for. One that takes a long, hard look at the things we have collectively allowed to pass into the status quo, and that invites us to rethink how we approach the value of music, what musical genres actually mean in practice, and what makes a musician. One that could also provide a valuable antidote to the restrictive concept of music and musical excellence that shuts a broader variety of people out of joining in; an antidote to the kinds of music history that enshrine a string of totemic 'big name' geniuses to the detriment of the broader context of music-making.

In *Duet* we'll undertake an odyssey through a small fraction of artful music's greatest hits. This book is for all those who are interested in the ingenuity of human intervention in all its sounding forms, whether they are a seasoned professional musician or a knowledgeable listener who cannot play a single note. It cannot, and does not, hope to provide a comprehensive overview of all the ways in which the musical and the visual have been entangled, but it offers an insight into the sheer variety of ways the visual has been integral to music throughout history.

We'll delve deep into the prehistoric caverns where the first music-making happened, and encounter some of the intricate operations that went into inventing graphic signs for musical notes. We'll create musical scales out of colour and perfume, and we'll change the world with a book of sheet music. We'll ship a clockwork organ to Istanbul where it will delight audiences, only to be dismantled ten years later. Spanning from 35,000 BCE to the present day, *Duet* reveals an assortment of ways that the seen and the heard have been in an intricate, intimate dance, inextricably entwined. In turn, it unmasks a more inclusive, dynamic and fluid way of thinking about music, and one that is true to music's very evolutionary origins as a tool of communication and community. By examining a cross-section of moments when music made meaning through a visual language, my hope is that *Duet* can allow us to revitalise our understanding of ourselves as music-making beings.

Music is a thing we built together, as a community, across continents and across time. It is a toy, but it is not trivial. It didn't develop in a vacuum, but through the ingenuity of people who used its visual power as well as its audible meaning.

𝄞

To return, then, to that enormous golden dragon, and the indulgent orientalism that formed my first stage. A whole performance life is before us. Hush descends; take a deep, well-supported breath. The curtain rises. The adventure begins, waiting for you and for me.

DUET

1

Curtain Up:
The Stage

Our breath plumes out in frosted clouds.

In the Christmas market in Dóm Tér (literally, Cathedral Square) in Szeged, Hungary, the temperature hovers just above freezing. Lingering all around us is an icy mist better suited to a horror film than a festive concert. Its soupy density has given it the uncanny ability to magnify and dissipate any light, so the entire space of the square is penetrated by daubs of bright candy colours from the fairy lights strung around. Clutching polystyrene cups of mulled wine and cider, shivering in our concert blacks, we wait to be let into the warm embrace of the space where we'll be performing.

To say we are dismayed when we discover that the theatre is made out of the haybales standing to one end of the market is an understatement. Bone-chilled, grumbling, miserable, we shuffle in.

But something magical happens once we begin singing.

Enclosed by the stacked haybales, our audience using them as seats and huddling together against the chill, a spell descends as we perform one particular song.

It's a Hungarian folk song, traditionally sung at Christmas time. The lyrics tell the tale of a heartbroken girl jilted by her sweetheart who has 'frozen' towards her. At the end it closes with an image of a sleeping baby, a 'lamb of God', 'born out of love':

Zöld az erdő zöld a petrezselyem	The trees are green, the parsley is green
Benned rózsám meghűlt a szerelem	Love has grown cold in you, my rose
Nem csak meghűlt meg is fagyosodott	So cold that it is frozen
Víg szívemre búbánatot hozott	It saddens my heart
Falu mellett van egy házikócska	In a cottage at the edge of the village
Abban van egy rengető bölcsőcske	There is a cradle rocking
A lábával rengetgeti vala	And with his foot he rocked it
A szájával fúdogálja vala	And with his mouth he sings
Aludj-aludj Istennek báránya	Sleep, sleep, Lamb of God
Szerelemből jöttél a világra	For you came into this wide world today
Aludj-aludj Istennek báránya	Sleep, sleep, Lamb of God
Szeretetből jöttél a világra.	For you came into this wide world today.

The tune is simple, and we had learnt it fast. To give it an English choral twist and 'make it ours', our Director of Music suggested we could improvise harmonies for it when we performed. In rehearsal it felt, I won't deny, a little morally questionable: as if we were taking part of someone's precious culture and mangling it with our own versions of good musical style.

But as we sang those improvised harmonies, for just a brief moment, the penetrating cold melted away. We, and the audience, became one with that rustic, strangely intimate space, shielded from the eerie fog outside. At the end of the song, several of the audience members were visibly overcome with emotion, sobbing at what they later told us was the beauty of what we'd done with their folk song. There are moments when you can *feel* music working: the edges of your body melting away, boundaries dissipating, a togetherness so complete between audience and performers that you are one organism.

Christmas is so often packaged as being cosy, but it's not often that we have such a visceral reminder of what warmth meant in the context of the Christmas story (regardless of whether you see it as fiction, truth or something in between). Cosiness isn't chestnuts roasting on a roaring fire, but a desperate, weary woman in the early stages of labour, her husband looking for and finding some kind of shelter from the elements – even something as flimsy and impermanent as a stack of haybales. What we offered that audience was their own old, favourite song, laced with all the storytelling techniques that English Christmas carols – about hope in adversity, about coming in from the cold – had to offer. It was a gift that, on that ice-hazed day, enclosed by walls of hay, they wanted to receive.

The look and feel of a venue, and no matter how simply or elaborately it is decorated, is of huge importance to how we experience music. But all these spaces work on the assumption that they will galvanise the musical performance that takes place within them. Over millennia, special, chosen places have inflected the way that people experience music.

𝄞

Incredibly, some of these ancient chosen places have survived.

Another, softer mist lingers over the hills of the Périgord, clinging to the treetops above what will one day be the village of Les Eyzies. Through these hills, somewhere around 12,000 years ago, a shaman – let's call her Helis – strides with purpose.[1] Helis is a Magdalenian. Her delightfully named culture refers to that of the Upper Palaeolithic and Mesolithic in western Europe, and gets its name from the type site of Abri de la Madeleine, a village carved into a monumental rock face not far from Font-de-Gaume.[2] Perhaps Helis visits La Madeleine every now and then; perhaps she's more of a loner, as befits certain requirements of her profession. It's a hard job, looking after the barrier between your community and the supernatural. Deep in these hills is a cave with an entrance moulded in fantastical shapes straight out of a scene from *Star Wars*. This is where Helis is headed. She strikes a spark from a flint, lights a flame, and ducks into the dark.

She is a skilled artist, and image-making is a crucial part of her work. Her paintings, and those of her predecessors, adorn the surfaces at crucial points within the cave. Bison frolic across the roof, seeming to move in the flickering candlelight.[3] There are gazelles, horses, wild cattle and cave bears. There are more than twenty paintings of mammoths. Another series of paintings shows line-and-dot drawings, known as tectiforms, that seem to represent huts and larger shelters, covered with animal hides. There are handprints, the topmost joint of each finger truncated in a mysterious fashion.[4]

Ahead of Helis, as she enters the cave, is a protrusion of rock. The bulge of its curvature reminds her, precisely, of the powerful chest and front haunches of a bull. Carefully, she begins to apply her red ochre. The style of the Magdalenian paintings requires a special technique: in the absence of other binding agents like egg or oil, Helis mixes the pigment in her mouth with her own saliva and then blows it onto the rock, using her lips as her painting tool. These images are a capturing of breath, as well as colour.

For thousands of years, these paintings lay forgotten, slumbering beneath the rock. Then, on a Thursday in September 1901, the day still hazy with the warmth of summer, a schoolmaster by the name of Denis Peyrony ventured deep into the caves.[5] For years his pupils had been playing in a mysterious cave above the village of Les Eyzies-de-Tayac-Sireuil where he worked.[6] Four days earlier, Peyrony and the Abbé Henri Breuil, a local Catholic priest and amateur archaeologist, had officially 'discovered' 291 prehistoric engravings at the nearby cave of Les Combarelles. But Peyrony wasn't done yet. What about those interesting marks in the caves that the village children had been using as a playground for as long as anyone could remember? He edged into the delicious cool of its depths, lantern in hand.

That day, Peyrony rediscovered the first of the 200 polychrome paintings that would be uncovered in the cave, now known as Font-de-Gaume.[7] We still have his drawings, both of Font-de-Gaume and Les Combarelles: testaments to an uncovered world.

Just under a century after they were rediscovered, I saw these paintings myself. I remember watching as the red ochre images seemed to undulate as we moved, the way they had been skilfully rendered to catalyse with the form of the rock on which they were painted to become bigger than the sum of their parts: pulsing as though breathing. I remember the acoustic experience of being down there in the gelid deep, as though held in the craggy interior of some primordial meringue. It was so very, very quiet. And yet, whenever anyone spoke, their voices would bounce back at us: warm, enriched like honey, resonant without being booming. I felt cushioned by the sound, engulfed gently by a soft, firm voice that seemed both deep in my head and everywhere.

Recent research is beginning to show that these decorations were not just there to aid visual communion with the sacred: they had a musical purpose too.[8] Evidence that music was a part of Magdalenian culture survives only in morsels, but there are a relatively large number of these scraps from that period, compared to the scant pieces from only a few thousand years later. We have no precise guide to when music was performed, so acoustic archaeologists have had to be creative with their analysis, looking to modern cultures that use similar objects. A conch shell horn, dating back 18,000 years and found in the entrance of the painted cave at Marsoulas, some 180 miles further south, has served as a useful clue. When it was first discovered in 1931, it was labelled as a ceremonial drinking vessel or loving cup. Conch shells are strong at their most tapered point, so whoever assumed that it had broken off by accident, rather than been deliberately shaped for a purpose, was making a bold move.[9]

Traces of red dots are visible just inside the aperture, similar to the painting technique used to render bison inside the cave at

Marsoulas (see plate section).[10] Such strong visual resemblances could suggest that the conch shell horn wasn't just for your regular Friday night soiree, but rather for ceremonial purposes, to be played beside the painting of the bison itself. The seashell's proximity to the cave also implies that these could have been musical spaces.[11]

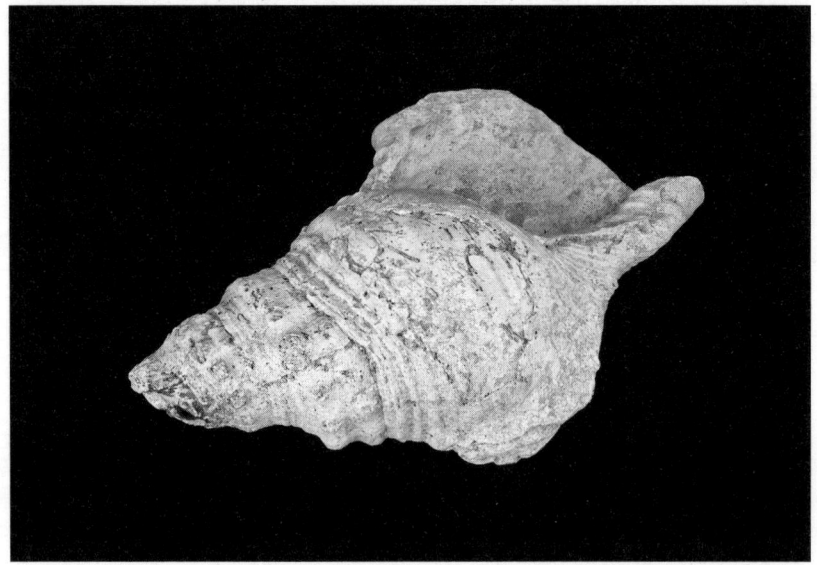

Conch shell horn from Marsoulas cave, c. 16,000 BCE.

Objects found at Font-de-Gaume include a 'bullroarer' whistle: a flat, perforated piece of wood or bone attached to a piece of cord, similar to an instrument used by Australian Aborigines to imitate spirit sounds. When spun in a circular motion, it creates a whirring sound. There was also a phalangeal whistle, a flute-like instrument made of a pierced phalanx bone, played by blowing over the top of the hole as you would a modern-day transverse flute. Really, though, the best evidence we have is the caves themselves. Music archaeologists have conducted performance experiments to identify the contextual sound effects of these spaces. In the case of the Marsoulas conch shell and the cave, this meant playing a 3D-printed resin replica of the instrument on the edge of the ravine outside the opening of the cave, and inside the cave in various positions including near certain paintings.¹² Observers of the experiment noticed that the sound of the seashell 'filled the cave', but without any of the eerie reverberations and phantom 'warblings' or 'throbbings' of tone recorded at other cave sites, as in the stone galleries at Chavín de Huíntar in Peru.

No one has yet conducted performance experiments at Font-de-Gaume, but they have at the nearby and now more famous site at Lascaux, discovered in 1940. It turns out that what I heard all those years ago wasn't just the result of youthful overwhelm. French acoustician Daniel E. Commins and his fellow researchers described the soundscape of the cave with a not inconsiderable pinch of delight.

> Early visitors of the original Lascaux cave were impressed by some unusual acoustic effects ... the soundscape gives the impression that some animals are shouting, running, talking... This phenomenon can be revealed by an experiment. In the Hall of Bulls, a spot marked by traces of candle drops has been identified as the possible position of ceremonies. One may assume that a lit candle was placed at that spot. Emission from the same position of hand clapping provides the illusion to people present in the Hall of Bulls that the bulls are running![13]

Commins and his team found that focal points, marked by the location of paintings, had spectacular echoes that couldn't be found elsewhere in the cave. Their own experiments in the Hall of Bulls in 2019 and 2020 found a long reverberation comparable to those found in a contemporary symphony hall. Spoken and sung words were entirely intelligible, and the acoustic allowed music to 'expand with elegance'.[14] The space also had a resonant frequency similar to a frequency component typical of the bellow of contemporary bulls. If you ever visit one of these painted caves, you'll discover exactly why those cold, hard scientists were waxing lyrical about a mythical ambience.

These ancient spaces might very well have been the first music venues. And right at the very beginning of the history of humans making music, there is the visual, amplifying the meaning of the sound. What researchers found at Marsoulas and Lascaux has been repeated across the world – each cave with its own idiosyncrasies, but with clear acoustic properties we now associate with Gothic cathedrals and modern symphony halls.[15]

Studies have, in fact, found that these spaces often have a link between visual motifs and resonance.[16] A 2017 statistical analysis found that motifs in prehistoric sites are mostly found in positions where there's a strong balance between reverberation and clarity, where words, for example, could be clearly heard.[17] The relationship isn't systematic – that is, the presence of a painted or carved image doesn't automatically signify an area with a good acoustic, and we can't assume that areas were painted just because they sounded good. Some motifs seem to be more likely to appear in resonant areas: the archaeologist Ìegor Reznikoff has observed that niches and recesses painted with red dots like those used to represent the bison at Marsoulas, and that decorate the mouth of the conch shell horn, tend to resonate strongly.[18] Chronologically, these also tend to be the earliest images to appear in cave art, followed by animals and geometrical forms.

Of course, it's likely that the use of caves shifted over time. Perhaps their role as a site of music performance became less important; perhaps they were dedicated to the sacred, or for community. We don't know for certain, but the implications are astounding – these caves might have been the Gothic cathedrals of their day, visited as key spaces of heritage that may contain the memory of a way of performing music. In these spaces, the air still seems thick with the presence of shamans like Helis, standing amid her paintings made of breath, red ochre, charcoal and saliva. It's possible to imagine her, only just out of hearing, oscillating her bullroarer and creating unearthly music as part of a ritual whose meaning we have lost.

Human beings still love caves as musical venues. The popularity of The Caverns in Grundy County, Tennessee testifies to that: deep underground, now lit with a rainbow splay of lights, host to shows and festivals where you can camp outside after the music ends, or hire a yurt if glamping is more your style. Outdoors or rather 'outdoors' and immersed in nature, it's tempting to think of such spaces as wild. But that would be missing the point. The seduction of spaces like The Caverns, like Marsoulas, Font-de-Gaume and Lascaux, is precisely their balance between the wild and the man-made: carefully, subtly shaped, decorated and cultivated to be not-quite-natural. In this way, these places tell us something vital about music and how we have wanted to experience it over the years. It is a natural thing, our brains tell us; it is enhanced, somehow, by being surrounded by sea or trees or rock. Even in the case of those Magdalenian Cro-Magnon cave painters, for whom modern-day concepts of indoors and outdoors are anachronous, the idea of total immersion in nature seems to have been important.

From antiquity until around about 1700, the people of Europe and the Near East believed in the music of the spheres: that humanity was actually indelibly stitched into a continuum with the natural world, and that music was the closest way to activate this connection. Here's Shylock showing Jessica the music of the spheres, in William Shakespeare's *The Merchant of Venice*:

> Sit, Jessica. Look how the floor of heaven
> Is thick inlaid with patines of bright gold:
> There's not the smallest orb which thou behold'st
> But in his motion like an angel sings,
> Still quiring to the young-eyed cherubins;
> Such harmony is in immortal souls;
> But while this muddy vesture of decay
> Doth grossly close it in, we cannot hear it.

Everything emitted a song – *musica mundi* – that reverberated with any music humans could make, and with the music that made our bodies function – *musica humana*. Venues like Marsoulas, Font-de-Gaume and Lascaux imply that some of the ideas behind the music of the spheres had been lingering for much longer than we have recorded history.

𝄞

Even where the venues themselves no longer survive, other evidence can allow us to piece together the fragments of the places where music was once performed. Although the gardens of Timurid and Safavid Persia are largely lost to history, illuminated miniatures give us a glimpse of what they might have been like. The opulent surfaces of these images often depict music-making deeply immersed in nature: a group of musicians tucked to one side of the perspective, among verdant trees.

A single sheet from a manuscript that has been broken up depicts a floral field where Sufi mystics perform a ritual ceremony known as the *sama*, to forge a connection with God; some dervishes are engaged in the celestial dance element of the ceremony, encircled by a ring of others who play music to accompany their movements. At the top of the image, probably illustrated by the painter Kamāl ud-Dīn Behzād around the year 1480, the trees drip with blossom. At the bottom, those overcome by the dance collapse onto velvety grass embroidered with white, red and blue flowers.

A similar dynamic is at play in an illuminated illustration from Amir Khusrau Dihlavi's *Khamsa* (Quintet), a poetic account of the historic ties between the city of Herat (in modern-day Afghanistan) and the Persianate world. It was owned by the Mughal Emperor Akbar, who ruled the Indian subcontinent in the second half of the sixteenth century. In the book, a princess tells the story of the youth of Rum, who imagines meeting a fairy queen and her entourage nightly in the garden. The illustration, painted by the Hindu court painter, Manohar Das, depicts rainbow-winged fairies clustered on the left-hand side, serenading the youth and fairy queen on a *dilruba** and tambourine. Blossom wafts luxuriantly in the background, and lush green spreads in each direction as far as the eye can see. Here, the natural world is the most harmonious stage set: curated into artfully shaped shrubs and trees, a rill guiding the water through the form of the perfectly managed garden. Perhaps there is ambient birdsong, the gentle trickling of water, the softest rustle of breeze through leaves.

Sufi mystics or Dervishes dance as part of the *sama,* from a Divan of Hafiz (c. 1480), opaque watercolour and gold on paper.

All this is a million miles from the primeval drama of Font-de-Gaume, Marsoulas and Lascaux. There is one image, though, that captures some of that elemental force, although in a rather calmer register (see plate section). The record of who painted and

---

* A form of sitar played with a bow.

Manohar Das and Muhammad Husain Kashmiri, *The Youth of Rum is Entertained in a Garden by a Fairy and her Maidens*, from a *Khamsa* of Amir Khusrau Dihlavi, 1597–8.

calligraphed this beautiful miniature has been lost, but we do know that its text was first copied in 1411 in Shiraz, Iran.[19] This particular miniature shows an episode from the Persian poet Ferdowsi's *Shahnameh* or Book of Kings, the foundational book of Persian identity, written at the turn of the eleventh century. It describes a mixture of the mythical and historical past of the Persian empire: Alexander the Great is on his way to invade India, and presumably just about to destroy Persepolis. He pauses by the banks of a river, where he spies on a group of young women swimming and making music as they bathe – the fifteenth-century precursor to every wild-swimming girl squad. The sense of Alexander's intrusion is clear from his posture – see him laying his finger on his lip and peering from his horse, as though he has never seen a woman before. But take a closer look at the image: the way the swirls of water fill two-thirds of the page, almost threatening to wash Alexander away. The river holds the women. It cradles them and protects them. And there, at its topmost edge, where water meets land, are the two women holding musical instruments: one a flute, the other a tambourine. Visually, the music is part of that containment, part of that cradling. Music and water make a harmonious atmosphere, a literal safe space for the women – for now.

In each of these miniatures, cultivated natural spaces are presented as luscious venues for musical performance. Very few of the gardens from Timurid and Safavid Persia survive, so these illuminated miniatures are precious resources. Yes, it's likely that they show an idealised space where blight and mildew, aphids and caterpillars never have the chance to wreak havoc and devour buds before they can flower. But they offer us an insight into what performers and audiences of the period wanted from a musical space. Surviving accounts tell us that music was predominantly performed at court, or in the exquisite gardens shown in the illuminated miniatures; it was accompanied by dance, imbibing of wine, discussion of poetry and all the best conversation that fifteenth-century Herat had to offer.[20] In the lost garden of Jahānārā, the Timurid ruler Soltān-Hosayn Bāyqarā had built a Qasr-e Tarabafzā or 'euphoria-inducing palace' specifically for musical performance.[21] It must have been a spectacular place. And in the illuminated miniatures we can see one of the vital images of that music-making culture, and the desire for a performance space that cocooned performers and listeners in undulating patterns of carefully curated flora and fauna, breathtakingly close to nature.

𝄞

Around the same time, several thousand miles north, a different sort of musical venue was being constructed. This one would also resemble a cave, but unlike Font-de-Gaume, Marsoulas and The Caverns in Tennessee it would be flooded with natural light.

Like the music that would be performed here, this monumental edifice would be an offering to the divine.

Construction began on 25th July 1446, with the laying of a single stone. The person who performed this action, with a great deal of ceremony, was Henry VI, King of England (and, so he claimed at this point, of France). Ever in the shadow of his illustrious father, Henry V, he was not the most lauded of medieval monarchs. But he was still a king and a force to be reckoned with nonetheless. The stone he laid was the first of a chapel intended to be the crowning glory of the Fens, and his key architectural legacy as a monarch. Auspicious days were often chosen for such occasions. In the Western church tradition 25th July is the Feast Day of St James,* the hot-headed fisherman of the disciples, who was beheaded by King Herod Agrippa I only eleven years after the crucifixion of Jesus. He is the patron saint of pilgrims, his symbol a single scallop shell. In this case, the auspiciousness of the day seems to have backfired somewhat. Not long after these events, Henry found himself a pilgrim of sorts, dethroned in the tempestuous events we now know as the Wars of the Roses.

Watching the stone-laying was Reynold Ely, who was probably what we would now term the architect of the chapel. Although medieval England didn't have a concept of solo authorship of design, he was the master mason and so roughly fits the label.[22] He had been commissioned to find workmen for the chapel around two years earlier, and had also been tasked with building the library staircase in Peterhouse, the venerable college just down the road. Initially, plans were for the ceiling to be constructed out of a lierne vaulting – a kind of starlike array of interlocking ribs, named after the Old French term, *lierne*, for the clematis flower.

Not long after Reynold set to work, Henry began to have the mental breakdowns that would prevent him from ruling. Fifteen

---

* In the Eastern Church tradition, the Feast Day of St James falls on 30th April.

years later, he was deposed by his cousin, Edward IV. Forty years after the laying of the first stone, the chapel remained unfinished; in the meantime Edward had died and his brother Richard had been deposed by Henry Tudor. Money appeared, money ran out. New plans were proposed, amended, abandoned. In fact, the chapel wouldn't be finished until 1515, and its stained glass windows wouldn't be done until 1531. But the building went on regardless, slowly, painstakingly. Such petty considerations as the death of kings were nothing to the kind of music that would happen within the walls of King's College Chapel, Cambridge.

For eight years, I passed this building day in, day out. I was studying at the smaller, shabbier college next door, which was looked down on for being a mere whippersnapper (imagine being founded in the 1470s rather than the 1440s? *Shocking...*) and for having stolen its land from its grand neighbour in some murky dispute, the full details of which have long been lost. On my way to lectures, it was easier to cut through the quad that it towers over than to tackle the tightrope-narrow pavements, traffic and busloads of tourists on Silver Street, especially if you had rolled out of bed at *precisely* 8.50 a.m., prepared for an eight-minute walk. I'd often pass the crocodile of the boy choristers in top hats and miniature gowns, on their way to rehearsal; in the afternoons I'd sometimes hear the organ groaning, or the faint strains of the choir running through evensong repertoire. When things got too much – and they often did – I'd slip into its cool stillness, lie back on one of the pews and gaze up at the hypnotic, lacy firmament that constituted its ceiling.

The ceiling, constructed between 1512 and 1515, is the masterwork of John Wastell.[23] Reynold Ely was long dead by this time, but perhaps that's all for the best, because without Wastell we would never have ended up with the largest fan vault in the world. Wastell was already known around Cambridge; he completed work on the gatehouse of King's Hall, later Trinity College, and Great St Mary's, the grand church opposite King's

John Wastell's fan vaulting on the ceiling of King's College Chapel, Cambridge, 1512–15

Chapel. But it's undeniable he was something of a maverick: rather than being defeated by the model that Ely and his successors had left behind – vault supports intended for a lierne vault, upper bays that simply didn't allow for his new scheme – Wastell remodelled, patching over brick structures with pieces of tracery, inserting new wall arches, cutting things out to squeeze the necessary structural elements in.

The fan vault at King's is so skilfully done that it has still, to this day, never been repaired or restored: it is just solid. Quite how Wastell managed to construct something that looks so delicate and yet is so stable remains a mystery. Architectural historians think he might have focused on getting the central pieces in first, and might have used the antechapel section as an experimental model, but without dismantling the thing there is likely no way we're ever going to know. What we do know, though, is that Wastell had a very clear idea about how he was going to set *this* stage. It would be imposingly enormous, a gobsmacking monument to the medieval Christian God. Part of the illusion of the ceiling is the way that it emphasises the distance between it and the floor with detail – an opulently filigree pattern that snags on your eyes, goading you to lean closer, *closer*, even as your neck cricks and strains. Art objects like this are all about manipulating how you look, making your eyes complicit and – in this case – reminding you how very small you are in comparison to the deity who dwells far above this airy canopy of stone.

As a piece of sculpture, a heft of material that is tactile and experienceable in three dimensions, the fan vault is also astounding. It is made up of a rock-solid tessellation of stone, sturdy enough to support the weight of several human beings. I can testify to that because I have walked along its underside (that is, disconcertingly, its topside), far above the chapel floor. The void between the eaves and the top of the ceiling is bizarrely moving: inscribed with centuries of graffiti, quiet and cavernous in its own special way. The space is still sizeable, and the convex curve of the ceiling makes it feel as though you are walking across the back of a great slumbering beast, a dragon ossified by some sorcerer's curse. You can walk its length along the central spine, which spans between two windows, and peer down at the people moving hundreds of feet below you through a tiny peep-hole just over the choir stalls. *What does evensong sound like from way up here?* I found myself wondering. *What does it* feel *like, lying with the inverse of that colossal vaulting against your back?* It's another version of that seductive backstage view: the workings laid bare, the invisible made visible.

Fan vaulting is one of the big hitters of Gothic architecture; one of its most distinctive features, inspired by the Islamic rib vaults seen by crusaders in the eleventh and twelfth centuries, brought back as an innovative amalgamation between structure and decoration. Not that people have always been so taken with the Gothic style. The posthumous edition of John Evelyn's *Accounts of Architects and Architecture* (1707) announces that Gothic was 'a certain Fantastical and Licentious style of building

The underside of the fan vaulting at King's College Chapel.

... [a] congestion of Heavy, Dark and *Monkish Piles*, without any just proportion, Use or Beauty compar'd with the truly *Antient*.' Personally I'm rather a fan (pun intended) of fantastical and licentious monkish piles, particularly where they entail fan vaults. They are named after the fan shape made of ribs organised radially. Often these ribs were masterfully cut from the same

Centuries-old graffiti in the window
of the space above King's Chapel ceiling

stone as their webs, meaning that the entire vault is a single-surface web of spidery, interlocking tracery. Originally the ribs had a structural function, helping to hold up the building, but by the time the ceiling went up in King's College Chapel, the ribs were nothing but decorative texture and elaborate pattern.[24]

If you're ever lucky enough to hear a concert or evensong in the chapel, I urge you to look up and try this optical experience for yourself. Quite how the visual of this intricate surface amplifies the way I hear music is a mystery to me. But on an acoustic level it's not so mysterious: Gothic tracery is now known to assist the resonance of music, and particularly the sacred music designed for the spaces of chapels and cathedrals of this period.

If you've ever been in a cathedral built in the Gothic style, you will almost certainly have noticed the incredible acoustics of these spaces: any word you utter ricocheting back at you. If you've sung in such a space, you might also have experienced how disconcerting they can be – sometimes the resonance of the stone and space is such that you can barely hear yourself at all, and have to trust that you are balancing the sound right. In the best cases, though, it's like singing in the shower times a thousand: a blossoming reverberation of pure, curated noise, rich and smooth as aural brandy. The music of the period – by composers like Guillaume Du Fay, Josquin des Prez, John Dunstable, Robert Fayrfax and Robert Wylkynson – is written to be heavily line-driven, with interlacing melodic lines that wrap around each other, rather than clearly discernible harmonies. It is perfect for such spaces that allow the overlap of resonating tones.

This is a music venue that is still used for the purpose that it was built for, centuries ago. Barring disaster, it will be standing many years after you and I are dead, whether still inhabited by humans or reclaimed by the slow creep of nature. It calls back, across the centuries, to the other cavernous spaces – Font-de-Gaume, Les Eyzies, Lascaux – and stakes its claim of timelessness. For many people, the sight of a boy chorister illuminated by a single, wavering candle in its interior is the signal that Christmas Proper has begun. On YouTube or the BBC there it is, every Christmas Eve. This annual broadcast has made King's famous. But in a town of so many choirs, it's a bit of an open secret: yes, musically, it's good, but there's another chapel choir that, by a consistent hair's breadth, produces a better sound. That accolade goes to St John's College Chapel Choir, who sing in a lovely but rather more homely Victorian number.* King's, on the other hand, has the full package. There's no doubt that the architecture of the chapel itself is doing a lot of the heavy lifting in its musical fame: a gorgeous masterpiece of a building that would beautify whatever happened within its walls.

So much has been absorbed into those stones, along with all those centuries of graffiti. Wastell couldn't possibly have known, when the final block of the fan vaulting was lowered into place, the sheer variety of purposes the space would be put to: from a training ground for military exercises under Cromwell's New Model Army during the Civil War, to a twenty-first-century silent disco filled with the drone of hundreds of people singing along, often tunelessly, to three different channels of music pumped out through their lollipop-coloured headphones. That fan vault would also go on to inspire the curling lines of the Cambridge Central Mosque in 2019, constructed to glorify a different manifestation of the Abrahamic God. In very little time these musical spaces become living, breathing entities of their own; we cannot control how a venue will be imagined or used, or what it will come to symbolise.

One painter revelled in the mercurial knottiness of musical spaces, and his favourite stage came to define his entire oeuvre. The impressionist Edgar Degas was fascinated, throughout his life, by what it meant to depict music. He would come to find his ideal subject when he eventually insinuated his way backstage at the Paris Opéra, first at the Salle Le Peletier and then, after

---

* By one of those odd coincidences that life seems to abound in, the organ that now occupies pride of place in St John's College Chapel was moved six years ago from the church where my school carol concerts were held.

that venue's destruction in a fire started by its trailblazing gas lighting, at the Palais Garnier where it remains to this day.

Many years after Le Peletier went up in flames, elements of its architecture would return, ghostly, in Degas' paintings. As his eyesight slowly deteriorated, bringing about his characteristic loose, impressionistic renderings, he delighted in showing unusual perspectives of these venues – the rehearsal rooms, the view from the wings (as we have already seen from *Dancers, Pink and Green*) and other contorted backstage perspectives – beyond what could be viewed as a member of the audience. Musical spaces dynamised his art, allowing him to challenge his viewers to rethink what it meant to see.

Throughout his career, Degas revealed the stage as a space that is simultaneously familiar and eerily uncanny. Exposing its workings, the forms of the dancers and musicians draw our eyes in unexpected ways. They are the physical, intellectual effort that goes into the performance, as well as the polished product that the audience sees. Some paintings (such as *The Ballet from 'Robert le Diable'*, painted in 1871–2 and 1876, and *Blue Dancer with Double Bass*, 1891) depict the image of ballet on the stage pierced by the oblique upright necks of double basses or the bodies of bassoons, as though viewing straight from the belly of the stalls at the edge of the orchestra pit. In *Orchestra Musicians* (1870) the orchestra takes up the entire bottom half of the canvas, large chunks of black and the chestnut of the string instruments in comparison with the gauzy swoops of green, white and pink in the top half. The idea of the stage – specifically of the Paris Opéra, but also of the stage in general – was intensely inspiring for Degas. Each of these paintings is an experiment in perspective that challenges us, even today, to focus on what it means to be seeing music in such a venue.

My favourite example takes this a step further (see plate section). It dates from 1879, and is on a black silk background that Degas has left visible across large swathes of its surface. Its fragmentary design is painted in monochrome watercolour with highlights of luminous silver powders and thin washes of tin- and gold-tinted brass powder. The pearly lustre resembles East Asian lacquerware and its Western imitation, Japanning; the glints of silvery and golden tones specifically recall a kind made in China by layering sheets of gold and silver foil beneath the lacquer in a technique known as *jinyin pingtuo* or 金銀平脫.[25]

All in all, it is a shimmering masterpiece. The metallic tones mean that the composition constantly appears to move, as different elements catch the light, flaring briefly with lustre and shifting to the next glowing golden form. A classic Degas, ballet dancers are the theme. This time, though, it takes its visual perspective from the flies, that is, the upper part of backstage where stage crew can hoist or 'fly' scenery and stage effects through a system of pulleys, ropes and counterweights. The effect is of a bird's-eye view, over the billowy clouds that now resolve from abstract forms into the shape of hanging scenery. The floor of the stage takes up the entire left-hand side of the image, punctuated only by a sprinkling of silver powder to imitate the shimmer of the stage lights.

Degas was heavily influenced by the Japanese artist Watanabe Shōtei, who had arrived in Paris for the International Exhibition in 1878, one of the first Japanese artists to visit the West.[26] Shōtei caused quite a stir, and Degas had seen him doing a demonstration of his painting technique at the exhibition. Here, the hazy, light touch of dripped ink, stains and delicate blurs echoes Shōtei's approach.[27] There's that cluster of figures at the centre, picked out in a stunningly restrained few golden filigree lines, blurred as though by accident: visible only as you move around the image, allowing the metallic paint to crystallise with the light. Some say they are audience members. To me, they look more like the corps de ballet that often stand on the sidelines of the stage during set pieces: yet more watchers.

But by telling you about its composition, I'm doing this strange little painting a disservice. It is tempting to see art objects as static things that hang on walls, stand in corners, are looked at, and that is that. Many, though, were designed with a practical purpose, to the extent that the division between what we might think of as the decorative arts and the fine arts is tissue-thin. And this object is about seeing music down to its very core and function.

You might have noticed that it's a slightly odd shape – in fact it resembles nothing so much as a fan. That's because it is, and it could have been very simply adapted to be fully functional as one. Fans as an art form were all the rage among impressionist painters like Degas, another part of the mania for an orientalist aesthetic.[28] Some were simply mounted. This is what the painter Mary Cassatt did with hers, in some ways the twin of the Degas fan. Sometimes they were carried around, taken to fashionable gatherings, used to flirt and cool oneself. Cassatt's *Woman in a Loge* (c. 1879) depicts an *à la mode* Parisian showing us how it's done: she sits in the theatre, brandishing the fan fully splayed so that its golden metallic highlights become the centre of the composition.

If we substitute Degas' silken black and gold fan into the place of the one in Cassatt's painting, this suddenly becomes a play on visibility: the watching of a ballet (a visualisation of music) from a perspective it is not designed for, translated onto the fan of a watcher of ballet, displayed prominently for all other surrounding watchers. Degas was at pains to emphasise this context: he painted the fold lines to create the illusion that the fan had been used before it ever left his studio, raising up the composition on what appear to have been the struts of a fan and dribbling the paint into its pleats.[29] The pearlescent sheen of its silver powders and tin and brass wash are perfectly designed to be visible in the low lighting of the audience during a show at the theatre. As its owner fanned themselves, it would have flashed, capturing the eye with every powdery pinprick of starlight. This fan was designed to be seen at a musical event: a musical event at which the perspective it presents is essentially unseeable and made visible only through the artistry of its creator. It is a symphony of seeing.

Inspired by a physical performance venue, Degas has transmogrified an elegant accessory into a stage in itself, delighting in the changes that the slightest shift in viewing angle or context can make to a musical space.

𝄞

The fundamental capriciousness of a space made musical is a conundrum that has reoccurred throughout history, and that particularly afflicted our next example.

Deep in the Amazon, Antonio Jose Fernandes Júnior has had an idea. He will create his own 'jewel' in the heart of this rainforest: the Teatro Amazonas, an opera house for the city of Manaus. It will be a beacon of civilisation and will establish the city of Manaus as a hub of arts and culture. There's only one problem. Júnior's money, and that of his compatriots in the Manaus House of Representatives that year of 1881, is pretty filthy.

The thirst for rubber has not abated since Christopher Columbus first brought a fascinating bouncy ball – one of those used by the indigenous Olmec people to play the Mesoamerican ball-game variously known as *pitz* (in Classical Maya) and *ōllamaliztli* (in Aztec) – back to Europe. Now, with the industrial revolution and the need for flexible but durable elements in machinery, the appetite is greater than ever. Júnior is a rubber baron, and his fortune comes from trees: vast rubber plantations from cleared areas of the Amazon.

But the rubber boom in the second half of the 1800s brought with it a labour shortage. The rubber barons looked north, to how their friends in sugar, cotton and indigo had managed, and rather than actually trying to hire people for their work, they took a leaf out of their book. They introduced the concept of 'slave raids', in which teams were sent out to capture and enslave vast swathes of the indigenous population of Brazil, Bolivia, Colombia, Ecuador, Peru and Venezuela, who were then forced to tap the rubber under threat of death.³⁰ Tribe chiefs were used as examples: if they did not harvest enough rubber, or if they refused to work, they were violently murdered. The brutality of these rubber plantations was such that in some places ninety per cent of the population was wiped out. What we now know as the Putumayo genocide was still going on in 1912, perpetrated by the Peruvian Amazon Company and facilitated by intermediary management comprising workers from Barbados, themselves often the descendants of freed slaves: the rubber barons had also learned the 'divide and conquer' maxim.

Interior of the Teatro Amazonas.

We cannot separate the money and the culture and even the very idea of the Teatro Amazonas from the barbarity of what made it possible. Júnior's push to establish a civilised hub of arts and culture was entirely at the expense of another civilisation, and a result of ethnocide.³¹

Initially the state legislature did not put forward enough money for what Júnior envisioned but, by the end of the following year, a larger budget was approved and construction began in earnest in 1884. The plans were designed by the Italian architect Celestial

Sacardim, and combine a heady mix of European architectural styles from across the previous three centuries – the baroque, the Renaissance, neoclassical – all crowned with a dome that looks as though it was stolen from sixteenth-century Persia, and which serves no structural use whatsoever. The dome was covered with 36,000 ceramic tiles, all decorated in the colours of the newly minted Brazilian flag.[32] Of all the things that might have caused controversy at the time, by all accounts it was the dome and its decoration that led to the most uproar, because people thought it was rather tasteless. Decoration inside was overseen by the artist Crispim do Amaral, including an ornately painted ceiling scene of nymphs and cherubs frolicking in the clouds, and a stage curtain depicting the goddess Iara at the meeting of the waters. Finally, the dome and its sweeping external staircases were painted rose pink, making a blockily synthetic flower in the cityscape.

It looks like the Belle Époque on steroids and, looking at it, you might imagine you were in Paris, or Spain, or Italy or Portugal. Manaus became known, during this period, as the 'Paris of the Tropics' and 'Paris of the Jungle', and it's not hard to see why.[33]

Ceiling of the Teatro Amazonas.

What were these men actually trying to do? There is a considerable whiff of delusion about the entire Teatro Amazonas project. The simple idea that people would be willing to don full evening wear to attend the opera in a city so close to the equator, where temperatures frequently reached forty degrees Celsius with ninety per cent humidity, is laughable. Superimposing a gigantic image of another culture, from another climate, over such a space is unbelievably jarring. Even that title 'Amazon Theatre' carefully glosses over the fact that the land on which the theatre now stands was once covered in rainforest. It's a queasy inversion of all that our Cro-Magnon shaman did in establishing a place for music deep in nature.

Not long after the Teatro opened in 1896, the rubber trade in Brazil collapsed. Seeds from the rubber tree had been smuggled out of the country and shipped off to Europe and in turn to South-East Asia, where aspiring rubber barons established plantations of their own. The Brazilian rubber monopoly was over, and the market disintegrated. The Teatro Amazonas fell into disrepair and disuse, closing in 1924. Those pink walls were painted blue, and then grey, and then returned to their original hue. Although it reopened in 1990, it is marked by that first hubris; it was briefly forced to close again due to a scandal over accessibility, and didn't begin scheduling regular concerts until 1997, a century after its doors first opened.

That's not to say that the Teatro Amazonas didn't achieve some good. It launched the career of Carlos Gomes, the first New World composer to garner attention in Europe; a bust of the composer and a painting of his opera *Il Guarany* adorn the ballroom today. It is now an exciting and dynamic music venue with a diverse programme (and fully accessible!). But its successes and its failures can tell us a lot about what we collectively expect from a music venue, and where this chafes against reality.

Music venues all over the world are littered with small architectural failures: for example, the 'mushrooms' or fibreglass acoustic diffusers that had to be installed in the Royal Albert Hall in London to combat the echo produced by its ceiling coving; and the last-minute switch of the auditorium and the concert hall in the Sydney Opera House to fit within the famous sails, which resulted in an oddly dead acoustic in both spaces. The Teatro Amazonas, on the other hand, broadly works as a performance space, and it's undeniably beautiful. But its beauty was, first and foremost, funded by the destruction of a people and their environment, and its beauty was intended for the entertainment of a tiny, moneyed minority at the expense of much else. No matter how transcendental a musical performance within its walls might be, it cannot be separated from the violence that was part of its creation.

Some musical venues sit empty and unused for decades, seemingly dislocated from the performances that should have been staged there. And then there are venues that, even many years after their ephemeral parts have been dispersed, destroyed and repurposed, continue to enchant, infused with the essence of productions long past.

Another show is about to start. Here, in the wings, lingers a man, his face intent, watching carefully, quietly. He is Serge Diaghilev, art critic, patron and general impresario. He is also the founder of the Ballets Russes, the dance company that would go on to change the course of theatre. Born in Selishchi, south-west of St Petersburg, Diaghilev *loved* music. He composed as a child and as a young man; at the St Petersburg Imperial University he studied music with the composer Nikolai Rimsky-Korsakov. But during his university years he realised he'd overlooked his true passion: art. In his twenties he put on a series of exhibitions of contemporary artists: British and German watercolourists, Russian and Finnish artists, Russians at work in Germany. He set up a magazine, *Mir iskusstva* (*Мир искусства* or *World of Art*), with his friends, and turned his eyes abroad. Not only would he raise awareness of contemporary art in Russia itself, he would also promote Russian art throughout the rest of Europe. In 1906 he organised a twelve-room exposition of Russian art and sculpture at the prestigious Salon d'Automne exhibition in Paris. France was rapt. What *would* this guy do next? But all the while, music, that early, fiery love of his, had been bubbling away at the back of his brain. Russian music – that was what Europe needed.

Something else had been bubbling away, too, closer to home. Increasing numbers of the Russian population were unhappy with the way that Tsar Nicholas II was running things. At the time a huge number of indentured workers, known as serfs, worked on the land in terrible conditions. Although reforms during the previous tsar's reign meant that the serfs were no longer 'owned' by the landowners on whose property they lived and worked, they earned very little money and had few rights. Despite the huge ethnic diversity across Russia, a policy of Russification was in place, meaning that other national minorities did not, for example, have the right to vote.

In January 1905, things came to a head: the tsar's soldiers opened fire on a crowd of protesting workers, led by the controversial Russian Orthodox priest Georgy Gapon. Between 200 and 1,000 people were killed. Mass strikes ensued, with around half of European Russians and a whopping 93.2 per cent in Russian-held Poland participating. Things briefly simmered down when the tsar agreed to the founding of a Duma, a parliament subcommittee with extra powers of governance; but he had inadvertently set in motion a series of actions that would result in his own execution, the murder of his wife and children, and the end of the Romanov dynasty (not to mention the turbulence in Russian politics and expansionism that continues more than a century later). For Diaghilev, whose major patrons were the tsar's first cousin and aunt, things were tricky to say the least. He wanted to show Europe the beautiful aspects of Russian culture, while

Russia itself was imploding in slow motion. More dangerous was the fact of his sexuality: despite homosexuality being illegal in Russia at the time, he was openly and comfortably gay, having had relationships with his star dancer Nijinsky and Prince Lvov, his aristocratic patron.[34]

Fortunately, Misia Sert, professional pianist and friend of Coco Chanel, stepped in and offered her rather substantial financial assistance to handily require Diaghilev's presence outside of Russia. Together they rented the Théâtre de Châtelet in Paris in 1909, putting on the very first season of the Ballets Russes, and the rest is history.

Despite that early foray into composition, Diaghilev wasn't a creator himself. He was an organiser. His great skill lay in bringing together artists, dancers, musicians and patrons to combine their work into an opulent whole; getting his collaborators (some of whom were notoriously tempestuous) to compromise, and to work together in a way that allowed no single aspect of the art form to take centre stage. Diaghilev wasn't the one who came up with the idea for productions like the cubist ballet *Parade* (1917). It seems to have been dreamed up by the surrealist Jean Cocteau and the composer Erik Satie. But Diaghilev was brought in to hold everything together and manage the delicate balance between Léonide Massine creating the choreography, Misia Sert stumping up the money and Pablo Picasso designing costumes that transformed dancers into skyscrapers, boulevards and a 'Chinese' conjuror.

By all accounts, though, Diaghilev wasn't especially interested in ballet. 'Anyone with no special wit can enjoy it,' he is recorded as saying; 'there is no sense of subject in ballet.' But what ballet offered was the chance to experiment with the symbiosis of music and art, his twin passions. For the next two decades, he would commission the most avant garde of composers to write the scores, and artists to design the sets and costumes for the Ballets Russes. This rotating firmament included Chanel, Henri

Natalia Goncharova's costume for the eponymous golden chicken in *Le Coq D'Or*. Wikimedia. Public Domain.

Matisse, Pablo Picasso, Laura Knight, Georges Braque, Sonia and Robert Delaunay and Jean Cocteau, with the artists Léon Bakst and Natalia Goncharova as regular, scintillating fixtures who would repeatedly contribute to the visual splendour of this theatrical powerhouse.

Securing Goncharova in particular was quite a coup. In 1913 she was hailed as the 'leader of the futurists' in Russia.[35] She was a giant of the avant-garde art scene who had already exhibited a full retrospective of her work including paintings, works on paper, designs for theatre, costume, fashion, textiles and wallpaper. Bakst, a Jewish-Russian artist who began as a painter of portraits and watercolours, had been responsible for the graphics in the magazine Мир искусства, and so was an old stalwart of Diaghilev's.

Together, they produced something remarkable. It was a crucible of intense creativity. Each of these figures worked at the cutting edge of their respective art forms, expanding accepted ideas about what could be done with clothing, costume, pattern, colour and perspective. Ballet required ingenious ways of cutting costumes so that they moved with the dancer; parts of the body needed to be exposed and free to move, and so what dancers wore needed to take different shapes and forms. The movement of the costumes would amplify the choreography, which was, in turn, evolving to complement the new styles of music. The dance would be a visualisation of music, one that picked out melodic phrases and textures and echoed them in movements encased by fabric, paint and sequins.

Dance is an art form, too, that has impacted my own life. One of the key *répétiteurs* – dance instructors – of the Ballets Russes was Enrico Cecchetti, an Italian choreographer, dancer and founder of the Cecchetti method of ballet. Retired dancers from the Ballets Russes would go on to disseminate his method throughout the world, including Ninette de Valois (founder of the Royal Ballet), Marie Rambert (founder of the Rambert Ballet School and Company), Alicia Markova (founder of American Ballet Theatre and the English National Ballet), the choreographer George Balanchine and the dancers who would go on to train both of my maternal grandparents before they joined the Borovansky Jubilee Ballet Company, later renamed the Australian Ballet. It was the dance style that I and my siblings would go on to learn as children. The strength of ballet training goes quickly, but the shapes linger. It's no exaggeration to say that the Ballets Russes haunts my every step and movement, sculpting almost every gesture and mannerism I have.

Diaghilev's approach to the marriage of art and music in ballet – and more than anything else, his decisions on whom to commission – transformed what music looked and sounded like.[36] Suddenly it was possible to be entirely experimental, to transform conventional theatre venues into spaces that resembled living artworks. The backdrops and stage curtains vacillated from cartoonishly luscious to impressionistically daubed. The compositions of Erik Satie, Sergei Prokofiev, Igor Stravinsky and Francis Poulenc provided the sound world of these spaces. Settings ranged from under the sea, in 1916's *Sadko*, to the towering interior of an Eastern Orthodox church in the never-finished, never-staged *La Liturgie* (1915), rendered in stylised fashion by Goncharova.

It was intensely whimsical, and the world in turn went wild for it. Soon enough it was inspiring new trends in fashion and interior design: all things Ballets Russes, in bright patchwork silk. All of the productions packaged up Russian culture as an exotic entity in a manner that appealed to the Parisian obsession with orientalism, yes. But Diaghilev and friends managed something that the tsar had failed to achieve: a coherent yet diverse picture of what it meant to be ethnically Russian, part of a country that stretched from the Baltic Sea to the borders with Japan, Korea, China, Mongolia and the historical countries of Persia and Turkestan.

Sadko and *La Liturgie* have to be my favourites for their sheer audacity. *La Liturgie* was a balletic reimagining of the life of Jesus from birth to crucifixion, taking the Gospels of the New Testament as its source material. It would be choreographed and designed in a style inspired by Futurism, the Russo-Italian art movement that revered modernity and technical innovation, thrumming engines and industrial machinery. The Futurist paintings of artists like Goncharova, Benedetta Capa and her husband Filippo Marinetti are angular and blocky, mosaics of opulently coloured segments combined into urban scenes and aeroplanes and locomotives in motion. You would have thought such an aesthetic would have been jarringly incongruous with a ballet staged in a Russian Orthodox church, but surviving accounts suggest that the concept, even if only in planning, was met with enthusiasm.

Ensemble of sea creatures for the Ballets Russes' production of *Sadko*, 1916.

As for *Sadko* – its plot following the eponymous hero as he is drowned by the Sea Princess and taken to an enchanted underwater kingdom presided over by the Sea Tsar – I'm frankly stunned the idea didn't catch on. Only its jewel-toned costumes survive, but photographic evidence (like the image above) suggests that its sets were also cartoonishly sequined, graphically inspired by new ideas about form and colour to be found not just in Goncharova's paintings but also in those of her cubist contemporaries Marc Chagall, Georges Braque and Marie Laurencin. *Sadko*, like *La Liturgie*, didn't endure as a production; it premiered in New York and went through only a few performances at the Manhattan Opera House before being laid to rest.

This philosophy – let's produce beautiful things, use them five times or perhaps not at all, and then move on – might seem stunningly profligate. But that's to impose a very different, and I would argue impoverished, view of what it means to put on a musical production to the one held by Diaghilev and the Ballets Russes. For them, each production was an experiment. Money wasn't the goal. It didn't matter if a production failed to make a profit or was met with lukewarm reviews, because each one was part of the cumulative effort that moved the whole art form towards greatness. Today, if a production fails to bring in money, that approach is cut short. I like Diaghilev's way better: more optimistic, more brave, altogether more adventurous. Music, in all its manifestations, benefits from being ushered gently into the world, not judged too harshly on its first profits. It was true in the first decades of the twentieth century, and it holds true today. Creating sequel after sequel of financially successful formulas doesn't encourage creativity or interesting musical expression.

The Ballets Russes certainly succeeded in cultivating ground-breaking musical expression. Before they burst onto the scene, ballet music had become rather predictable and uninspired. Endless variations on the works of Richard Wagner were the order of the day. Wagner constructed his music with cells of melody to 'represent' certain characters or moods, which he constantly modified and regurgitated. It was an episodic way of writing, which has its place, but was overused to the point of being stultifying. Recycled pieces, or structures of pieces, resulted in repetition of potential visual interpretations into dance: a limited sound palette led to a limited approach to steps, forms and movements.

By commissioning pioneering composers, Diaghilev opened the floodgates to different ways of entwining music with art. Claude Debussy's reimagining of the musical canvas as a space where lingering, sinuous lines of chromaticism (broadly, notes outside the key or scale a piece is composed in) could unfurl without the thumping high drama of Wagnerian motifs gave birth to an explosion of musical creativity by his younger contemporaries Satie, Maurice Ravel, Stravinsky, Prokofiev, Shostakovich and my own guilty favourite, Poulenc. These composers pushed the limits of what music could do: its harmonic language, how it could tell stories, and how it could offer up opportunities for new styles of visualising music. Without their work, we wouldn't have such radical and varied ideas about how to showcase musical colour – the individual tones and texture of each instrument – and dissonance, ideas that have pervaded from classical music into jazz, pop, funk, rock, metal, 1980s synth and beyond. That means no meandering opening riff to The Who's 'Baba O'Riley', no shifting semitones in Billie Eilish's masterful 'Bad Guy', none of the synth beats of dubstep.

Diaghilev is buried on the cemetery island of Isola di San Michele in Venice, his plot not too far from Stravinsky's. When I visited it in the summer of 2015, his grave was still covered in weather-beaten, grizzled pointe shoes, their ribbons tied around the pilasters of his marble monument: generations upon generations of ballet dancers still coming to pay their respects to the great maestro almost ninety years after his untimely death. Diaghilev set the stage in a way that catalysed some truly explosive interactions between the visual and the musical. He and the Ballets Russes, and their motley crew of designers, composers, costumiers and cheerleaders, pushed the boundaries of what staging music could look like. Often, they came up against the limits of possibility; sometimes this happened when they were already deep into the planning process. It didn't matter. They'd learnt things about artistic expression, about what worked in the meshing of art and music and what didn't. They had moved closer to understanding the intricacies of their art form, and that in itself was enriching.

𝄞

Some venues are planned to be entirely ephemeral: one-time, one-chance productions, like so many of Diaghilev's. But these spaces have a way of taking on lives of their own, and in some cases, they endure far beyond their original brief scope and context.

Wind blusters around the headland, wafting the scent of crushed bracken and mingling it with the aroma of seaweed, buttery gorse flowers and salty air. Waves thunder somewhere below the edge, just out of sight. The year is 1932; it is late summer. A woman named Rowena Cade and a group of players from her tiny Cornish village are putting on their long-planned production of one of William Shakespeare's late (and most musical) plays, *The Tempest*. Their production will be in a rocky gully on the granite outcrop overlooking the sea that forms part of Cade's garden: it will be performed against the backdrop of those restless waves, alternately slate blue and turquoise. The Minack Theatre is born, in a space where all seems on the verge of 'melt[ing] into air', the 'baseless fabric of this vision' whisked away by the buffeting wind, leaving 'not a rack behind'. It is a venue made of sky, sea and stars.

The press were enchanted. 'Standing lightly on a rock above the blue waters of the Atlantic, there is Ariel,' the *Cornishman* newspaper reported, 'singing her beautiful little lyric to a melody that steals upon the ear and makes one think one has stepped like Alice, through a looking glass, and stumbled upon some island inhabited by fairies and pixies.' There was also, hypnotically, a full moon on opening night. *The Times* also sent a reviewer, who pondered that, 'short of securing an island and wrecking a ship on its coast, there could be no more ideal setting for *The Tempest* than the cliffs a few miles from Land's End.'

The edge of the stage at the Minack Theatre, complete with Rowena Cade's designs carved into the concrete.

The name 'Minack' comes from the Cornish *meynek*, a rocky place. Visit it now, on what you hope might be a clear, dry day (and which might miraculously end up being so, despite the lingering mizzle one bay over, such is the fundamental whimsy of the Cornish climate), and you'll see for yourself. The sheer labour that went into its construction is mind-boggling. Cade herself, along with her poor gardeners, Billy Rawlings and Charles Angove (what on earth did they think they'd signed up for, when they applied for the job?), dragged much of the material that went into its making up or along the cliff face to her precipitous garden. Rather charmingly, she describes Rawlings as cutting up the boulders 'by hand, much as the English cut butter'.[37] She decorated the place herself, too, carving the names of past performances and the patterns of intricate Celtic knotwork into the drying concrete with a screwdriver. Well into her eighties, she could still be found pottering about the site, hauling bags of sand and, on one occasion, twelve fifteen-foot shipwrecked beams up the cliff, keeping her precious Minack spick and span.

Performances at the Minack take place whatever the weather. Rain, hail, blistering sun or a moderate gale are all part of the atmosphere and the show that is being performed. Legend has it that during that first, foggy 1932 performance, a barque* crashed into the rocks that cascaded down behind the stage. The fate of the barque – did it sink? Did anyone call the coastguard? Or did it only briefly founder and then sail merrily away again? – remains unknown, if indicative of what the general atmosphere of performances is like. Bring an umbrella, suncream, a walkie talkie, a torch, a raincoat and a thick jumper: you need to be prepared.

Before she embarked on building the Minack with Rawlings and Angove, Cade had not done a single day of manual labour in her entire life. She was no architect, builder or set designer; up until 1931, her only experience lay in making some costumes for amateur dramatic societies. Nor would building theatres go on to be her career: she had the Minack, and the Minack had her. It was her life's passion. She was born into a relatively privileged family in Derbyshire in 1893 and had been raised to be a respectable lady. Her move to Cornwall, along with her mother, was precipitated in part by the death of her father, and partly by the aftermath of the First World War. The site cost the two women the ridiculously low sum of £100 – just under £5,000 in today's money. She was soon joined by her sister Katharine, along with Katharine's two small daughters. From the Minack headland, Katharine wrote dystopian and utopian fiction, reimaginings of the world without restrictive gender norms.[38]

---

* A small boat.

It's a beguiling image. Two sisters, at the very edge of land and sky, creating worlds – one from words, one out of enormous chunks of granite, elaborate designs etched into concrete, and the spoils of shipwreck. The two sisters and their mother lived on their beloved Minack headland for much of the rest of their lives, writing and building and summoning out of nothing, with a monumental theatre at the cliff edge at the bottom of their garden.

We are back where we began: spaces crafted from rock, and the scantiest of makeshift shelters from the elements. The Minack, like Font-de-Gaume and Lascaux and that theatre of haybales in the Dóm Tér in Szeged, is a musical space that *works*. These spaces recognise the power that comes from the fragility of performing in such spaces, and how that ephemerality can be a crucial part of the enchantment of the experience of music. The Ballets Russes left us only designs, costumes, pieces of set, but no full trappings of a single ballet – we cannot judge whether the settings of their productions would still work as musical spaces, but we know that they altered the way that music was composed and dance was choreographed, and what performances could look like, forever.

Plenty of people have striven for the same goals as the Ballets Russes with varying degrees of success, but perhaps their closest descendants working today are the Berlin-based 1781 Collective. Founded in 2018, their self-described mission is 'to reclaim music' by 'exploring new listening and performance methods' and to 'offer an alternative to the traditional music industry for both audiences and creators'.[39] Their *LABYRINTH: The Cabinet of Curiosities* festival is structured around ten rooms, which the audience can wander between. Ten audience members are allowed in each room at any given time, and the performances switch every ten minutes. The 1781 Collective is named after the year that Mozart left his role as court organist for Count Hieronymus Colloredo, Archbishop of Salzburg. Sick of the controlling and limited traditional system, Mozart set out for a life of freelance composition and performance, producing many of the works that we know and love today. And the Collective's philosophy is simple, as their founder Chris Lloyd states it:

> The music's not boring. The context of a traditional setting is boring, and therefore people don't want to engage in it. The traditional classical music industry has always gone on about how they need to attract new young people, but they actually don't want new young people. They want new young people to come to their concerts and experience it like they're old people.[40]

Not so much bums on seats as incinerate the seats and see how the performance looks from a trapeze. It's an ethos that resonates with me. I've been back to Glyndebourne several times since I was on stage there; like several venues in the UK, it's part of the '£30 under 30 scheme', so when I was younger it was astonishingly cheap. But on these visits, I've frequently been met with the assumption from fellow audience members and stewards that this must – *must* – be my first time there; there is a belief that someone like me couldn't possibly belong there. The decision over who is permitted to occupy musical spaces has always been policed, but – bourgeois though he most certainly was – Diaghilev would likely be spinning in his grave that this still holds true in the twenty-first century. The Ballets Russes and the 1781 Collective show us another way: musical performances staged explicitly as invitations to allow audiences to make their own meanings, to interact with the music both physically and mentally as best suits them, not just sitting through two-hour recitals but dancing, lying down, moving in between pieces, choosing their own sequence of music.

Music venues, whether they are carved into the cliffside above a roiling ocean, deep underground or a skewed reimagining of fairytale spaces, are always about escapism. However, the balance between this otherworldliness and the denial of context is delicate. The Teatro Amazonas shows us that it's all too easy for a music venue to go too far in removing itself from the environment that has created it. It was intended to be the 'jewel' of the Amazon, and there it stands to this day, created by the spoils of enforced labour and the destruction of rainforest. I don't believe that this should prevent us from enjoying the rather zany beauty of the theatre, or the musical performances that it commissions and hosts. But it's important that we are fully aware of the history of such spaces, so we can construct a better, cleaner legacy for their future.

Spaces like the Minack, Font-de-Gaume and Marsoulas pull off this high-wire act. They create a landscape apart from the everyday world, and allow the sound to transport us there. The experience can be extraordinary: we emerge, blinking, as though from darkness into bright sunlight. I've seen it from the other side. When an audience is truly immersed in your performance, they don't clap when it finishes – not at first. Instead, there is a dazed, astounded silence, a collective sense of breath held, as though the music has briefly suspended the need for oxygen.

A venue is only one ingredient in the recipe that makes music radical or conventional – but it has a way of laying bare any absurdities. Sooner or later, the look of a place insinuates itself into the musical meaning. Seeping through the cracks and gaps, the dead space of waiting for a performance to begin, when your attention drifts as you listen, suddenly, there it is: the visual appearance of these spaces, amalgamating with the sound and transforming, suddenly, into another world entirely.

2

Feather on the Breath of God:
Writing the Notes

Four pairs of sloe-black, haughty eyes glare out at us with not a little belligerence. God, this is so boring. Mum, why are you making us do this? Four sullen adolescent faces, suspiciously examining each and every one of our flaws and finding us wanting. Each expression has a slightly different flavour: contempt, disparagement, superciliousness. The middle boy is uneasy and secretly desperate to please, to contain the imminent insurrection brewing in his sister's face – but the overriding thought in this sibling hive mind is clear. Insolence comes off the canvas in waves. To me they look like nothing so much as the sixteenth-century version of the noughties emo/pop-punk band My Chemical Romance, the picture of teenage disaffection.

The two eldest boys are nonchalantly holding a pair of books. One is scrawled with musical notes, visible even upside down; as you move closer to the canvas it becomes clear that you can read them. This music book, in fact, has an entirely recognisable piece of music in it. Its presence in this painting will change how people think about English musical culture, and how music travelled.[1]

The other book looks – *looks* – as though it contains notes. But when you look closely at this one, you see that these marks are nothing but a clever pattern of swoops and dots: an impression of music notation.

Curled in a window seat of the wood-panelled library of my college, I lean back from the screen of my laptop. It gradually dawns on me that I have been holding my breath – that this painting has momentarily sucked the air out of my lungs. I am a few months into my PhD, and the process of trying to narrow down what I want to explore is overwhelming. At this stage in my research career, where every figure and idea emits a seductive, overwhelming tug (focus on *me* – no, *just* on me, all 80,000 words, *me*), this is the image that slices through the noise and refines my consciousness and my planning like a whetstone. Think you know what you're looking at, it taunts, think you know how notation works? Music – and the graphic marks we call writing – will never look the same again.

Behold, the painting now known as *Four Children Making Music*. We know little about its creator, the artist enigmatically known as the Master of the Countess of Warwick. Even their gender is up for debate.[2] What is clear, though, is that they did something radical in this painting: they transformed a vanilla portrait of four disaffected siblings into an optical trick, a masterful undermining of the idea of visual symbols for music.

Master of the Countess of Warwick,
Four Children Making Music, c. 1565.

From a distance, the scrawls in the music books are nothing but an interlacing pattern that echoes the embroidery on the girl's sleeves and the filigree of the feather in the youngest boy's cap. It's not clear that the notations are different: that in one book they are entirely legible, while in the other they are a pastiche of legibility.

It's a visual ruse that lays bare the paradox at the heart of the very idea of musical notes, and, perhaps, of art itself. Musical notes are revealed as nothing but visual marks: scrawled symbols that have gained meaning only due to consensus built up over thousands of years. *Four Children Making Music* is, in a very real sense, a hymn to the arbitrariness – and beautiful, hard-won collaboration – that goes into the making of musical writing.

Musical notes are demanding: eye-, ear-, and imagination-snatching, flooding our brains with visual, aural and spatial information. But, as we shall see, they also have an uncanny propensity to play dead, in a way that stubbornly, actively refuses to be passive.

𝄞

When, how, where, does the metamorphosis from mark to musical note happen? What alchemy occurs to transform a graphic symbol into curated sound; a song; a symphony; a chorus?

Here is a brief story about how it might begin.

Let us imagine, for the sake of argument, that you are five years old. The year is 2013, and your entire world is about to be turned upside down by a song. The riff of four simple piano chords has been seared, glittering, into brains the world over.

Musically speaking they are a masterstroke. Most music written in the Western classical tradition follows certain expected patterns, with a set number of directions, moods and finishes as neat as tying the ends of a ribbon into a bow. Here, though, is a turbulent progression that refuses to settle harmonically, scorching itself into our memories as an instantly recognisable tune. You don't hear it as the journey from F minor to D-flat, to E-flat, to B-flat minor, though: to you it is fretful, restless.

The camera zooms in on a desolate, snowy mountainside, a single figure marching doggedly onwards, dragging her skirts. Snow flurries around her.

She's a princess, afflicted with a magical curse – and this time it is not sleep (inflicted by apples or spindles or otherwise), it is not a mermaid tail, it is not the terrifying animation of household objects: it is ice in her hands.

In the space of three minutes and thirty-eight seconds, that snow and ice will be harnessed by the power of the song, a manifestation of Elsa's power, as she constructs a frozen palace on the mountainside. The crystals that she shapes become a visualisation of her song.

They aren't musical notes – not quite. But they are the first step towards the idea that sound can become visual, an introduction to the concept that there is a way of making music into something we can see with our eyes.

For the rest of your childhood, as you trundle down the street after your parent or carer, as you ride your bike around the park, fly on the swings, bounce on your bed, this piece of music will be the words on your lips, like an enchanted amulet of comfort and promise, the theme tune to your youth. And so, safely equipped, you are off on your lifelong odyssey through all the ways that music can be visualised, and all the ways that art can sound.

Because this is more than a song. It is a way of seeing: it has its own shimmering visuals that teach you a lesson about what music looks like. You learn the other half of this lesson in school – the squiggly little lines and the dots that can be translated somehow into sound. This half, though, is never fully articulated, though you let it in and it becomes inscribed deep in your bones, in how you will listen and perform and dance and think about music for the rest of your life.

This piece of music, in case of doubt, is 'Let it Go' from the 2013 Disney animation *Frozen*, the film that launched a thousand rainy afternoons and the imaginations of small children and karaoke enthusiasts the world over. Previous generations had *Beauty and the Beast*, *Anastasia*, *The Prince of Egypt*; the marvellously camp *The Slipper and the Rose*; *The Sound of Music* and *Snow White*. But *Frozen* and its eighty-person animation team, led by Lino DiSalvo, Tony Smeed and Becky Bresee, have done something different. The film also, subtly, artfully, harnessed an ancient idea in sparkly new clothing.

Your ears might be bleeding by now, but – if you are one of those people who have been forced to listen to this song approximately three billion times by children, grandchildren, nieces, nephews, friends and the juggernaut that is twenty-first-century Disney – I want, briefly, to take you back to that first moment you experienced it. With fresh eyes and fresh ears, it's possible to appreciate the musical finesse that thrums through the way it was conceived, aurally and visually.[3]

At the heart of *Frozen* and its sequel, *Frozen II*, is the story of an indigenous culture – the Northuldra, loosely based on the Sámi, the original inhabitants of large swathes of Scandinavia including Sámpi or Lapland, Finland, Norway and Sweden. Scandinavian culture appears throughout both films – from the ancient art of *kulning*, a vocal technique or herding call that manipulates the voice to carry far into mountain pastures, to *rosemåling*, a form of decorative painting based on abstractions of floral shapes with C- and S-shaped curves, which became popular in the folk art of Sweden and Norway from about 1700 onwards. In 'Let it Go' and its musical sequel of sorts, 'Into the Unknown', Queen Elsa's first power ballad in *Frozen II*, the rosemåling becomes a way of marking ice and snow with Elsa's magic, showing it is magically formed. When first her sister, Anna, and then Elsa herself become frozen, they are covered with rosemåling-like snowflake patterns, the hallmark of the enchantment.

The rosemåling-snowflake is also, as both films progress, a way of visualising Elsa's music. 'Into the Unknown' closes as the wind spirit's melody, performed by the singer AURORA, crescendos on the note known in Western classical parlance as a C_6. This is vertiginously high, the top note professional sopranos are expected to be able to reach. As the wind spirit reaches this showstopper of a note, the night sky explodes into glittering diamonds of ice, each inscribed with rosemåling-like snowflake symbols signifying earth, fire, water, air. Elsa's song, her music, her magic, are all responsible for maintaining a kind of cosmic harmony between all living things. In *Frozen*, rosemåling patterns become ways of visualising music – separate phrases and separate notes, all in iridescent fireworks of ice.

Although they repurpose traditional artforms such as kulning and rosemåling, *Frozen* and *Frozen II* are packaged in a clean, computer-animated aesthetic geared directly for the early twenty-first-century eye. The way they portray the relationship between the visual and the musical, however, harnesses a desire that has resurged time and again, stretching back throughout history.

There are plenty of lavish examples of the ways that humanity has turned music into a visual art. But it is worth lingering on possibly the most boring: the musical note. You'd be forgiven for wondering if a note even really counts as a visual object. Almost everyone knows what a musical note looks like, yes. But really, what can there possibly be to learn about them? They are *dry*. They radiate a forbidding aura of highbrow complexity. They are intimidating to those who do not read them. To those who can read them, they are more or less transparent: you look at them, you transform them into the sound they represent, and they disappear. But, as this brief quest through some of their manifestations seeks to show you, they epitomise the ways that we have entangled the visual and the musical.

Duet

Here's one of the musical note's current manifestations. In British English it is known as the crotchet, from the French *crochet*, meaning to hook on, and, yes, etymologically related to the needlework technique that fashions art out of wool.* In US English, it's a quarter note (because it is quarter of the basic musical note of medieval tradition, the semibreve or whole note). If you've picked up this book, in all likelihood you are familiar with its bulbous bulge and the elegant flick of its tail. There are variations, of course, but this is the basic building block of written music. It can be hollowed; it can be elongated; it can be shorn of its tail, or its tail given extra flicks; it can be dotted, bisected.

All these details give the musical reader information about how to interpret it and turn it into sound. The Persian *koron* or کرن is one of my favourites – looking a little like a flag, it means to lower the pitch of a note by less than a semitone (if we're being strict, to flatten the note by roughly a quarter tone, or a half flat – but really it's up to you). But how did we arrive at *this* basic shape? This shape of all others? It seems utterly improbable.

To me they resemble tadpoles – I suspect because one of those first music workbooks I was given, back in the nineties, depicted crotchets as the aquatic larvae. Throughout history they have gone through many different forms, but it seems particularly fortuitous

---

* 'Crotchet' is also, rather delightfully, a synonym for an unfounded whimsy.

that they ended up like this: teardrops, or the lobe shape of a pear-cut jewel.

Whether or not you read music, it is likely that you recognise this, the basic beat of the four-time bar, the first note children tend to be introduced to. And in its current manifestation, it is, surprisingly, only about 200 years old.

Faced with the totemic force of the twenty-first-century crotchet, you could be forgiven for being slightly bewildered by its youth – who is this little whippersnapper with such pretentions to authority? But there have been more ways of visualising a basic musical unit – pitch, rhythm, general shape – than there are minutes in a day. Each of them had its moment in the sun and then fell out of use. A few have lived on, far past their expected lifetimes. Each of these manifestations offers an insight into our own embryonic musical and visual cultures; they show how our ancestors chose certain graphic shapes and forms, and ways of making music that we simply cannot hear any more, because we have lost the art of extrapolating their visual meaning into sound. The effect is disconcerting and somewhat daunting to someone like me who has invested so much of their life into deducing such traces: the past, whispering back, songs of all the things that it knows that you and I do not.

Notes are also not *just* about extending people's memories of a tune so it can be more easily reproduced. Among the many reasons that we have collectively reached for an image of music, the urge to record music in graphic forms so it can be shared, adapted and performed again and again is one of the most compelling. What this really boils down to is the attempt to fix sound into something tangible. Reaching back into human history to periods that have left nothing more than mysterious fragments, we have spun signs out of pure air, the sheer ungraspable matter of sound, to see what was once heard.

Sound, indisputably, came first.

Visualisations of music arrived in the chasm left by the fleeting nature of sound; our ancestors sought to pin it, any of it, down. And so came the serpentine lines, the dots, the dashes, the coils. We can't literally see the music we hear, but if we could, it would look like this line, dot, coil – went the reasoning, perhaps. Thousands of trials as people slowly invented ways of making music visible. These acts are indistinguishable from those of the painters, sculptors, weavers, goldsmiths and ceramic artists who attempted to represent the more tangible things in their art: the notes are just suggestions where other painted, sculpted marks are filled out into less abstract, less brief forms.

Musical notation came not from a single source, but in fits and starts all over the globe, hot on the heels of its older, more swaggering cousin: writing. Writing wasn't invented by a single culture, but fizzled onto the world stage independently from approximately eight main hotbeds, percolating out from these centres. It was created by the Sumerians in Mesopotamia in around 3300 BCE, Egypt around 3250 BCE, the people of the Indus valley in 2500 BCE, Crete and Greece in around 1400 BCE, China in 1200 BCE, the Phoenicians in around 1000 BCE, the Zapotec of Mexico in 600 BCE and the Mayans some time before 2500 BCE. All of these cultures shifted gradually from line drawings to abstract or pictographic forms, capable of conveying increasingly complex information. They all used a pointed implement known as a stylus to carve, paint or scratch a surface with its forms. Initially writing was about commerce and accounting, but soon became used for religion, government and law – all part of the intricate web of instruments needed for the maintenance of power. People didn't have to be able to read it in order to understand a considerable chunk of its meaning, and this was part of its sorcery: its power was tied to its visual appearance, its visual presence, and it was a language that all could understand.

Writing, it seemed, could do almost anything. Within the bewitching swirls of its properties, why shouldn't it preserve that most evanescent of things, music?

The threshold that divides word and picture is tissue-thin. The very earliest instances of musical notes, from Sumeria in ancient Mesopotamia, are enough to show us the truth of this enduring fact. We know, from the context of where these tablets once stood, that they were not intended to be used for performance. Instead, they were like enormous posters plastered on walls and monuments, advertising the intimidating might of the Sumerian government. Most people couldn't understand them: this kind of music notation wasn't designed to be read by the masses – but it was designed to be seen. There is also the tantalising evidence of the earliest surviving compositions by a named composer, the Sumerian princess and high priestess named Enheduanna. A crucial part of Enheduanna's role was to ascend to the top of the ziggurat in Ur and ceremonially exalt the gods in song.[4] In this hyper-visible position, she would have declaimed lyrics like those of her own 'Hymn to Inanna', goddess of love, fertility and war:

> In the van of battle, all is struck down before you.
> With your strength, my lady, teeth can crush flint.
> You charge forward like a charging storm.
> You roar with the roaring storm.
>
> You continually thunder with Ickur.
> You spread exhaustion with the stormwinds, while your own
>   feet remain tireless.
> With the lamenting *balaj* drum a lament is struck up.[5]

Faced with lyrics like this, it is clear: visualising music in Mesopotamia was a way of exercising power.[6]

In the history of music, Enheduanna's 'Hymn' offers us a cautionary tale about the nature of political power and its fundamental ephemerality. Almost 200 years after we began to rediscover the traces of this culture and its cuneiform script, we still have no fixed idea of how to interpret it. Performed versions of these compositions vary wildly to the extent that they are almost unrecognisable as being related. What the original music sounded like is anyone's guess.[7] Powerful as musical notes might be within an individual culture, it is not until a consensus on interpretation is reached that they can spread through time and space.

Tablet with Temple Hymn in cuneiform, c. 1800–1600 BCE.

Unfortunately for ancient Sumeria, and Enheduanna, the link between these visual signs and their specific meanings has been frayed and hangs by the flimsiest thread.

Feather on the Breath of God: Writing the Notes

The Seikilos epitaph, first/second century CE.

Another ancient example has fared better. This is the Seikilos epitaph, and it is the oldest complete song in the world. It was looted in 1883 from the ruins of the ancient Greco-Roman city of Tralles, in the hills above the modern city of Aydın in southwest Turkey, and it commemorates, in music, someone lost and loved. It was uncovered by a man named Edward Purser, tasked with building a railroad through the site. His wife was so taken with the column that she elected to take it back to England to serve as a flowerpot stand.[8] The base was a little wonky, though, so really there was nothing she could reasonably do other than have it sawn straight across, destroying a good proportion of the bottom line.* Mercifully, a copy was taken beforehand, so we do have the complete text. Here are the words:

---

*   It is uncertain if Mrs Purser ever wondered whether she should have, instead, commissioned a stand for the base, arguably a less destructive way to stop it from wobbling.

Duet

ΕΙΚΩΝ Η ΛΙΘΟΣ / ΕΙΜΙ · ΤΙΘΗΣΙ ΜΕ / ΣΕΙΚΙΛΟΣ ΕΝΘΑ / ΜΝΗΜΗΣ ΑΘΑΝΑΤΟΥ / ΣΗΜΑ ΠΟΛΥΧΡΟΝΙΟΝ // ΟΣΟΝ ΖΗΣ ΦΑΙΝΟΥ / ΜΗΔΕΝ ΟΛΩΣ ΣΥ / ΛΥΠΟΥ ΠΡΟΣ ΟΛΙ / ΓΟΝ ΕΣΤΙ ΤΟ ΖΗΝ / ΤΟ ΤΕΛΟΣ Ο ΧΡΟ / ΝΟΣ ΑΠΑΙΤΕΙ // ΣΕΙΚΙΛΟΣ ΕΥΤΕΡ

I, the stone, am an image. Seikilos placed me here as a long-lasting sign of deathless remembrance.

While you live, shine
Have no grief at all
Life exists only for a short while
And Time demands his due.

Seikilos to Euterpe.[9]

It's a poignant image: a man in around the first or second century CE, commemorating the ephemerality of kinship through music. The song remembers the life of a woman named Euterpe, perhaps his wife, lover, sister or daughter – although there's also a school of thought that it could have been written for a man named Euterpes, his father. But this also could have been a lament by Seikilos for his *own* mortality. Euterpe is the Greek muse of music, so Seikilos, perhaps a musician, might have composed this as his own epitaph. The musical elements are above the words themselves. Those swoops and dots represent ways that the words should be manipulated into song. Look closely, and you can make them out: the alphabetic signs 'C', 'Z', 'K', 'I' tell us the pitch, while the linear symbols tell us the duration. The dots are called *stigma* (*stigmē* in the singular). We still don't really know what they're for, but an ancient musical manuscript called the *Anonymous Bellermanni* refers to stigma as being for '*arsis*', which could mean upbeat. 'Arsis' might also mean a kind of rhythmical emphasis.

There is something deeply moving about it: Seikilos, the man, the musician, making his pitch for immortality with an image of music. The body of whomever he sought to memorialise has long since been lost, but his words and his music live on. Some have said that the lyrics are a little trite or sentimental. For me, though, that more or less misses the point. The sentiment might have been repeated over and over in the thousand years since the Seikilos epitaph was made, but that doesn't reduce its power. A man felt an emotion strongly enough to record it in music and in image. And, despite the centuries that have passed, the cultures that have risen and fallen and the empires that have gained and lost power, you and I can recognise it. If it is banal, that is precisely *because* it is timeless.

And right there, in one of the earliest remnants of our desire to picture music, there is a problem. It is all so *slippery*. Look at the way the epitaph describes itself:

> I, the stone, am an image. Seikilos placed me here as a long-lasting sign of deathless remembrance.

It is an image, an *eikon* – a work of visual art. Not music; not a song. And yet. Musical notation, in ancient Greek culture, was for performers and not really intended for a wide readership or audience. Troupes of musicians would encounter it as they came to entertain at a banquet, but it wouldn't typically appear in such a public place for everyone to see. Like the Sumerian notation, most people would have encountered it as a picture, rather than a picture that made sound. Seikilos is making quite a statement: he is showcasing his power, his ability to read what most people couldn't, but he is also displaying his powerlessness against the march of time that will take away his ability to perform the song.

As classicist Robert Rohland observes, the Seikilos epitaph is thus both song and stone, both performance and text: 'the notes, permanently silent in the graveyard, create a *silent requiem* for *carpe diem.*[10] It is unique. And yes, it is the same as every picture of music that has come before and after, for the way that it epitomises the relationship between music and image. Deliberately placing music notation on a tombstone – in other words, on an object that seemingly deprives it of its function – doesn't just render that visualisation useless. Rather, the use shifts, subtly: it reveals what is left after the performers are gone, and that what is left is also a kind of music.

The success of what Seikilos aimed to do with his epitaph is clear, even today. Classicists, archaeologists, musicologists are still trying to piece together how precisely to perform the song, debating the meaning of that swoop, of that 'arsis'. As recently as 2018, classicist Armand D'Angour suggested that the lyrics were inseparable from the way that the song had been composed melodically – an argument that would have been unthinkable only ten years before.[11] We are still trying to battle the ultimate powerlessness that Seikilos warned us of; still trying to assert our insignificant selves against it. We continue trying to make Seikilos' epitaph into music, spurred on by that 'image' of 'deathless remembrance'. So yes, the notation on the Seikilos epitaph is about memorialisation. But it is also about inviting people *in*: about giving people a prompt, and seeing what sound they make out of it, what meaning. It has transcended the limits of what it claims to be, 'an image' and a song, to become something fundamentally between, at the very edge of possibility. Thousands of years later, we are still grappling with the same conundrum at the heart of this alchemy, with the same tantalising possibilities.

𝄞

In a convent along the banks of the River Rhine in Germany, a document is being put together under the watchful eye of the Mother Superior. She is a force to be reckoned with, and more than this: she has mystical visions, and her close connection to

God gives her an aura that few, it seems, are able to deny. She is Hildegard von Bingen, alias St Hildegard, the Sybil of the Rhine. Hildegard was the author of several books; this one, now known as the *Dendermonde Codex* and produced in around 1176 CE, was one of her last. It contains her *Symphonia Harmoniae Caelestium Revelationum*, her collection of songs including sixty psalms and canticles, complete with notation. It would be almost a thousand years after her death before musicologists realised that her musical contribution went beyond the sound of the songs themselves: the way she had written the notes was also a gift to posterity.

Most medieval chant notation doesn't indicate any rhythm or tempo (speed) and, until recently, it was assumed that Hildegard's chant was no exception. It is written with note shapes called neumes* which illustrate the contours of a melody or line of music but don't necessarily relate to a specific pitch or rhythmic content. By the eleventh century, when Hildegard was born, the neumes were 'diastemic', which meant their writers had developed graphic signals for showing the relative pitches between neumes. The *Dendermonde Codex* appears to use this system. But then, in 2004, musicologist Barbara Stühlmeyer noticed that the neumes Hildegard had used followed comprehensible and consistently traceable rhythmic principles. In other words, the visual note shapes were even more loaded with meaning than scholars had previously thought.[12] They were far more innovative than Hildegard had been given credit for.

Hildegard had invented a whole new way of writing music, and one so ahead of its time that it took over 900 years for musicologists to decipher its genius. This shouldn't necessarily come as a huge surprise when considered alongside the rest of her output. Restricted by the confines of the Roman alphabet, she had invented an alternative alphabet known as the *litterae*

---

* The word 'neume' seems to be a melding of two Greek words, πνεῦμα, *pneuma*, 'breath' and νεῦμα, *neuma*, 'sign'.

Duet

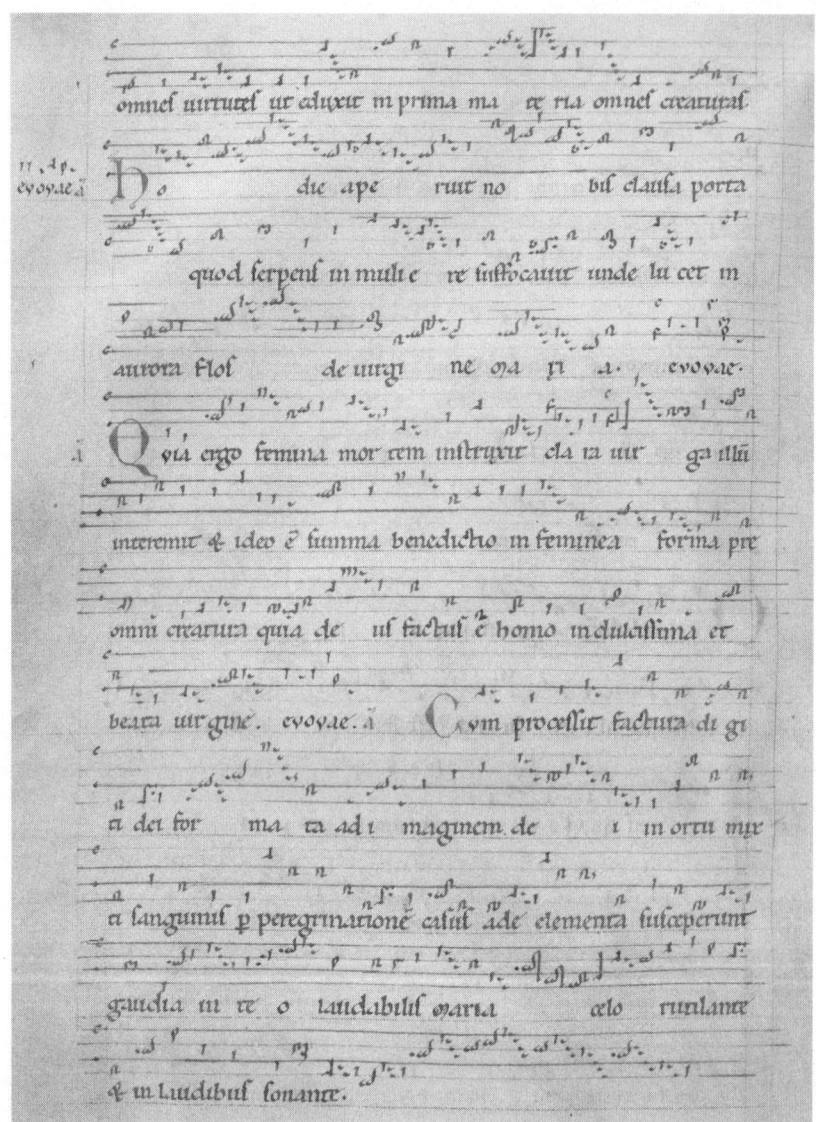

An example of Hildegard's notation
from the *Dendermonde Codex*.

ignotae, to go with her *lingua ignota* or unknown language, which she used for mystical purposes.[13] She never says as much, but her work suggests that she was enchanted by the possibilities of visuo-graphic signs and pictograms, by what could be visualised and how, and by the limits of visual and aural communication.

For her, music was about recapturing the original joy and beauty of paradise, invented to forge deeper and greater connections with the divine. It was incredibly important to her: music, and the vision of the choirs of angels, was one of the foundational mystical experiences she recorded in her book *Scivias*, accompanied by an exquisite illustration carried out under her direct instruction or perhaps drawn by Hildegard herself.

Hildegard's vision taught her that there had originally been ten choirs of angels. One day, the choir led by the angel Lucifer broke away from the rest, believing their beautiful voices had nothing to do with God. In that moment, their skill vanished, and they plummeted to hell like lumps of lead. God called upon humanity to form a replacement choir, and so music on earth was born. In Hildegard's conception, though, music was about words: 'Underneath all the texts, all the sacred psalms and canticles, these watery varieties of sounds and silences, terrifying, mysterious, whirling and sometimes gestating and gentle must somehow be felt in the pulse, ebb, and flow of the music that sings in me. My new song must float like a feather on the breath of God.'

The *Dendermonde Codex* gives us a fleeting glimpse of that feather, that song, set into motion by the voices of Hildegard's nuns and set adrift on the breath of God. We would not have her music without the unique, carefully considered way she saw it and wrote it down. It sounds trite to say this, but it surely doesn't lose its power for its simple truth. And more than preserving her music, the way that Hildegard visualised it gives us an insight into how her mind was working, how she saw that powerful connection with the pulse of the music that sang deep in her bones. Normal letters, and normal musical notes, do not offer her ample shape or expression for what she wants to sing and what she wants to say. She needs to bend and twist these marks to their absolute limit. The new signs she made, both for words and for music, would form a new textual and musical language for use in her monastery at Rupertsberg, for the use of her hand-picked

Hildegard's illustration of heavenly music, from the *Scivias*.

community of nuns. Although her music would end up being disseminated to a few choice contemporaries, it's important that we remember that this music, celebrating female sainthood and devotion, was written for these women alone.

Hildegard was writing music relatively early in the life of the graphic forms that would become Western classical notation. At this point in the history of music, notation wasn't yet a way of consistently marking pitch, duration and rhythm. Pieces of music were recorded and intended to be 'read' in a manner far closer to the graphic scores of the mid-twentieth century than the kind of scores you can buy from a traditional music shop today. It was a framework over which the performer could erect their interpretation, because the distinction between improvisation and composition was extremely blurred, as it would continue to be in the Western tradition, well into the sixteenth century. But notation was slowly shifting towards an agreed form that people from different nations and communities could interpret.

At this stage it was available only to professional performers, and to monks and nuns dedicating their lives to God. It is not clear whether much emphasis was placed on building a bridge between the visualisation and the sounds it could produce: Hildegard herself stated that she was never taught notation or singing. However, notation was slowly cementing its future, unlike its earlier Sumerian cousin. It was aided in its battle for survival by one key feature: it was diagrammatic. Japan, Palestine, India and Korea had all joined the music notation party by this point but, unlike these other systems from across the globe, Hildegard's method was pictorial. It relied on a visual system of signification.

This trait had been inherited from all seven of its direct ancestors: the Palaeofrankish, the Frankish, the Breton, the Lotharingian or Messine, the Aquitanian, the Old Hispanic and the Nonantolan styles of notation, all of which had developed between 800 and 900 CE in scattered hotspots across Europe, with their own distinctive idiosyncrasies. For example, the Lotharingian or Messine style of notation is calligraphically stylish: its sign for a single note is a short, angled stroke that twists up towards the right, with a little flourish. Aquitanian notation has a high volume of dots, used for a variety of meanings which alter dependent upon their placements. But all six have the same basic principles. All of these notations place their notes above the text. They all adopt a metaphor taken from antiquity and classical writings about music, that assumes an acoustic space where sounds are positioned as though in a physical space. Shrill sounds are 'higher', and placed accordingly; heavy sounds are 'lower'. These are the tiny, embryonic beginnings of our modern scale (of which more in Chapter 3).

For now, the basic idea was that if a pen-stroke moved upwards, this implied the shift to a 'higher' sound; strokes that moved downwards implied the shift to a 'lower' sound; and horizontal strokes implied that the pitch remained the same. But still, this European neumatic notation had kinship with other forms that were developing across the world at the same time. Other notation types suggested directions. Chinese *qin* notation maps out music by describing the movement of the fingers over the *guqin*, or qin instrument that gives it its name. Qin notation comes in two forms. One is *wenzipu*, which is a verbal description of the music. The other, *jianzipu*, is tablature, meaning that it roughly maps the form of the instrument with a column for each string, and notation to indicate finger positions rather than pitch. But qin notation is a little different from other kinds of tablature. It has an extra layer because Chinese music is concerned first and foremost with timbre (the *textures* and *colours* of a sound). The notation *Yen*, for example, means hitting the string downwards. *T'ui ch'u* or 退出 means pressing down and pushing the outermost string and releasing it; its other meanings are 'to withdraw, to retire', and also, for a more twenty-first-century flavour, 'to log out of your computer'. *Chin, fu*, means to slide along a string from left to right. All of this information can be deduced by following the order, top to bottom, left to right, inside to outside.[14]

Qin notation symbols might look like regular Chinese characters, but they're actually composite simplifications of earlier qin styles of notation that were gradually outmoded over the Tang and Song dynasties (roughly 600–1279 CE) and largely driven by the famed qin player Rou Cao. Compared to a regular Chinese character, the modern symbol for qin contains a sentence-worth of instructions in Classical Chinese, and is far more internally variable. Chinese culture values penmanship immensely: children are taught to paint before they can write, and each stroke is loaded with meaning and named after an object from nature, such as the 'plum tree branch' and the 'little drain between fields'. Each brush stroke, and the movement it preserves, is highly eloquent. This is allied with a philosophy that is precisely about rescinding personal power, about embedding oneself in nature and transcending worldly needs, epitomised by the poetic accompaniment to the eleventh-century qin score *Liezu yu feng*:

> I do not know whether the wind is riding on me
> Or whether it's me riding on the wind

Notation also often included pictures to aid understanding of hand positioning, as in the *Taiyu Yiyin* (1413), which illustrates hand positions like 'the lonely duck looking for the flock' and 'a crane calling in the shade'. So qin notation is a kind of choreography, allowing the performer to create a painting of their own, upon a different sort of surface. None of the notation concerns rhythm or tempo. The strings of the guqin instrument, crafted from twists of silk, become a terrain to be navigated, to dance or fly across at a pace determined by the skilful player.

These days the guqin is taught in teahouses, and at conservatoires and art institutes for those who are particularly skilled. Traditionally, though, it was aristocratic and seen as only for 'the Superior Man', and most certainly not to be played in 'a drunken and noisy atmosphere'. Preferred settings, according to early sources by the likes of the third-century poet and musician Ji Kang, were outside, having climbed a mountain; resting in a forest; resting in a valley, or in a quiet hall or Taoist abbey, if you absolutely must. Despite its accompanying philosophy, then, qin notation was just for the powerful, and a way of performing the refinement that came with power. Back then, the notation was usually calligraphed by (elite, probably male) masters and passed down to their (aspiring elite, probably male) apprentices.

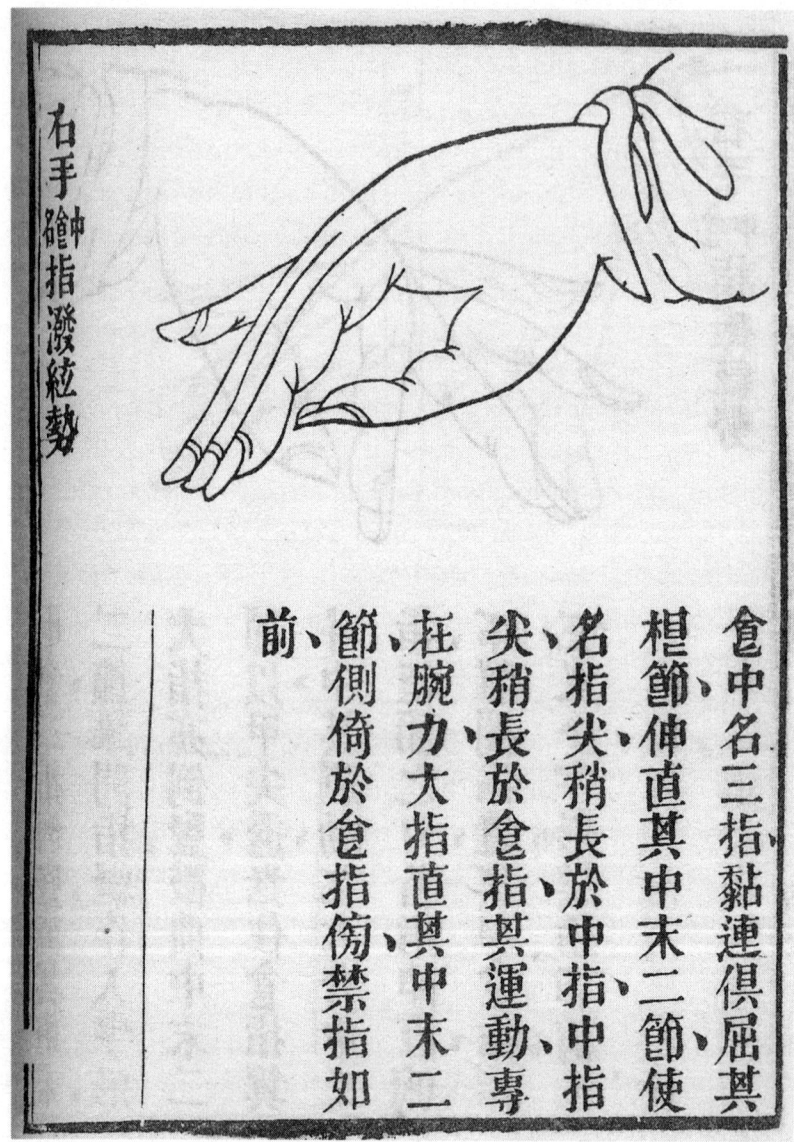

Instructions for hand positions for playing the qin.

This isn't to say there were no female qin players or composers – Madame Zhong's *Sizhaitang Qinpu* (1620) has survived, complete with 'Heartfelt Words on Going Through Bitterness', composed by the lady herself.[15,16] But this, sadly, is the only securely-attributed collection of qin notation by a female composer.[17]

Feather on the Breath of God: Writing the Notes

Madam Zhong's 'Heartfelt Words on Going Through Bitterness', from *Sizhaitang Qinpu*, 1620.

It's possible that the names of female composers simply haven't been preserved alongside their compositions. Surviving visual depictions like the tomb figures buried with the Marquis Zeng of Suizhou in the fifth century seem to suggest that women, often courtesans, tended to be qin players, rather than composers.

Zhong herself was a concubine of a prince and also known as Queen Zhao of Chong, so was in a position of relative privilege. We are lucky that her notation has survived.*

The earliest surviving qin notation is a piece called 'Solitary Orchid in Jieshi (or Stone Tablet) Mode', believed to be by Qiu Ming and written down in around the seventh century.[18] Much like Hildegard's neumes, they were points of departure: prompts so the performer could gain the general outline of the piece of music and inflect it with their own artistry. All of this was ingrained in the visual forms of qin notation, the ways that its sounds were made visible.

𝄞

Throughout the history of music, language has been the pinch of spice that makes the full flavours of the musical note sing. Language has shaped the note's visual forms, and how each culture has imagined the notes' ability to represent sound. Musicologist Susan Rankin suggests that the reason all of those early European neumes looked so similar is because they were used to write music for the same texts, in the same language: Church Latin.[19] Think about it. Imagine that I gave ten people the same text in the same language, and asked them to write music for it. Chances are that there would be considerable similarities in the way they shaped the sound to match the words. There are conventions in the way that a language is pronounced, such as where stresses are placed in a word (*dish*washer rather than dish*wash*er, *gar*dener rather than gar*den*er), or whether it rises or falls in pitch at the end. Such things seep into the way that we think a text should sound musically. But Latin was not the only language that was being used to disseminate those texts at that point.

---

* Incredibly, one of her qin instruments also survives, and is in the collection of the Chinese National Academy of Arts in Beijing.

Across the Red Sea, not too far from where the action of the Bible took place, Ge'ez is the language of Christianity.[20] Ge'ez has had a huge influence on the way humans have seen music across the globe; it is the language for which the illuminated manuscript tradition was invented, the source of the idea of sumptuous texts lavishly embellished with gold leaf and pigments made of powdered jewels. Once adopted by medieval Europe, it led to objects such as the Book of Kells and the Lindisfarne Gospels.[21] As a language, Ge'ez originated in what is now Eritrea; it is not strictly what we might term a living language, but it *is* the main liturgical language of the Ethiopian Catholic Church, the Eritrean Catholic Church, the Beta Israel Jewish community and the Ethiopian Orthodox Tewahedo Church. This last is the oldest, and was first officially recognised in the fourth century CE; to give you a sense of just how old it is, it was around this time that the Roman Catholic Church was first officially recognised.

Tewahedo or ተዋሕዶ means 'united as one', referring to their ancient belief that Christ's divinity and humanity existed without separation and without confusion. Because of how early it split away from other Christian denominations, the Ethiopian Tewahedo Church maintains the service structure of the ancient church: the unbaptised and those preparing for baptism attend until the reading of the gospel and sermon, after which the Anaphorae (the Eucharistic Prayers) are conducted. Music is integral to the service. The tunes, according to legend, were composed by St Yared in the sixth century CE; as a group they are known as the *deggua*. Let's say you are a *däbtära*, one of the cantors who leads the service.[22] Outside of church you are responsible for exorcisms, providing traditional medicine and white magic like protective amulets, a kind of spirituality that the Western church lost its connection with around 300 years ago. But within the church, your role is musical. You sing, you dance, you guide the chant. Everyone joins in the singing – they

Illuminated Gospels from the Amhara region of Ethiopia, late fourteenth/early fifteenth century.

clap their hands, move to the rhythm and shake, tap and sound musical instruments in time with the chant.

Like the worshipping communities of western Europe, the Ethiopian Tewahedo Church needed notation to record its music. Luckily for the church, St Yared was also a dab hand

The nativity scene, from Illuminated Gospels from the Amhara region of Ethiopia, late fourteenth/early fifteenth century.

at picturing music, and so part of his legend is that he not only composed the music but also created the visualisation: so as you sing, you are gazing down at an illuminated manuscript.

Like its Western counterpart, Yared's way of seeing music didn't signify exact notes or rhythms but the general shape of the piece. By 1500, though, a new, more nuanced form had developed: *melekket*, literally meaning 'sign', capturing an array of performance dynamics that were simply not available in Western notation at the time. On the face of it, melekket is *not* immensely visual; it doesn't illustrate the contour of the melody. Like other examples of notation that we've seen, it wasn't designed to be read by everybody: it was for the cantors, and decoding it required special training. Even today, when an aspiring däbtära begins their training at the Zema (the special school for liturgical music), they master the oral aspects before they learn how to read the visual aspects.[23] But take a look at some of melekket's signs and instructions. This sign, ⌣, is *kinat* (or ቅናት in Ge'ez script). It describes an upward glissando, a smooth, sliding movement over multiple pitches. This, ⌢, is *difat* (ድፋት) and means 'to go down an octave'. ⎯ is *hidet* (ሂደት), meaning accelerando (speed up) and crescendo (get louder).

Only men can train to be däbtära, and you typically have to be from a family of an existing däbtära in order to be chosen. They are as feared as they are revered. The ability to read this notation goes hand in hand with the perceived ability to bring spiritual ill-health, or even black magic. Scary as this sounds, it's a bit of a double-edged sword: däbtära are itinerant, always held slightly outside the community. As superpowers go, the ability to read melekket has its weaknesses along with its power. Nevertheless, for the wider community of the Ethiopian Orthodox Church, melekket has its benefits: cultivating a separate musical language from the Western elements of the church has given the Ethiopian Orthodox Church a power of its own.

In this way, melekket encapsulates an entire music-making culture, one that engages the eyes just as much as the ears. It is all too tempting to think of musical notes as things that evaporate the moment the music is performed. But Ethiopian melekket is more like a mirror: it reflects the musical culture of the Ethiopian Christian Church back at the reader, offering a glimpse into the fourth century and its beginnings. Like those rosemåling ice crystal forms in *Frozen*, melekket signs are visually appropriate to the world that they transform into song.

𝄞

Western classical notation, in the meantime, had gradually settled into the shapes that we recognise today. But, ever restless, people continued to experiment with notes, to enhance them and curate the ways that they were written.

It is Saturday, 4th March 1820. Fanny Mendelssohn, fresh-faced and hopeful, just shy of fourteen-and-a-half years old, begins to preserve her compositions in a musical album. Her annoying little brother Felix copies her and starts his own three days later. Family friends are in no doubt, though: Fanny is the big talent in the family. Writing to Goethe in 1816, the composer Carl Friedrich Zelter had declared: 'she could give you something of Sebastian Bach. This child is really something special.'[24] But in July 1820, just four months after Fanny began her musical album, her father burst her bubble. 'Music,' he wrote to her, 'will perhaps become [Felix's] profession, while for *you* it can and must be only an ornament.'[25] They fuck you up, your mum and dad. I'm sure Daddy Mendelssohn thought he had Fanny's best interests at heart, however difficult it might be for us to understand what was going through his head. Women like our old friend Hildegard, like Francesca Caccini, Barbara Strozzi, Maddalena Casulana, Raffaella Aleotta, Elisabeth Jacquet de La Guerre, Marianna Martines, Maria Szymanowska (some of whom were women of the Mendelssohn family's social class) had managed to live as musical professionals over the centuries before this, and particularly in the decades leading up to Fanny's birth. Clara Schumann, a mere fifteen years younger than Fanny, would go on to have a successful and generally untroubled career. It was an odd, cruel thing to dictate, even then.

Two decades later, in the sultry summer heat of Rome, Fanny and her husband, artist Wilhelm Hensel, embarked upon a collaboration that would marry their talents; it would also offer a new way of visualising music.[26] *Das Jahr** (1841) is structured around a cycle of piano pieces representing the full calendar year, with a short poem and illustration from Hensel at the beginning of each piece. Looking at these pages from the collection, you'd be forgiven for wondering, *Are these truly musical notes?* Their visual element initially appears simply decorative: a marginal component supporting and framing the substance of the music notation. But this division is deceptive, and it's not true to how *Das Jahr* works in practice as a musical object.

In *Das Jahr*, there's a sense that Fanny Hensel Mendelssohn is turning that moment of paternal disapproval on its head, transforming her virtuosic music into an ornament itself (see plate section). The pages for each section were tinted in their own separate delicate colour: pastel pink, peach, green, yellow, blue, allowing easy navigation between pieces, but also adding an extra visual theme. They are graphic strategies comparable to those achieved by more conventional musical symbols, such as vibrato signs, crescendos, diminuendos. They invite a specific way of engaging with the piano compositions with the eye as well as the ear; their colours evoke moods, scenes and atmospheres that Hensel Mendelssohn hoped would feed into the way each of the pieces would be performed. It's clear that *Das Jahr* was of immense personal importance to her. Writing from Rome, while she was composing the collection, she enthuses:

> I have been composing a good deal lately, and have called my piano pieces after the names of my favourite haunts, partly because they really came into my mind at these spots, partly because our pleasant excursions were in my mind while I was writing

---

* The Year.

them. They will form a delightful souvenir, a kind of second diary. But do not imagine that I give these names when playing them in society, they are for home use entirely.[27]

Like a delightful second diary, full of secret reminiscences of her favourite haunts in Rome, the visual elements of *Das Jahr* gather together and catalyse the aspects of Mendelssohn's compositions that traditional Western classical notation was not capable of capturing. It might not be quite as radical-looking to our eyes as it seemed at the time, but it still exercises a pull against the limits of what can be visually represented when it comes to musical sound.

Hensel's illustrations are in the margins of each sheet, dancing around Fanny's music notation and framing it. Years of artistic convention have trained us that what happens in the margins is subordinate to what takes place in the centre of the page. The artfulness of this visual strategy is, in fact, in this very sleight of eye: of course it's there to frame and support what's going on in the centre, and this is why it's so important. It's a relationship of equals, rather than main and bit-part character.

Even before the era of smartphones and website popups – *Would you like some cookies? Sign up for our mailing list? Are you sure? Before you go, remember you looked at this?* – attention wandered, and there were techniques our ancestors used to tackle this cognitive drift. Hensel's delicately rendered illustrations allow the eye to stray to a different part of the composition, before guiding it back to Fanny's piano compositions. The relationship between the illustrations and the notation, between the decorative margins and the centre, isn't unique to *Das Jahr*, either: the origin of the English word 'ornament', *ornare*, comes from the Latin and Greek for equipment. These margins are tools, designed to aid the performer's ability to see and to read. They leave things open to the performer's discretion and interpretation; they take music beyond its traditional notational space, allowing it to spread across the page; and they approach music as a visual entity, independent of sound. This latent visual potential has always existed, waiting for us to reach for it and let it sing all over again.

𝄞

Das Jahr shows us that notation can be a visual thing independent of sound. Our next example takes that one step further. It's a form of musical note that is only connected with the *idea* of music: intended to make viewers think of music, but not ever to be fully performable. It reveals that, no matter how dubious the status of an artefact, the emergence of musical notation that appears to hail from certain mysterious, ancient cultures tends to spark a furious excitement that is inseparable from our deep hunger for new ways to understand how something visual can unlock sounds from our deepest past.

In 1937, at the height of Egyptomania, a couple of papyrus fragments came to light. They were inscribed in a mixture of Coptic, Persian and Greek, with phrases like 'Sacred Hymn Singer', 'Spiritual Symphony' and 'Beginning' and 'End'; they featured hieroglyphic-style illustrations, seemingly of musicians performing; and they were covered with a series of coloured circles. They appeared to show an old, lost style of notating music – one that used colour to correspond to pitch. Supporting this incredible implication was another inscription, above two vertical columns of coloured circles to the far left of the fragment, that read 'Key'.[28] In other words, it seemed to be an ancient manifestation of the long association of music with colour (which we'll see more of in the next chapter). Ever so briefly, ever so tantalisingly, it looked as though this might, perhaps, be the earliest remnant of Christian written music found to date, inscribed in a mysterious and lost visual language. But all was not as it seemed.

We now know that these seductive little fragments were a hoax. It is still unclear who created them, but the most likely candidate is the man who found them, Aram Gulezyan, an Armenian-American whose family had fled ethnic persecution in the dying days of the Ottoman empire. Gulezyan claimed to have discovered the fragments among the flotsam and jetsam of his late father's and uncle's possessions, nestled with things that they had carried over the Atlantic to the United States. It's possible he did, in fact; but they certainly couldn't have been brought over from Armenia. When the fragments finally underwent testing some seventy years later in 2006, the conservation scientists discovered that they had been painted with modern pigments: Prussian blue, first produced in 1704; synthetic ultramarine, first produced in 1830; and, most damningly, titanium white, which wasn't available until the end of the First World War – in other words, well after Gulezyan's family had reached the US.[29] These paints weren't remnants of a more recent restoration, they were the only pigments present. This colour notation from fifth-century Egypt was, in fact, a forgery produced between 1919 and 1937: an invented notation from early twentieth-century America, not ancient Egypt.

Despite the fact that they are forgeries, these papyrus fragments reveal a startling truth about musical notes, and what we collectively believe they are capable of doing. Ancient Egyptian music notation was something of a 'holy grail' at the time the fragments emerged, and had been since the seventeenth century.[30] A string of gentleman scholars had chased after it, convinced that it would unlock deeper understanding of the very nature of music. According to this school of thought, musical notes were far more than representations of sound: they were the key to the untapped essence of music's deepest secrets, and the relationship between sound and vision. The strength of the desire to find such a source was enough to prevent several well-respected Egyptologists from noticing that this colour-music didn't quite add up – not just on first inspection, but for over fifty years.

Once you look past the dubious origins of these fragments, they reveal just how important the visual appearance of musical notes has been for our collective psyche, when all else – specific contexts, idiosyncrasies, even the ability to play the music they supposedly represent – is stripped away. These supposedly ancient colour notes play right into the zeitgeist of the early twentieth century:[31] the mania for all things ancient Egypt fuelled by archaeological finds such as Howard Carter's discovery of Tutankhamun's tomb in 1922, and the bright, jewel-like flashes of colour and arabesquing lines associated with orientalism.[32] The desire for a source like Gulezyan's fragments was lingering in the air, and heavily informed by what people thought an Egyptian music score might look like: lustrously pigmented, hieroglyphic, strange yet familiar, a precursor that would, after some deduction, make sense to the modern musical world (see plate section). Imagine the fragments as a vital clue in a film along the lines of 1934's *Cleopatra*, the original *The Mummy* (1932), or one of the archaeological whodunnits by Agatha Christie, and it fits perfectly. These colour notes, masquerading as ancient Egyptian relics, were designed for modern eyes.

For me, though, the ancient Egyptian context of this forged colour music notation is not the most interesting part of the story. Christianity came to Egypt very early, it's true, but there's another ethnic group and community that plays a vital, if unspoken, role. Gulezyan claimed that these fragments came via Armenia. This wasn't simply a random detail: closer inspection reveals that this particular aspect offers a potential key to unpicking what lies behind this bizarre story. Gulezyan was from the Armenian diaspora, and music – and musical notes – were a crucial aspect of Armenian national identity. Armenia represents one of the very oldest branches of Christian culture: it was, in fact, the earliest nation in history to adopt Christianity as its state religion, in 310 CE. Like the Ethiopian Church, it developed its own distinct Christian culture and manner of devotion, not governed by the approaches of the Roman Catholic Church. Along with its distinct alphabet, Armenia also had its own style and set of devotional chants, and its own music notation, known as *khaz*.

Khaz has been in use since the eighth century CE and, like melekket, is deeply entwined within its musical culture. Like melekket and Hildegard's notation, its forms are neumatic, meaning that they do not correspond to precise pitch but instead to the billows and swells of a melodic line. Unlike those two notations, it was overhauled and simplified in the nineteenth century to ensure that it could be learned with ease and that it would be more likely to survive as a musical form. In modern khaz, there are now forty-five different symbols that indicate pitch, with fourteen possible notes per octave. Instead of a sharp sign, Armenian notation uses a tilde or ~ to alter pitch.

Through centuries of rule under the Ottoman empire, through persecution and the Armenian genocide of 1915–17, which saw more than a million Armenians sent on death marches through the Syrian desert and slaughtered in the name of ethnic cleansing, khaz endured. Incredibly, it's still in use today. Perhaps it also lived on and mutated in the mind of Gulezyan, born an ocean away but saturated with the inherited memory of what it meant to visualise music in notes, and keenly aware of the special legacy of the Armenian Apostolic Church – a music-making tradition that didn't look or sound like any other. We don't know what Gulezyan's motivations were in creating this frenzy-inducing fragment; he died at the turn of the millennium, just before his fragments underwent testing. But looking more closely at the context, it is possible to see tiny morsels of what inspired him. He wrote Armenia into the story, along with ancient Egypt. Armenia, he claimed, is where his father and uncle packed away these pieces of papyrus, stowed carefully among their belongings as they fled. Might have this been an attempt, in the aftermath of the genocide, to remind the world of how important Armenia was to our collective musical history? To emphasise that, while Egyptomania gripped the world, another venerable nation had also been colonised by the Ottoman empire, and had played

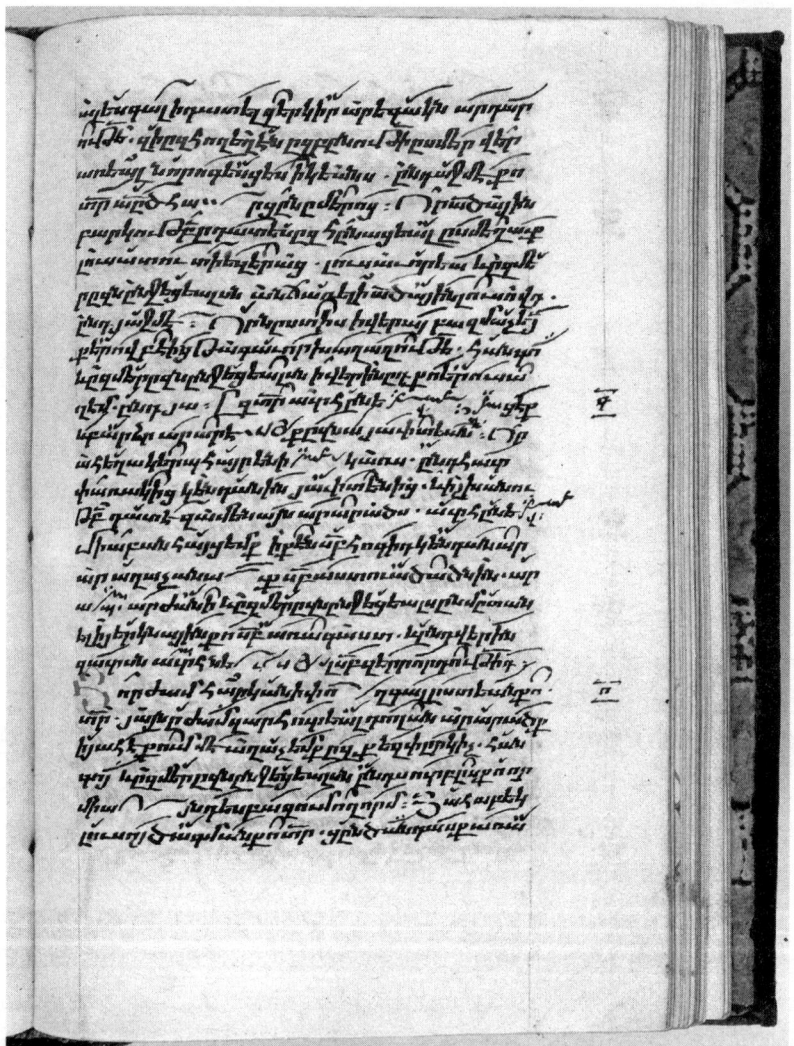

Khaz notation in an Armenian hymnal, 1679.

a crucial role in the early Christian Church? Or perhaps to feel a connection with a culture that placed so much emphasis on its own remarkable history of visualising music in notation?

We'll never know. What is clear, though, is that this bizarre episode demonstrates just how much we have yearned to weave sound and vision together as a single story. These musical notes, however deceptively, offered a portal into another world and a lost, rainbow-tinted musical culture, just waiting to be decoded. Even where they have no actual relation to pitch, rhythm, melodic line or anything performable, musical notes have a way of sparking our desire to infer musical meaning.

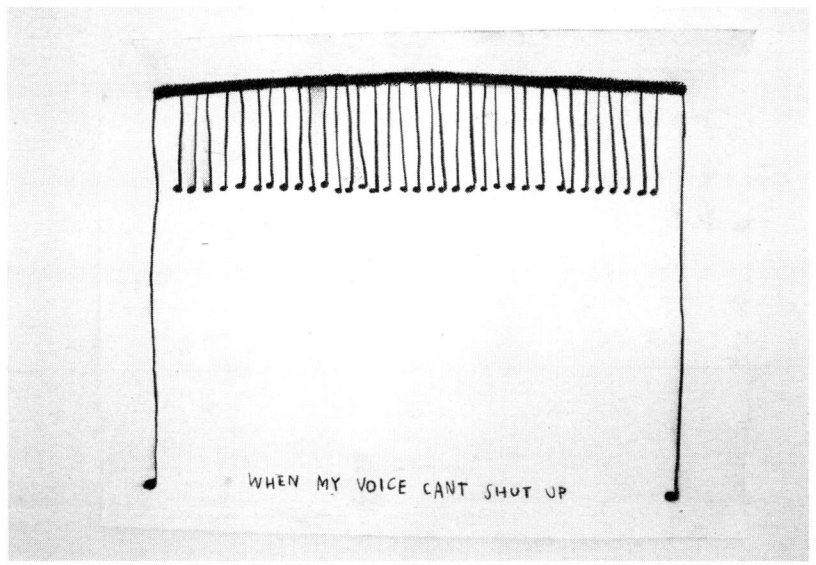

Christine Sun Kim, *When My Voice Can't Shut Up*, 2015.

Musical notes are not static. New musical notes are still being invented to this day. Frequently, they are more associated with visual art than their predecessors, which suggests that perhaps we've known, all along, that sound and vision are both parents of our musical language.

Korean-American artist Christine Sun Kim has been profoundly deaf since birth. She has also been fascinated by sound, and by her experience of music. She was struck by the way that people with hearing could not conceive of how deaf people could experience music or the 'social currency' of sound.[33] Her artworks *How to Measure Loudness* (2014), *How to Measure Quietness* (2014) and *Waiting in a Line at a Grocery Store* from her series *Six Types of*

Waiting in Berlin (2017) use Western music notation symbols like *f* (forte, loud) and *pp* (pianissimo, very quiet), playfully subverted, to capture how it feels to live deaf in a hearing culture.

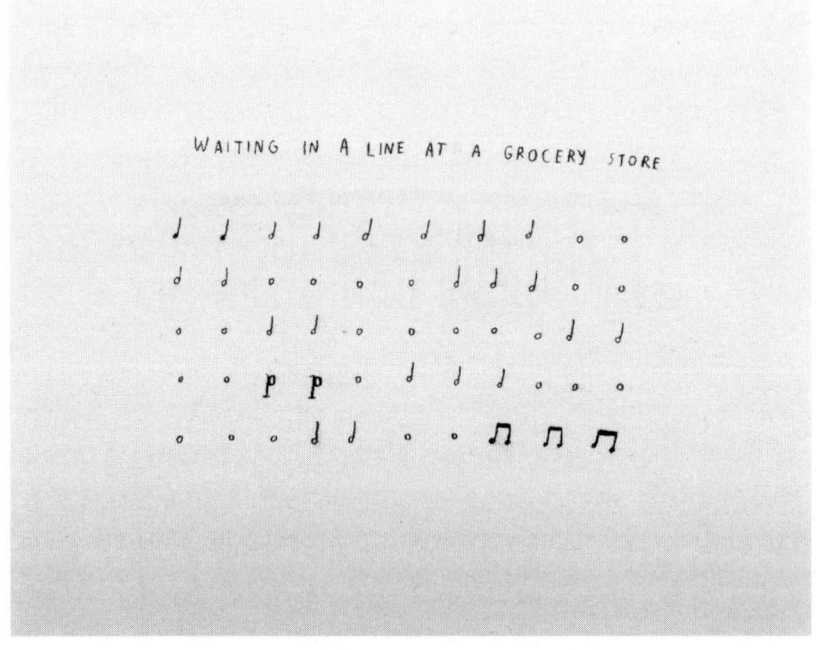

Christine Sun Kim, *Waiting in a Line at a Grocery Store*, 2017.

In her hands, musical notes become a malleable material, stretching off the page and into the fabric of everyday experience, whether you are deaf or hearing. The cognitive dissonance of the ascent from '*mf* – sleep' to '*ffffff* – argue in limited ASL' to the paradoxical '*ffffffff* – voice lost in oblivion' encapsulates the struggle to express oneself across a language barrier, from, say, English or French or German to American Sign Language (ASL), from sound to image. They also reflect the fact that regardless of whether or not a person can hear, they still have to learn what Kim calls 'sound etiquettes' such as 'Don't slam the door!', or 'When you're eating, make sure you don't scrape your utensils on the plate.'[34] Her images offer us the opportunity to construct their own narrative, their own direction and thus their own soundscape.

However, it's her American Sign Language-based notation that truly pushes the boundaries of seeing music. Kim describes her works *All. Day.* and *All. Night* (2012) as being 'like a piece of visual music', the result of approaching ASL 'through a musical lens'. They are perhaps best thought of as acts of sensory translation, because their forms are so intricately related to the gestures of ASL, and Kim's desire to establish ASL as a serious form that serves as a 'vehicle for my voice'. In this way, her artworks allow her to assert the power that her deafness imbues her with. In a world geared towards the able-bodied, it can be tempting to see disability as a form of powerlessness. Kim demonstrates that this isn't so. It provides her with another way of seeing, of experiencing music, even of hearing. 'Music,' she notes, 'is so full of social value, respect, and recognition, and so rich in research, and has a very clear place in history. I can honestly say the same for ASL, but people often treat it as a "cute" language for deaf people that often battles with stigma. ASL is highly nuanced and functions almost like music, except that it does not have sound.'[35]

Accordingly, *All. Night* and *All. Day.* encapsulate the visual rhythm of ASL and its grammar of hand-shape, palm orientation, position and movement. *All. Day.* combines the sign for ALL-DAY (where the right arm with a flat hand-shape takes a semi-circle movement, imitating the rising and falling of the sun, over the left arm that lies horizontally and still), with A LONG SLUR (which takes the image of a musical slur and magnifies it to enormous proportions, extending it from the bottom left corner of the image, stretching across the entire height and width of the artwork to the bottom right). In *All. Night* these movements are inverted. Kim's works are both the visualisation of these signs, and the performance of them; the marks of the ink record the movement of her hands in these gestures.

Kim gives us yet another way to think about musical notes. The notes we have explored – written by Seikilos, Hildegard and Yared – take sound for granted, as something that we can experience or imagine through our ears and memory. In her 'visual music' drawings, Kim shows us ways of experiencing sound and music beyond our ears.[36] Visual cues like rhythm, gesture and pattern offer notation under a whole other aspect: how to approach silence as a musical device, when 'silence' is all you can hear; how to express your voice in image, rather than sound; how to capture the aspects of music that survive without hearing. The graphic forms of notes, in themselves, are a kind of music.

𝄞

Music notes might have begun as mnemonics. But even where their purpose was to prompt memory, their visual forms did more than briefly activate a sonic memory. They weren't transparent, and they didn't dissolve like sherbet upon consumption. Their visual forms endured, and became innate to how music was conceptualised, enunciated and performed. When our ancestors chose to start preserving their songs for posterity, their eyes and their ears worked together in symbiosis. We could even say they worked in duet to produce the musical cultures that, through their twists and turns, became the ones that we have inherited today. I've shown you the merest fraction of the different ways that musical notes have been written over the thousands of years of which we have a record of how music was made. What they all have in common, though, is an interest in creating a picture that is appropriate for its corresponding sound: a fit between eye and ear, and a recognition that the materiality of these signs is important to the music that they record.

Sometimes, as with melekket, notes were used to glorify a deity. Sometimes they were used to experiment and to extend the limits of an existing visual system, as with Hildegard's. Sometimes they were used to commemorate, as with Seikilos' mysterious composition. Once music is in a material, visual form, it can be reproduced. It can travel. Regardless of whether you can read it, it has a meaning and that meaning is both musical and political.

People often assume that music, especially classical music, should be apolitical – art for art's sake.[37] The twists and turns in the tale of the musical note show us that this is impossible. Our word 'political' comes from the ancient Greek word *polis* or πόλεις, meaning city, both the physical buildings and the people who make up its inhabitants. If we accept the concept that music is driven by a succession of genius composers and performers, isolated on their pedestals, untouched by lowly mortals and their paltry attempts at music-making, perhaps music could be apolitical. But you and I know better. Music is nothing if not communal: a musical note has not performed its primary function if it is used by only one person and has remained indecipherable to everyone else. Likewise, a musical note's success doesn't have to be tied to one way of reading, or one way of meaning. Unlike other forms of 'writing', musical notes can dance across the threshold of image and text and back again, can be for our brains to comprehend as well as for the apparently simple pleasure of our eyes.

This plurality is what makes music so pervasive. The ways that we make music together, as a community, are inscribed in each one of these visual forms. For every St Yared or Christine Sun Kim, there are thousands and thousands of people who have taken the musical notes they left behind, and made them work and live and breathe and *sing*. The politicality – the communal nature – of music is key to its endurance, even as it shape-shifts into an ever-increasing variety of visual forms.

The history of music did not begin with musical writing and musical notes. The advent of the musical note, though, marked the beginning of a way of thinking about music that inflects how we perform, listen to and visualise music today. It is the beginning of the entangled, messy romance between art and music.

3

The Hand of Guido:
Mapping Musical Pitch

Spring 2007. Downtown Beijing whips past the windows of the minibus in a blur. Communist Youth League members are sauntering in CCP uniform and lurid Nike Zoom Blazers like my own, smudging into neon shop signs, banners and dilapidated store fronts. Slowly, in fragments, the city gives way to countryside. Evocative ruins loom – all faintly stained pink, from where they had been wrapped in red paper during the Revolution. This landscape of otherworldly monuments is occasionally punctuated by half-finished constructions like a long-abandoned Disneyland resort, and by the freakish partial forms of the National Stadium, known as the Bird's Nest, and the National Aquatics Centre, known as the Water Cube, built for the 2008 Olympics. Both the rosy, ornately carved blocks from the past and the tangled metal and glass from the future look as if they are disintegrating, as though we are simultaneously in the present moment, one thousand years in the past and one thousand years in the future.

This unstable sense of time could possibly be frightening, but my siblings and I are otherwise occupied. Our parents have brought us to China in the hope that it might help us better understand our heritage. Our journey to this part of the country is a bit of a fudge already: our actual connection is to long-destroyed villages scattered around Macau and Hong Kong on the south coast and now, presumably, filled with pink-stained ruins or possibly even still wrapped in red paper. People keep coming up and touching us, particularly our hair. To them, we look so un-Chinese that it's a bit of a joke: why have we, who look and sound nothing like them, come *here* of all places to understand our heritage?

Deliriously jet-lagged and disorientated, we are singing *The Sound of Music* to our grandmother. Everything flabbergasts her. She is fluent in Mandarin and Cantonese, but both languages have evolved so fast that anything she says sounds quaint and antiquated to the people we encounter, her speech littered with the equivalents of 'thee' and 'thou' and 'betwixt'. Being here is as strange for her as it is for us. *The Sound of Music* is one of her favourite films, and we started singing because we wanted to cheer her up. At least, that was the theory. A good twenty minutes later, we are still going.

Our parents, sitting in the front seats of the minivan, are pointedly trying to ignore us. *DOoooooo, a deer, a female deer, RE, a drop of golden sun, MI!!!!! a name, I call myself, FAaaaaaa, a long long way to ruuuuuun...* We take it in turns to improvise or sing the tune, occasionally warbling deliberately bad harmonies or mixing in segments of random pop songs. *Teeeeee, a drink with jam and bread!* interjects the elderly man hired to drive us around, bobbing along to the song. This is the only indication he has given us that he knows any English. My father places his head in his hands and sighs deeply.

All this might sound like frivolous escapism into the comfortingly, mind-numbingly familiar in the face of so much strangeness. You'd be right. But, years later, I can't separate the memory from the poignancy of the song we'd chosen. 'Do, Re, Mi' is more than an excellent musical theatre classic, one of the best works ever to come from the pens of Richard Rodgers and Oscar Hammerstein. It's a clever riff on an old, and ingenious, way of mapping music: the inheritance of a thousand years of thinking about visualising pitch, a musical bridge that marries our English and our Chinese heritage, the very thing we'd flown 5,000 miles in search of.

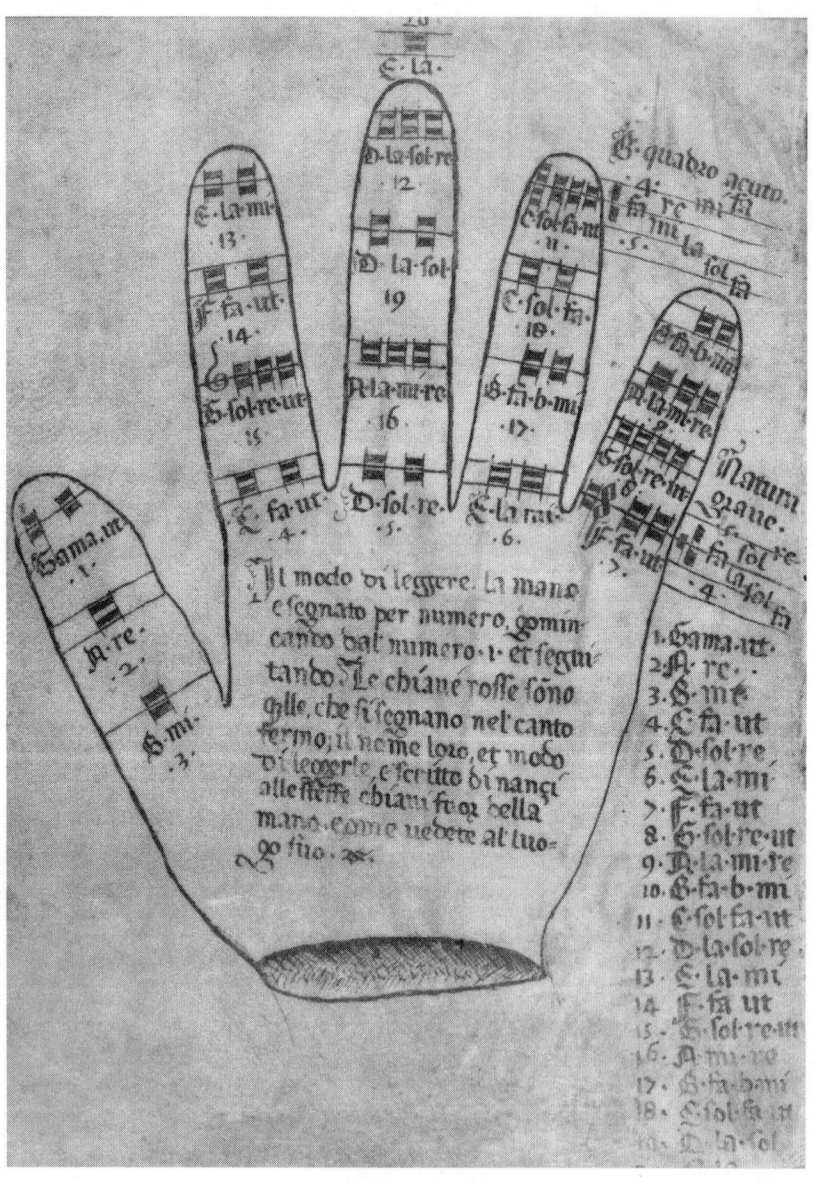

Guido's hand.

The Hand of Guido: Mapping Musical Pitch

The story of the musical scale has many beginnings, but one of the most important took place in a cathedral in Tuscany, around the year 1028 CE, with a man painstakingly delineating each letter, swoop and slash on a piece of parchment. It's close work, and he is fastidious. You have to be, when you are translating the imaginary onto ink and paper. His name is Guido. He himself is most certainly not imaginary, but several aspects of his story *are* mythical.

Guido is a Benedictine monk, and by this point he already seems to have been making waves in the world of medieval music. Bishop Tedald of Arezzo has hired him to oversee the training of singers for the Cattedrale in Arezzo. For that, he has a rather special trick up his sleeve (or rather, at the end of one of them): his hand.[1] It's uncertain how much of this idea should be credited to Guido; it is possible he was just responsible for perfecting it.[2] The story, though, has him as the creator of the technique: using the hand to memorise pitch space – the intervals between notes. Once this had been memorised, the hand would help the aspiring musician navigate the notes with increased agility, better equipped to improvise and appreciate the relationship between pitches that make up some of the most important building blocks in any musician's skill-set, even today. It's neat; it's catchy; and it's visually striking.

The principle is simple: Guido's hand is a sight-singing tool, which maps the joints of the fingers onto the first note of each of the six phrases of the hymn 'Ut queant laxis'. The words are as follows, in Latin on the left and in translation[3] on the right:

Ut queant laxis **re**sonare	So that your servants may, with loosened
Fibris **mi**ra gestorum **fa**muli tuorum	voices, resound the wonders of your deeds
Solve polluti **la**biis reatum	Clean the guilt from our stained lips
Sancte Johannes	Saint John

The first syllable of each phrase in turn was used to form the sounds of a six-note pattern (or hexachord) that roughly corresponds to our modern scales – 'ut', 're', 'mi' and so on, which you might recognise as the predecessors of that famous song from *The Sound of Music*, and which are known as 'solmization syllables'.

Dividing pitch into six notes was, in many ways, a purely arbitrary aesthetic choice; some East Asian and Indian equivalents divide it into five, and some, like Mēlakartā/Thaat and Gongche, into seven. The hexachord didn't depict a fixed pitch, but one that could be positioned relative to the pitch at any given starting pitch, or root note. Each finger of the hand represented a hexachord; each joint was a point where you could 'mutate' (or, in modern parlance, modulate) to a different hexachord. When a music master instructed their singers, as Guido did at the Cattedrale, they would point to different bits of the hand, and the singers would sing the pitch indicated. The master would move across the hand to help the singers memorise other routes across the full range of notes, known as the 'gamut'. It didn't even need to be the master's physical hand: a picture of the hand could suffice too. Eventually, the singer would internalise the visual image of the hand to call upon whenever they were performing. Music, generated by image, guiding sound.

In most other places across the globe, people learnt how to read music through the image of an instrument, just as many people read guitar or bass tab today: a qin in China, a lute or *tambura* for Mēlakartā music in southern India, or a *shamisen* in Japan. In medieval Europe, it was the image of this hand. Its use spread like wildfire out of Italy to Scandinavia, France, Germany and Spain. Examples of what became known as the Guidonian hand could be found even in that provincial backwater, England. Images of the hand exist from before Guido's lifetime, so it seems he was the person who popularised or refined its use, rather than the one who invented it. Nevertheless, the legend lived on, and the visual image of the hand, carefully held in the minds of musicians across Europe, ushered in a series of musical innovations and styles that forever changed what music could sound like.[4]

It's hard for you and me, so steeped in the legacy of this invention, to appreciate just how ground-breaking it was. So much of modern musical culture is built on the logic of Guido's pitch space. Once a musician had a clear map of where they could

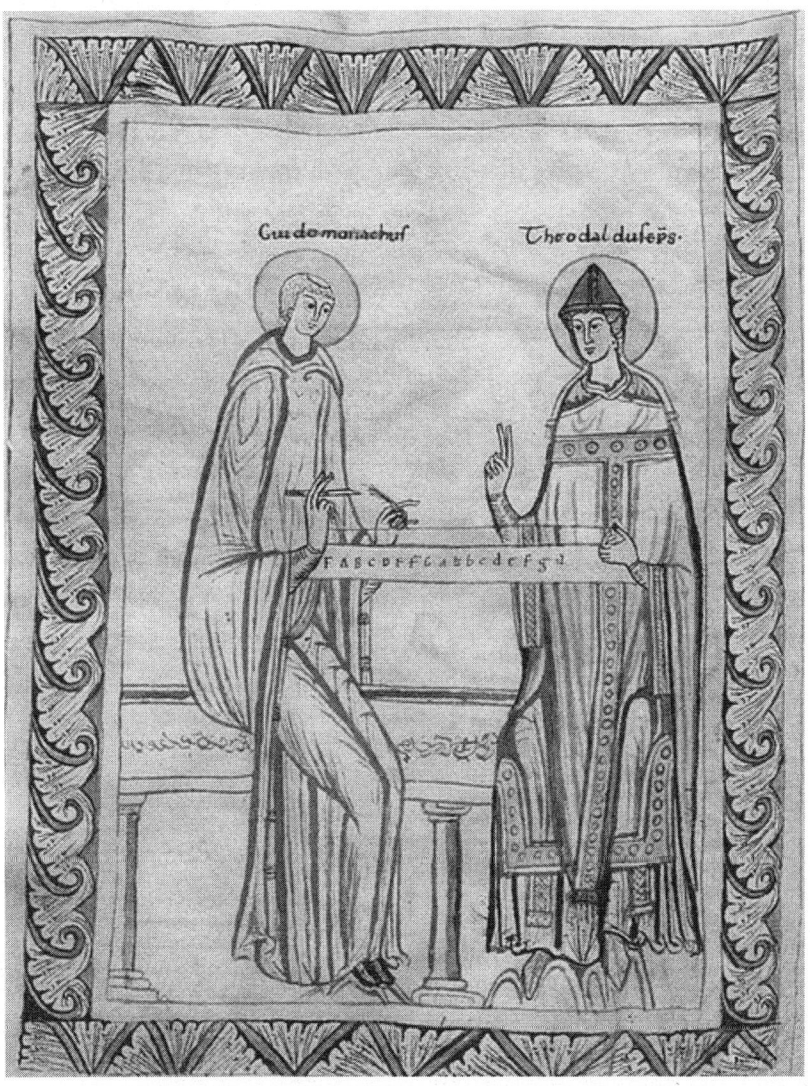

Guido shows Bishop Tedald his scale.

move across pitches, and which ones work best (like fourths: '*some day* my prince will come'; and fifths, the *Star Wars* theme tune interval: '*Da, daaa*, da-da-da daaaa-da'), they had a route towards composing harmony. Where earlier music was based on monophony – a one-line melody – now multiple lines could weave in and out of each other, complementing each other, and creating the dense body of sound so characteristic of late medieval music.

We've seen how integral place can be to the visual experience of music, and how complicated the messages that venues bring to a performance sometimes are. But physical venues aren't the only spaces that feed understanding of music. For over a thousand years, human beings have used imagery to map pitch, to understand how musical notes relate to each other, to write their music and to preserve those pieces of music for other people. Generalising wildly, today they are known as scales.

I know, I know. Scales are enough to make many traumatised ex-budding musicians run a mile and I promise, I hated them too. *Really*, raged my teenage brain, *why should I be practising musical scales every week, let alone every day?* I *knew* that a piece with seven flats was in the key of C-flat minor and that five sharps was in the key of B major: so what was the point of proving it to the ether and some omnipresent, perpetually disapproving but fundamentally ineffectual God of Music every single morning before school??? This is an extremely stupid question: rehearsing scales is about increasing the musician's dexterity, building up muscles in your hands and your fingers and your diaphragm which will, in turn, allow you to articulate pitches with greater skill. If I'd dedicated any sort of time to practising singing scales, there's a reasonable chance I might have noticed my nodules much earlier and thus done much less damage to my voice.

Musical scales, without exaggeration, change the way we can imagine music. Before we envisioned them, music held far fewer possibilities. They're like maps, cartographical diagrams to help us navigate the landscape of all that can be heard.

Robert Fludd's 'temple of music', showing the musical scales, 1619.

Over the years, Guido's hand evolved into another form of diagram: the ladder-like scale that you might be more familiar with. The scale gets its name quite literally from the Latin words *scala*, ladder, and *scandere*, to climb: up and down, rather than across. For several centuries, the ladder and the hand coexisted happily as diagrams of pitch space. There was a brief trend for imposing Guido's hand on organ pipes, to get a sense of how the notes related to each other, but largely it had become a chart of an abstract, dreaming space of music. The natural philosopher Robert Fludd even envisioned it as a fully coordinated building – a 'temple' of music, constructed with bricks made of Guido's solmisation syllables, stacked in hexachords one on top of the other. But the dominance of Guido's mind's eye of music couldn't last forever.

I know now that what my child-self needed to appreciate scales was a bit of spiciness. If someone had told me of the strife and intrigue of the origin stories that lay behind the rise of Western classical musical scales, I would have been hooked.

And so, here is one of those stories. Brace yourself, because it is a tragedy: it's the rise of the modern scale, modern tonality, the snappily-named 'twelve-tone equal temperament' (stay with me), and the loss of the flexible mind's eye of music.

𝄞

For years the Guidonian hand reigned supreme across Europe.[5] Nevertheless, it was failing to keep up with the way that music was evolving: the image of musical pitch space it had given birth to was full of contradictory theoretical hacks that were opaque for large numbers of people; its rules had to be broken as often as they were followed. The hand also didn't sit well with other developing bodies of knowledge, and where music was supposed to sit within them. Since the ancient Greeks, music had been seen as a sub-branch of mathematics. This was all well and good, but how, mathematicians wondered, were they supposed to rationalise that idea, when the musical system was based on a concept of pitch space so numerically convoluted that pitches were unequally spaced? Guido's hand needed an overhaul. Several people saw themselves as the one to fix the issue, and some were certainly more successful than others.

To the Shaolin monastery at Dengfeng, then, and the year 1574. Bring your torch.

A man sits bent over a sheet of paper, high in the sculpturesque mountains of Henan province, central China. It's the land of the Longmen Caves, where colossal, 2,000-year-old Buddhist figures tower over the landscape; where monasteries cling to the uppermost peaks of Mount Song, the ancient 'centre of heaven and earth' according to Chinese mythology, where the mermaid goddess Nüwa dwelt and created the first human beings out of yellow clay, to cure her loneliness; a land constructed out of fantastical geological formations lingering over the ochre waters of the Yellow River. Hunched over his desk, ink brush cramped in hand, the man is scribbling, tugging at his hair, throwing his brush down in vexation, sighing. By his side, though, is a musical instrument: a seven-stringed qin – the Chinese zither – which is the key that will unlock the solution. This man, aided by that zither, is about to work out how to transform the musical scale into neat, equal packages of twelve parts.[6]

His name is Zhu Zaiyu. He's a distant descendant of the Hongxi emperor, and a minor prince of the Ming dynasty.[7] But he hasn't been interested in titles since his father fell out with the emperor, had the title of prince stripped from him and ended up imprisoned when Zhu was only fifteen. He's a scholar, more keen to be known as a choreographer, composer, poet, mathematician and music theorist, than as a statesman and fearless ruler. His ideas will eventually travel across thousands of miles of land and sea to Europe, where they are so desperately needed.

Equal temperament was radical. It was more than just changing the division of music from six parts into eight. Without it, you could not reliably say what, for example, an A_4 – the A above middle C – sounds like. Depending on the performance venue, an A_4 could be far closer to the notes that sit either side of it, a

G-sharp or a B-flat, or perhaps something different entirely. It is a laudable aim, to ensure that all A_4s across the globe are created equal. But of course, the problem is that the music written and the musical venues constructed before this point were not designed with this purpose in mind. C_5 (the C above middle C) is generally accepted as being a soundwave that vibrates at a frequency of 523(.25) Hertz. In high Gothic Lichfield Cathedral in the English Midlands, constructed c. 1195–1340, however, it is a disconcerting 540Hz, almost a full semitone higher.*

The English organist, composer and Methodist Samuel Sebastian Wesley (1810–76) *hated* equal temperament: 'I own I do not like it ... I never enjoy playing on an organ where nothing is in tune, where simple triads produce the effect on the ear which dissolving views do to the eye before a picture has reached its full focus.' Almost *everything* alters pitch: the vowels you are singing the notes to, how cold it is, how wet it is, the proximity of the performer next to you, and what they are wearing. And there were plenty of alternative candidates for A_4 besides the 440Hz that equal temperament, via Zhu, eventually arrived at: the French government, in fact, decreed that A_4 should be tuned to 435Hz and, for a brief time, many opera houses across Europe followed suit.** 440Hz was officially adopted as a standard only in 1955, following the lead of the BBC, who had chosen it due to technological limitations, as 435Hz and 439Hz were much harder to record and faithfully disseminate than 440Hz.[8]

But all this was to come, and Zhu knew nothing of it. He just wanted to establish a systematically ordered map of musical pitch, a neat and predictable musical scale that musicians could carry around in their heads in place of Guido's hand.

Zhu sets out his system in his *Comprehensive Treatise on Music and Music Theory*, a collection of fourteen separate titles that

---

* That is, closer to a C-sharp than a C.
** British orchestras, ever contrary, tuned to 439Hz.

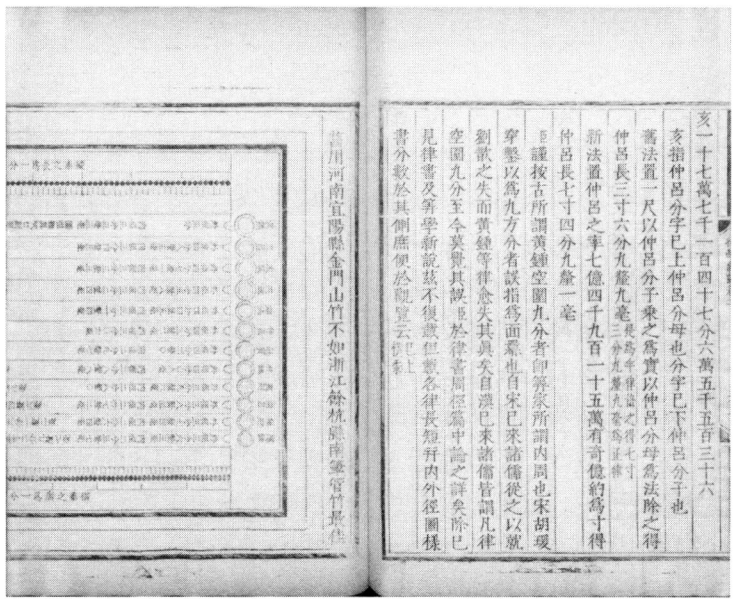

Zhu Zaiyu's calculation of pitch pipes and their relationship to measure, 1584.

he'd written c. 1580–1607. It was simple really, he wrote. You just divide the length of string and pipe by – look away briefly if you are allergic to mathematical equations – the twelfth root of two ($^{12}\sqrt{2} \approx 1.059463$)'. He conducted his calculations on an eighty-one-spindle abacus of his own invention (of course), which allowed him to keep count to twenty-four figures beyond the decimal point.

But this dry, technical account of figures and calculations and equations doesn't quite do Zhu's deductions justice. 'One dawn,' he writes, his excitement palpably leaping off the page, 'I suddenly had a perfect understanding of it, and for the first time I realised that the ancient sorts of pitch-pipes all gave mere approximations to the [true] notes ... Only the makers of the seven-stringed zither [qin] in their method of placing the markers at three quarters or two thirds [of the length of the strings] had as common artisans transmitted by word of mouth [the way of making the instrument] from an unknown source.'[9] Multiple things are going on in this description: a recognition of the need to visualise, in order to move towards the abstract image; the recognition of the use of the visible image of the pitch pipes; *and* the recognition of what cannot be visualised.

Dance is, among many other things, a visualisation of music. Some forms of dance, like ballet, *agbadza* (from Ghana), *kathak* (from India) and the lotus dance (from Vietnam), have gestures and movements so systematised that they are more or less a language in their own right, able to tell a narrative as clearly as a spoken or written word. Dance does something special, though, that words do not. It physically fills and traverses space. Many things are necessary for the making, breaking and remaking of a mind's eye of music. A good knowledge of music theory and of advanced arithmetic are key. But it is equally important to have the ability to work with space: to be able to project your analytical thought into space and imagine movements, structures, gestures and the interweaving of bodies. It is a very different form of visualisation to that which we might associate with mathematical calculation.

Zhu's combination of choreographic output and dance music gave him this expertise. His proposed mind's eye of music is the perfect collision of all of his spheres of knowledge: the musical (he knows how to play each of these instruments, how to manipulate their strings or pipes to produce a pitch), the mathematical (his knowledge of numerical ratio), and his recognition of the importance of space and the positioning of the markers. The visualisation, through the qin, enabled Zhu's deduction.[10]

Unfortunately, it would be several centuries before the full text of Zhu's work made it to Europe, so in the meantime another man was obliged to make the same discovery. Some twenty-five years later, over the dark waters of the canal, the light of a single lamp shimmers and ripples. It is cast from a window high, high up, beneath the eaves of Leiden. Look closely and you can just make out a figure, hunched over his desk, pen cramped in

The Hand of Guido: Mapping Musical Pitch

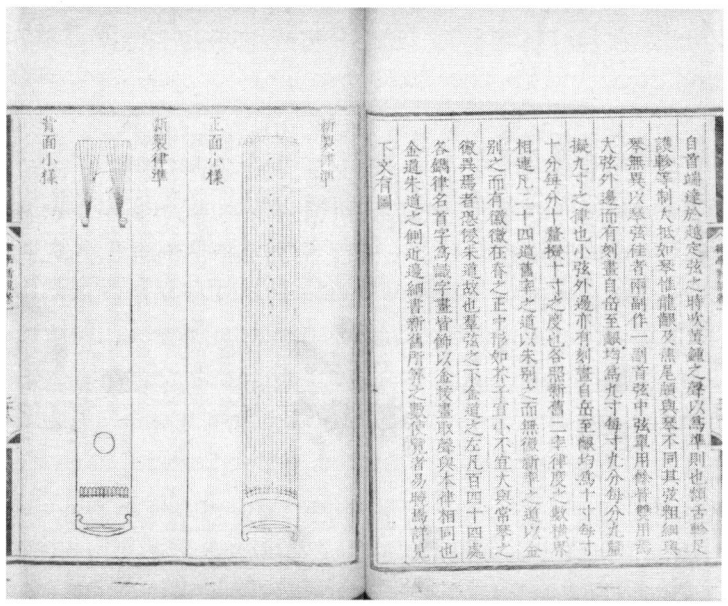

Zhu's proposed thirteen-string qin, to create equally-tempered music.

hand, scribbling, tugging at his hair, throwing his pen down in vexation, sighing. This man, like Zhu before him, is working to reinvent the mind's eye of music, the way that musicians pictured pitch space.

No matter which way he manipulated the numbers it made absolutely no sense: music did not fit into neat mathematical parcels. Why was the note B-natural not the same as a C-flat? Why should we accept that the musical scale divided into six, seven, eight uneven chunks? Why not ten? Why not twelve? At every turn, this beautiful, universal form that connected earth to heavens, body to cosmos, human to divine, resisted order and proportion. The scale shouldn't be a vague depiction, oh no. Those lines and spaces should be diagrammatic and represent precise boundaries between notes. *It should, it must,* thought Simon Stevin, *divide into equal sections* – a twelve-tone equal temperament or '12tet', as it has since become known.[11,12]

Some context is needed here. If you lived in the Netherlands around 1600 and you needed someone to unpick some mathematics or engineering, Stevin was your man.[13] Very little is known about his life, but he appears to have been born into a Calvinist family in Bruges in 1548, when many of the city states that made up modern-day Belgium and the Netherlands were part of the Holy Roman Empire. Much of Stevin's childhood was filled with conflict, as these states battled for independence from the empire. Following the founding of the Dutch Republic, Stevin moved to its heart in the city of Leiden, enrolling first at the Latin school and then at the University of Leiden, where he befriended Prince Maurice, Count of Nassau and son of William the Silent.*

The war in the Low Countries would continue to rumble on for eighty years but, for a brief period, the tension between the two sides created an ideal crucible for scientific innovation. Stevin was key to this effort: a mathematician, physicist and engineer who coined many of the technical mathematical words still in use in Dutch today. He believed that the Dutch language was a beautiful thing, far more able to capture complex operations than Greek or Latin:

> Dutch words [are] easy to understand and modest in appearance, but in reality [they possess] an infinite power. For if one considers the thing defined, in this case *everedenheijt* [equal temperament], it is like a definition of its substance, the mere ring of which, at first hearing, brings home to us and shows us that thorough understanding of equirationality was not found among the Greeks and their successors.[14]

This is from the middle of his unpublished treatise *On the Theory of the Art of Singing*, written in about 1605. Elsewhere in the treatise,

---

* William the Silent was the first *stadtholder*, or prime minister, of the Dutch Republic.

he demonstrates the truth of his argument with Dutch terms for musical language. Pitch division can be conducted like 'geometrical ratio', but instead of *'grootheyt'* (greatness) and *'cleenheyt'* (smallness) it is governed by *'groftheyt'* (coarseness) and *'fynheyt'* (sharpness or, more literally, sweetness, delicacy or daintiness) of sounds. Such fanciful language is out of character for Stevin, who is famed for his desire for plain expression. In any case, this moment gives us a useful insight into what was going through his head as he fought to divide up the musical scale into ratios like geometry, and to harness mental imagery into a new mind's eye of music to match the one that Zhu had come up with a quarter of a century before.

It's worth noting that, although these men were rough contemporaries – Zhu only a decade older than Stevin – they were working with incredibly different concepts of music. Zhu probably found the new mind's eye of music much easier to deduce because it was an entirely abstract concept for him. When he was working out his system, he didn't set out to rework and refine the hexachordal model, as Stevin did. It was a purely theoretical exercise: a mathematical mind puzzle, like a particularly knotty form of sudoku. Chinese music during this period wasn't structured around hexachords, and it wasn't quite as pedantic as the Western system: the interest was in the timbre or colour of sound, rather than fixing the gaps between notes to an absolute value. European polyphonic music was built on aligning harmonic and melodic intervals covering large parts of the 'circle of fifths',* and temperament was, notes musicologist Alexander Rehding, 'an urgent practical problem'.[15] In Chinese music, the division of the scale into equal parts had only a few practical

---

* The circle of fifths is a way of arranging key signatures in a specific order, and in a circle, where the key moves moves from a starting chord (for example, C) to the chord rooted in the *fifth* note in the scale of that first key (in our example, G), then on again (in our example, D). Famous examples of this include Jimi Hendrix's version of 'Hey Joe', which moves around the circle of fifths from C, to G, to D, to A.

applications. Zhu could approach it with more flexibility, without the expectation that music should sound a certain way, and not trying to rework the existing way that music was envisioned.

As you may have noticed by now, I am not much concerned with who discovered something first: the conditions that enable something to take off, or that lead people to try and invent something, are far more interesting to me. I think these aspects can tell us more about ourselves, as well as about the discovery, whether it is equal temperament, calculus, relativity, the quark model, Bayesian probability or the light bulb. In this case, it is possible that Zhu and Stevin arrived at the system independently.[16] However, it would be extremely disingenuous to deny that Stevin might have heard tell of Zhu's proof and have been attempting to recreate it.[17]

In the last decades of the sixteenth century there was a lot of to-ing and fro-ing between China and Europe in general, and the United Provinces of the Netherlands specifically, despite the perilous year-long voyage it took to navigate between them. The Portuguese first arrived on the south-eastern coast of China as early as 1513. Determined to establish a foothold for trade, they spent much of the next four decades weaselling their way into establishing a colony. The first attempt at diplomatic relations went badly. In 1517, Tomé Pires was accepted as the first Portuguese ambassador to Beijing, and a trading post in Tamão was granted by the Zhengde emperor. Pires's brother Simão de Andrade then messed things up by fortifying that trading post, which the Chinese court interpreted as an act of aggression; Pires was executed, and trade with the Portuguese was forbidden.[18] But the Portuguese didn't leave, merely moved on to various places along the eastern coast; the Chinese army destroyed each one of these settlements. Eventually, a truce came about when the two sides faced a common enemy: pirates. Together, the Chinese and the Portuguese joined naval forces to lessen the grip of piracy along the coast. As a token of gratitude, Portuguese traders were granted use of a port very near the villages where my ancestors lived until the early twentieth century. Macau* became a Portuguese colony in 1554, in exchange for a symbolic rent of 500 *tael* (兩).

China was 'the richest [place] in the world' according to Dirck Gerritszoon, the first Dutchman recorded to have travelled to China in the 1580s.[19] Spices, silks, silverware, lacquerware, gemstones and delicate porcelain were greatly in demand by the burgeoning European middle classes, as well as by aristocratic customers. Elizabeth I of England even attempted to write to the Wanli emperor (a distant cousin of the one who came to terms with the Portuguese) at least three times between 1583 and 1602, in the interests of establishing diplomatic contact and trade relations; alas, all her letters went undelivered.[20] Meanwhile, events in mainland Europe were having repercussions on the import of these valuable goods. When Philip II, Holy Roman Emperor (and ruler of the southern Catholic Netherlands), was made King of Portugal in 1580, all trade between the Dutch Republic and the Portuguese was brought to a startling halt, due to the conflict in the Netherlands. As a result, demand for these 'exotic' treasures became even more frantic.

When thinking about the sixteenth and seventeenth centuries, it is hard to overestimate the acquisitiveness of European traders, a flock of wingless magpies sailing the seven seas in quest of all that was shiny. Ideas about music were commodities just as much as decorative objects like porcelain and silk. Macau became a key outpost for Jesuit missionaries, seeking to Convert the Natives and serve as informal diplomats to smooth trade negotiations. The music theorist Gene Cho has argued that shreds of Zhu's ideas travelled back to Europe through the Jesuit missionaries returning from Macau, which enabled Stevin's younger contemporaries Marin Mersenne and René Descartes to arrive at the concept of musical scale that we use today.[21] While Stevin's own musical treatise wasn't published until the nineteenth century, it's very

---

* Probably an ibericisation of A-Má Gao, 'Bay of the Sea Goddess A-Má'.

possible that his theory circulated among people who dispersed its contents far and wide. It's also possible that Mersenne and Descartes used snippets of Zhu's work and Stevin's in combination – or indeed that whispers of Zhu's theory made it back to Stevin, along with the material goods being transported in a roundabout way to the United Provinces from China.

Other aspects of his work suggest that Stevin was very interested in China and in establishing a foothold there. In 1602, the United Provinces founded the Vereenigde Oost-Indische Compagnie, or Dutch East India Company, and set sail in a doomed attempt to take control of Macau from the Portuguese. Stevin's works such as *De Havenvinding* (1594)* explored how to determine the longitude of a ship via the magnetic variation of a compass's needle; and his fortification and architectural plans went on to assist the design of Dutch Batavia,** which was colonised in 1619. Both works were crucial to establishing a solid trade route between China and the United Provinces.[22]

So, against the backdrop of the Dutch efforts to establish a colony to rival Macau, there are many possible ways that Stevin might have heard of Zhu's theory, although none have left any concrete trace. The effect on music, in any case, of this cross-pollination of East and West was a scale of neatly-divided parcels of music, equal in size, but never quite right for using in performance. You'll know this feeling, if you play an instrument or sing yourself: that reaching for a way to bend a note to fit it better into the harmony and the spaces between the other parts – up a bit, down a bit, fractionally adjusting. This is where the phenomenon of so-called 'baroque' pitch comes in: taking the pitch down a semitone(ish), loosening its stitches, back to a map of musical notes closer to that older hexachordal structure. These days that shift is almost unconscious. We're still doing it, though – reaching

---

*   Haven-finding.
** Now known as Jakarta, the capital of Indonesia.

for a long-internalised image of music, a visualisation given to us by a pair of men working 5,000 miles apart, 400 years ago.

𝄞

The story of the scale doesn't end there. In many ways it was only just beginning. It took on a new status as time went by: as an organising chart to categorise sensory perceptions of an entirely different nature.

Welcome, friends, to the parfumiers Piesse & Lubin. It's located in a ritzy sandstone building at 2 New Bond Street in Mayfair, the luxurious London shopping district, a leisurely stroll from Buckingham Palace. From the shopfloor of their palatial premises, Messrs Piesse & Lubin are striving to anglicise and industrialise the fragrance industry. But below, in the basement, is where the magic happens: here lies the laboratory where the parfumiers house rank upon rank of flowers and bottles, jars and pots of scentful products for use in their aromatic confections. A man moves between the glittering transparent vials, struck, suddenly, by the visual resemblance to organ pipes. He scribbles it down on a scrap of paper – one for his book, *The Art of Perfumery*, soon to be submitted to his publisher.

His name is Dr George William Septimus Piesse, seventh child, one-time optician, latterly a research chemist at University College London, and finally co-founder and co-owner of Piesse & Lubin with the Parisian scent aficionado Wilhelm Lubin. For decades, perfume had been seen as a continental product – not a meaningful endeavour for the English market.[23] Piesse set out to change that by sparking interest in the newly available synthetic chemical compounds that replicated famous scents. He even invented the swashbuckling figure of Mercutio Frangipani to market some of his perfumes, allegedly a botanist on Columbus's second voyage to the 'new world'. According to Piesse, Frangipani caught the scent of Antigua before he saw it; he discovered frangipani, or white jasmine, on the island, and brought it back to Europe where it was cultivated and spread by his descendant, the Marquis de Frangipani. Piesse was a consummate storyteller, and weaving a mythology around his perfume was hugely successful: the Frangipani perfume became one of the most popular scents of the 1850s and 1860s in England, France and the United States.[24]

Perfume? I hear you cry, *it's invisible, just like music! How can it possibly be visualised?* But, of course, scent is made entirely from that which is visible, and which is often used as synecdoche to stand for that fragrance. Think of the rose, which by any other name would smell as sweet. Piesse's repurposing of the musical scale is visual, too, used to impose a visible logic on his argument. The image of music lingers behind the story Piesse wove out of how to structure a perfume, and the intricate work of his chosen craft.

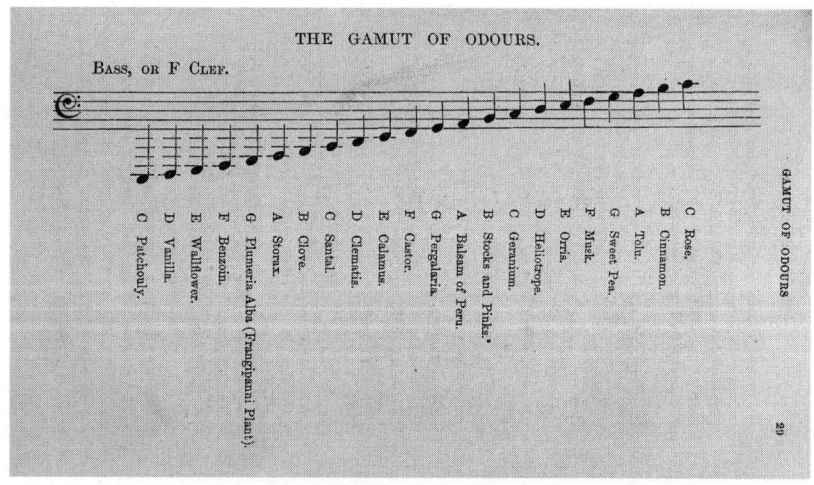

Septimus Piesse's perfume scale in bass, or F-clef, from *The Art of Perfumery*, 1862.

A key part of Piesse's storytelling technique was the publication of detailed, whimsical descriptions of his craft. He first proposes the analogy between music and scent, briefly, in the 1855 edition of his *The Art of Perfumery*, where he proposes the concept of the perfume octave in a description of how to imitate the essence of

The Hand of Guido: Mapping Musical Pitch

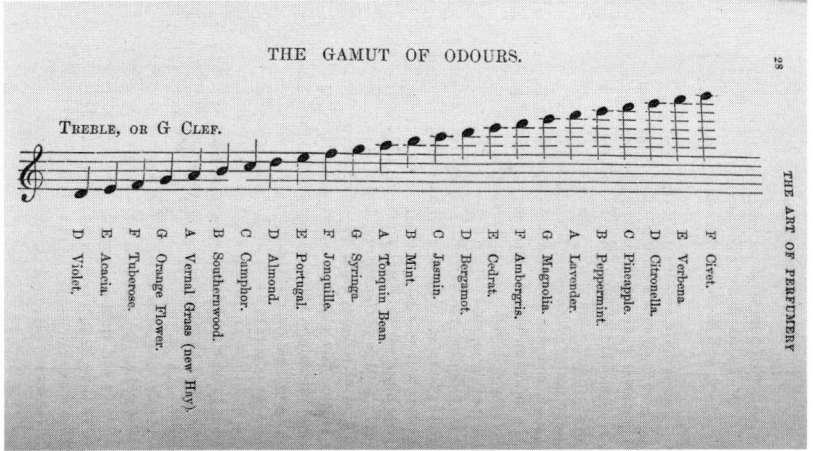

Septimus Piesse's perfume scale in treble, or G-clef.

sweet pea scent. By the revised 1862 edition, he had developed the metaphor into a fully-fledged series of diagrams, accompanied by an expanded explanation of the octave of odours. Later, his son Charles would describe it as an 'odophone': a full gamut encompassing some fifty odours.[25] Septimus Piesse's delight in the idea floods out of his writing like a heady perfume bouquet of its own.

> Scents, like sounds, appear to influence the olfactory nerve in certain definite degrees. There is, as it were, an octave of odours like an octave in music; certain odours coincide, like the keys of an instrument. Such [sic] as almond, heliotrope, vanilla and clematis blend together, each producing different degrees of a nearly similar impression. Again, we have citron, lemon, orange peel, and verbena, forming a higher octave of smells, which blend in a similar manner. The analogy is completed by what we are pleased to call semi-odours, such as rose and rose-geranium for the half note; petty grain, neroli, a black key, followed by fleur d'orange. Then we have patchouly, santal wood, and vitivert [sic], and many others running into each other.[26]

```
Bass.
  G  Pergalaria.    ⎫
  G  Sweet Pea.     ⎪
  D  Violet.        ⎪
  F  Tuberose.      ⎬  Bouquet of chord G.
  G  Orange Flower. ⎪
  B  Southernwood.  ⎭
Treble

Bass
  C  Santal.        ⎫
  C  Geranium.      ⎪
  E  Acacia.        ⎬  Bouquet of chord C.
  G  Orange Flower. ⎪
  C  Camphor.       ⎭
Treble.

Bass
  F  Musk.          ⎫
  C  Rose.          ⎪
  F  Tuberose.      ⎪
  A  Tonquin Bean.  ⎬  Bouquet of chord F.
  C  Camphor.       ⎪
  F  Jonquil.       ⎭
Treble
```

Septimus Piesse's bouquet chords.

Alongside these scales were perfume bouquets, tuned to different 'keys' and running downwards from 'bass' to 'treble'.[27] They were, as a later theorist would rather delightfully describe them, 'florichords'.[28] I can almost see it: an array of orange blossom, sweet peas and violets, laid out architecturally as though in an edgily modern flower arrangement. This fundamental plausibility, the fact that concepts like bouquets of chords are imaginable, is part of the intense power that fragrances or sounds exercise on our senses of sight, touch and taste. Piesse's description of how to construct a harmony of scent through a bouquet of chords makes intuitive sense. We can see how it would work, even if we are aware that the fundamental subjectivity of scent makes the analogy rather less scientific than Piesse claimed. As yet there is, sadly, no way of quantifying the sharpness and flatness of odours as the frequency of a given pitch does for sound; but that doesn't mean we can't imagine this symphony of fragrance, and feel it at the very edges of our sense of smell.

There are odours to which neither sharps nor flats are known, and there are others which would almost form a gamut in themselves by their variety of differences. The most numerous class of odours in nature are of the lemon character.

If a perfumer desires to make a bouquet from primitive odours, he must take odours as chord together [*sic*], the perfume will then be harmonious. In passing the eye down the gamut it will be seen what is harmony and what is a discord of smells. As an artist would blend his colours, so a perfumer must blend his scents.[29]

Piesse's chosen perfume bouquets were in the keys of C, F and G. Strikingly, this is a throwback to Guido and his three main hexachords, which were the C, the 'natural', F, the 'soft' and G, the 'hard'. The spectre of the hand, and the logic that had infused the old mind's eye of music, continued to linger. Lost ideas about how to structure and organise the ephemeral might seem a million miles from the way that people think about music today, but they are lurking just beneath the surface, ready to emerge in surprising (and, in this case, surprisingly floral, woody and musky) forms. This is a side of musical scales we don't often see: one that inspires and surprises, even as it imposes order.

Piesse never attempted to mock up a physical scent organ. Others did later, but this was too concrete, too frustratingly lacking in the phantasmagorical for a man who wrote about 'bouquets of primitive odours' and 'discords of smells'. This was the age that would give birth to Lewis Carroll's *Alice's Adventures in Wonderland*, an era enchanted by the magic of mathematics.

This isn't to say that Piesse's idea was universally well received. 'To arrange "smells", therefore, on a musical scale,' fumed one review in the *Journal of the Franklin Institute*, 'is a mere matter of fanciful and far-fetched analogy, without the shadow of a support in scientific fact.'[30] Of course there are problems. Piesse presupposes a reasonably high level of knowledge of the Western classical music system, in order to put together your own chord bouquet – otherwise you might, heaven forbid, put together rose with violet and verbena, or peppermint and pineapple. His obituary in the *Scientific American* is kinder: 'he, as do all men of original ideas, met with acrimonious criticism bordering upon abuse.' Although Piesse was roundly criticised in his lifetime, the idea of the octave of odours continued to excite people across the nineteenth century.

Musical scales, no matter how dry they might appear, no matter how many children they have traumatised, have inspired incredible feats of innovation. The way in which they play between what can be visualised and what can be heard has been remarkably stimulating for people seeking to capture the ephemeral. In need of a diagram, an abstract map of high to low, the musical scale was an ideal place to start. And the example of Piesse's fragrance octave reveals something striking about musical scales. Intangible though they are, musical pitches and scents seem to exist along a spectrum that has physical positioning: we intuitively understand that some are 'higher', some 'lower', some compatible and some discordant. The visual representation of the scale is a manifestation of this logic. The result is a mind's eye of music that tantalises and seeps far beyond the realms of what can be heard.

𝄞

It's 1894, some forty years after Piesse, and we're moving west. Deep in the smog of Victorian London, banging emits from 26 Kensington Park Gardens in Notting Hill. Behind the decorated stucco facade, powdered black with soot despite the leafy square it faces, there are the sounds of screws being tightened, widgets grinding, segments being hammered into place.

A man in shirt sleeves is kneeling before some kind of contraption of metal, wood, glass and a partly butchered piano, his frock coat abandoned and slung unceremoniously over a chair, mutton chop whiskers dishevelled. I'd like to think that he kept such toil to his workshop, but I suspect he was just not that kind of person – instead, much to the frustration of his wife and housekeeper, the components of the machine are probably spread out across the Persian rug in the drawing room, cogs and nuts rolling beneath the Chesterfield sofa and pinging off into the brocade of the drapes. Finally, a shout of triumph! From the contraption comes a bright flash of rainbowed light, briefly projected through the window onto the viscous grey smog.

The image of the musical scale continued to spark imaginations, and none more so than that of Alexander Wallace Rimington, an etcher, painter, illustrator, engineer and inventor who would later become Professor of Fine Arts at the Queen's College, University of London. He was the quintessential eccentric Victorian gentleman inventor, a tinkerer full of madcap ideas that perplexed large swathes of the population. What the world needed, he thought, what it *really* needed, was what he called a 'colour organ'. Here he is describing how it works, some seventeen years after he first embarked upon constructing the prototype, in his book *Colour-Music: The Art of Mobile Colour*:

> Colour and sound cannot, of course, be adequately described in words, nevertheless at this stage it may be as well to attempt to give some idea of the kind of effects produced by the colour-organ.
>
> Imagine a darkened concert-room. At one end there is a large screen of white drapery in folds surrounded with black and framed by two bands of pure white light. Upon this, we will suppose, as an example of a simple colour composition, that there appears the faintest possible flush of rose colour, which very gradually fades away while we are enjoying its purity and subtlety of tint, and we return to darkness. Then, with an interval, it is repeated in three successive phases, the last of which is stronger and more prolonged.

> While it is still lingering upon the screen a rapid series of touches of pale lavender notes opens with a Wagnerian trumpet-blast. The screen is at the same moment flooded by an intense orange which palpitates with the harmonic colours corresponding to a subordinate passage upon some of the other orchestral instruments. The blast ceases, there is a faint echo of it upon the violins while the screen pulsates with pale lemon and saffron, hardly discernible. Again comes the blare of the trumpets, and once more the screen flames with orange modulations.
>
> This is the opening, let us say, of a passage of pathetic character in which accidentals often intervene and the key tends to become minor. The colour scheme, without being a direct translation, sympathizes with this – it is low in tone and shows slight discords, and then gradually develops a more joyous character.[31]

Rimington was a man of huge ambition. This doesn't quite translate into his paintings themselves, which are too washed-out and sentimental for my own taste. It was the period of the Art Nouveau, of pointillism and the Arts and Crafts movement; by the time he published his book, cubism was on the rise. In the years when John Singer Sargent, Aubrey Beardsley, Vanessa Bell, Roger Fry and Laura Knight were experimenting with the possibilities of paint, Rimington's works seem surprisingly staid. His paintings seem entirely out of keeping with the man who invented the colour organ, an object so steampunk that it would fit seamlessly in a film by Jean-Pierre Jeunet or Wes Anderson.

At the heart of his concept is the idea that the colour spectrum can be mapped directly onto musical pitch. The principle is relatively simple: you press a key, or play a chord, and a colour or selection of colours will be projected onto a screen, offering a rainbow of music. Rimington had noticed that both colour and music work via 'vibration' (or, as we'd now say, frequency). So there must, he thought, be a colour octave to match the musical octave. He took the note C as a starting point. It was, he wrote, 'purely arbitrary' but it illustrated how he saw the colour octave working. The last note was violet, which, 'as it approaches the dark spaces beyond it into which our eyes cannot penetrate, ... tends more and more towards becoming purplish before it finally fades into a dark neutral tint' that, Rimington argued, became more red, thus closing the octave.

Although it's impossible to ascertain now, it seems not unlikely that Rimington had some degree of chromaesthesia, the form of synaesthesia that results in being able to see sounds as colours.[32] Plenty of musicians and artists have been recorded chromaesthetes, most recently the American musician and record producer Pharrell Williams, whose Lego animation biopic *Piece by Piece* (2024) explored the influence it had on his life and music.

Chromaesthesia was first recorded in the late seventeenth century. Traditionally it – along with all other forms of synaesthesia – was understood to occur as a result of increased brain connectivity across senses, but more recent research suggests that it's actually a matter of entangled concepts, as well as senses, and that the mechanisms at play can vary wildly from person to person. The music psychologist Caroline Curwen has demonstrated, for example, that the sound–colour association can be complex and context-related, shifting with key signatures as well as single pitches or just speech sounds.[33] Other studies reveal that chromaesthesia appears to be something of a spectrum, showing that a large proportion of otherwise neuro-typical people associate high-pitched sounds with light or bright colours, and low-pitched ones with darker shades (possibly due to the impact of lingering neural traces from the neonatal period of development, when babies initially experience intense connectivity across their developing brains).[34]

But chromaesthesia, like all forms of synaesthesia, is incredibly difficult to pin down scientifically. As well as the huge variation between people, there's no agreement, for example, on what looks or sounds or tastes or smells like what. This doesn't get any easier to quantify with high levels of musical training, either. There's a well-documented dispute between the Russian composers Alexander Scriabin and Nikolai Rimsky-Korsakov, who both experienced chromaesthesia but virulently disagreed about which colours corresponded to which sounds. Rimsky-Korsakov saw F-sharp as an 'indefinite gray-green colour'; Scriabin saw it as a 'bright saturated blue'.[35]

I myself experience something like chromaesthesia but I do not see discrete colours, more entire forms, shapes and images closer to the 'wild, almost crazy lines sketched before me' described by the painter Wassily Kandinsky.[36] They are incredibly contextual and do not map neatly onto musical pitches or keys. Sometimes they are less vivid, and I have no idea why. Very often I feel them more as a matter of movement or kinaesthesia, and I'm almost unaware of where sound, image and movement meet. The variance even in individual subjects is such that even today, the cognitive operations behind coloured hearing are poorly understood.

In any case, Rimington was far from the first person to draw an association between colour and music. The concept had been floating in the scientific ether since Aristotle, and for a time it was the favoured party-trick theory of the mathematics bros of Europe. Isaac Newton, that famous innovator, proposed a colour wheel with spokes that corresponded to notes of the musical scale in around 1665. The mathematician Louis Bertrand Castel proposed an 'ocular harpsichord' in 1725; evocative descriptions survive of coloured silks revealed and lit from behind by candles, but frustratingly nothing more than that. Benjamin Stillingfleet's *Principles and Powers of Harmony* (1771) included diagrams of colour/sound scales. Closer to Rimington's own time, the flower painter and art theorist Mary Gartside published 'An Essay on Light and Shade' (1805), which explored the idea of colour harmony with elegantly blended abstract blossoms of pigment in crimson, green and blue, nestled in billowing petals of their accent colours.

Gartside herself didn't depict a colour scale, but her account indicates that she saw the spectrum in this way. She wrote that 'to produce true harmony, must the *colours* be arranged, graduating from the extreme bright and warm tints to the extreme cold ones, for if one colour is out of place it destroys that harmony of colour, which is as pleasing to a nice eye, as true harmony in music is to a nice ear.'[37] The dye and pigment chemist George Fields published the same observation in a book titled *Chromatics, or, the Analogy, Harmony and Philosophy of Colour*; first published in 1817, it was expanded in 1845, complete with hand-coloured diagrams of the colour octave. Field, like Gartside, saw the connection between music and colour as inevitable:

> It is impossible, not to be struck with the entire resemblance and complete analogy of the two scales; nor will the philosophic mind of the artist find it difficult to carry these relations into figures and the forms of science universally. And as the acuteness, tone, and gravity of musical notes, blend or run into each other through an infinite series in the musical scale, imparting *melody* to musical composition, so do the like infinite sequences of the tints, hues and shades of colours, impart mellowness, or melody, to colours and colouring. Upon these gradations and successions depend the sweetest effects of colours in nature and painting, so analogous to the melody of musical sounds, that we have not hesitated to call them *the melody of colours*.[38]

Field's colour octave, though, started at blue rather than red, and he was invested in capturing colour's rhythmic possibilities – its 'breves and minims, quavers and semiquavers' – as well as its relationship to tone.

So Rimington's colour organ had a long, august pedigree – enough that you'd assume it would have been a hit with its audience. Initially the organ was silent, meaning that the 'player' had to accompany music rather than produce the whole show themselves. Over time, Rimington managed to modify the instrument to make sound as well. The colour organ had its maiden voyage at the now-demolished St James's Hall, Piccadilly, in 1895, with displays to accompany the music of composers Richard Wagner, Anton Dvořák and Frédéric Chopin; further performances took place at St James's again, and then at the Free Trade Hall in Manchester. Some were delighted with it. Others, not so much. 'The tints with which the screen was filled were often very beautiful,' the reviewer for *The Times* wrote on 28th June 1895, 'if rather suggestive at times of "crushed strawberry" and other colours of that style, but they seemed unsatisfying, and did not convey the same impression to the mind as the music.'

It's a shame that the colour organ never caught on, but I wonder if Rimington mistook his market. Listeners of high classical composers like Wagner and Dvořák probably weren't the ones who would most enjoy what the colour organ had to offer. The 1890s were the golden age of Gilbert and Sullivan and their cheeky little operettas like *The Mikado*, *H.M.S. Pinafore* and *Iolanthe* – all more plausible candidates for a performance that might benefit from what spectators described as 'flashes of colour like lightning'. Music halls were also of huge importance to the musical life of great swathes of the British population during this period. By pitching his colour organ as an instrument for so-called highbrow art music of the most traditional sort, ignoring the avant-garde and many of the other fashionable genres and forms of music, Rimington backed himself into a corner.

In any case, quite why he chose to pitch his colour organ as a high classical instrument is not entirely clear. His own account offers very little in the way of clues. Instead, in *Colour-Music* he states explicitly that his intention is to create a resource for artists that will increase their colour 'faculty', and train them to 'appreciate subtle harmonies in colour':

> Many artists wisely keep objects of beautiful colour in their studios in order to be able to bring their minds *into tune* with the beauty of colour in nature or art. Some choose Oriental china, others Limoges enamel, others the plumage of birds or collections of gems and minerals, others, again, Medieval and oriental draperies or stained glass. But the artist who has access to a mobile colour instrument – which it is to be hoped will some day take such a simplified form that it will be within the reach of everyone – can at any time sit down and obtain thousands of suggestions, almost at haphazard.[39]

That metaphor encapsulates all that Rimington sought to do: he sees the use of 'objects of beautiful colour' as a way of 'bringing minds *into tune*' with colour – the colour organ is a matter of bringing eyes and minds to the right pitch of colour, and ensuring a harmonious outcome. According to his logic, the visual image of the musical scale will help artists align themselves with a greater colour intelligence: a perfect mind's eye to map the relationship between shades on the spectrum. For me, this context makes Rimington's focus on traditional Western classical music even more mysterious. He's arguing for innovation and experimentation, 'almost at haphazard'. This approach fits far more closely with music by composers who focus on pioneering use of pitch, like Claude Debussy, Ethel Smyth and Igor Stravinsky – our friends from the Ballets Russes – than composers like Wagner, who focused on using music as a kind of narrative tableau.

The closer you look at the details of how Rimington describes his colour octave, the more intriguing it becomes. The visual system allows him to create a consistent vocabulary of colour, yes. But he knows that it will be imperfect, and that is part of what galvanises him to bring the colour out into the world: he thinks that once people develop 'colour sense', greater understanding of that vocabulary might follow. And so he reaches for a vaguer, looser approximation of where one shade of the spectrum blurs into the next. It's strikingly close to the loosely-stitched system of Guido's hand – a map of potential connections that can be refined to taste, choreographed by the performer, rather than a rigid sense of exact pigment or pitch. In his diagram of the division of the colour scale upon the colour organ, Rimington acknowledges that there isn't even a true consensus about what a discord in music is, especially in 'advanced modern music'. The colours, he states, 'could not be accurately represented in pigment', and so they cannot 'correspond more than roughly'.

> The colour sense has been so little educated as an aesthetic faculty as compared with the high cultivation of the musical one through past centuries that, although there is, perhaps, a general agreement as to certain pronounced discords, in colour – though even that is open to question – there is not the same general sensitiveness among most people as to lesser ones. Hence, although there may be a general agreement as to the discord between the juxtaposition of colours at the beginning and end of the spectrum-band, there will be less unanimity as to whether intermediate combinations are discordant, even supposing we have divided our colour scale correctly and started it from the right point. Opinion as to what constitutes a discord in music is, moreover, undergoing a change and becoming less definite in its pronouncement, as is evidenced by some advanced modern music.[40]

The visual potential of the musical scale, mapped onto the colour spectrum, galvanised Rimington's invention. Most fascinating, though, is the way that bringing out its visual role revealed the musical scale's limitations. Rimington is in no doubt that musical pitches are absolute: he talks about the octave as an exact, precise division. But there, creeping in at the edges, is that older mapping: context-specific, subjective and hazy.

The colour organ came heart-stoppingly close to widespread acceptance. Henry Wood, founder of the Proms,* hoped to showcase the instrument with a performance of Rimsky-Korsakov's colour–music antagonist Alexander Scriabin's 'Prometheus: A Poem of Fire' in 1914. However, the United Kingdom declared war on Germany on 4th August 1914, putting paid to those plans. Rimington's organ, denied the big mark of acceptance by the British musical establishment, languished. Rimington died four months before the end of the First World War, and without anyone to advocate for it, the colour organ was consigned to the status of Curiosity. The fate of the actual physical instrument is unknown, but it was probably dismantled and reused for parts – a sad but perhaps fitting end to a machine that sought to formalise colour and sound, both of which are so slippery and evade easy categorisation.

𝄞

A more successful attempt to visualise pitch in colour occurred around the same time, deep in the Welsh valleys, in the village of Dowlais. The mappings of musical space we have seen so far have been made of syllables, numbers, mathematics, colour, scent. This one is made of sound waves, of voice, of paint and of glass. Let me introduce you to the voice flower, the creation of Megan 'Margaret' Watts Hughes.

Watts Hughes discovered how to create these forms by accident, all on a golden afternoon in May 1885. She was a gifted singer – the local community had paid for her to study at the

---

* The classical music festival run every summer from the Royal Albert Hall in London.

Royal Academy of Music in London with the renowned singing teacher Manuel García, and she had toured with the 'Swedish Nightingale' Jenny Lind, one of the most famous sopranos of the day. Lind adored Watts Hughes, and once said of her that 'I have never met anyone so related to me in the art of music.' Ill health meant Watts Hughes had to leave the Royal Academy prematurely (nodules, my brain immediately flares, though there's no record of the true reason).[41] But music, and singing, continued to be her passion.

On that day in 1885, she had been using a rubber sheet and seeds to test the resonance of her voice. 'On one occasion as I sang,' she recalled, 'I noticed that the seeds which I had placed on the India rubber membrane, on becoming quiescent, instead of scattering promiscuously in all directions and falling over the edge of the receiver onto the table, as was customary when a rather loud note was sung, resolved themselves into a perfect geometrical figure.' At first this had been about measuring vocal prowess and helping her to improve her singing technique. Now, she began to construct an implement to track these visual forms and the interaction between resonant frequencies, waves of compression and rarefaction, and the images that they could create. It consisted of a tube, narrow at one end, with an elastic membrane 'such as soft-sheet rubber' stretched over the other, which was wide-mouthed and horizontal. The membrane was covered with pigmented glycerine (the thick liquid by-product of soap manufacture). When she sang into the narrow end, the glycerine would billow and ripple. She called it the Eidophone.[42]

The Eidophone allowed Watts Hughes to produce some incredible visualisations of music. Single pitches, sung into the implement, became ethereal patterns that preserved the geometry of standing-wave resonances. Psychedelic colours flood across the plates of glass in deep foresty green, gold, mermaid turquoise, sepia and murky teal. Each form resembles seaweedy petals, sea anemones and fragments of coral, refracted through deep-sea light. And curiously enough, the longer you spend looking at them, the more clear it becomes how they relate to the voice that produced them. You can almost hear her: the overtones, the grain of her voice and how it has manifested in fractals as she paints with song.

These 'beautiful crispations' were forgiving things, and could be attempted multiple times in order to get the right visual effect. Sometimes, Watts Hughes wrote in an 1891 article in *The Century* magazine, and 'possibly from the condition of the colour-paste', the 'first display of petals' can come out imperfect.[43] Never fear, she said, 'all that is needed is just to sing the same note again, but diminuendo [more quietly], and straightway all the petals will retreat into the central heap, as at first. Then the singer may try once more, and another crescendo will probably achieve the production of a perfect floral form.' Watts Hughes recommended exercising 'great care and delicacy' in singing to produce her voice flowers; they were, she thought, a great way of training a singer in the 'steady sustaining of notes in intensities from the softest pianissimo to a very loud forte'. They could also, she observed, produce visualisations of forms that seemed to map onto overtones; these are the extra frequencies found in every pitch but 'inaudible even to a well-trained ear'.

Not all of her examples were annotated, but by and large she focused on specific musical notes, and the interaction between them: '3rd interval E', 'B', 'C' appear carefully inked on some of the voice flowers. In 1904, she published her book *The Eidophone Voice Figures: Natural and Geometrical Forms Produced by Vibrations of the Human Voice*, complete with illustrations demonstrating that each note reliably produced concomitant patterns, depicted over a musical stave with simple song tunes, such as 'God Save the King'.[44] Such tunes were very far below Watts Hughes' level of skill, but they were easily accessible to others. The intention was clear: she wanted anyone and everyone to join in and create their own voice flowers.

At first glance the vocal flowers might look nothing like a scale, but suspend your disbelief for a moment and look closer at the way that Watts Hughes systematises her forms. She certainly saw them in this way: one pair of diagrams in her book depicts a series of diatonic scales – that is, scales organised by key – with

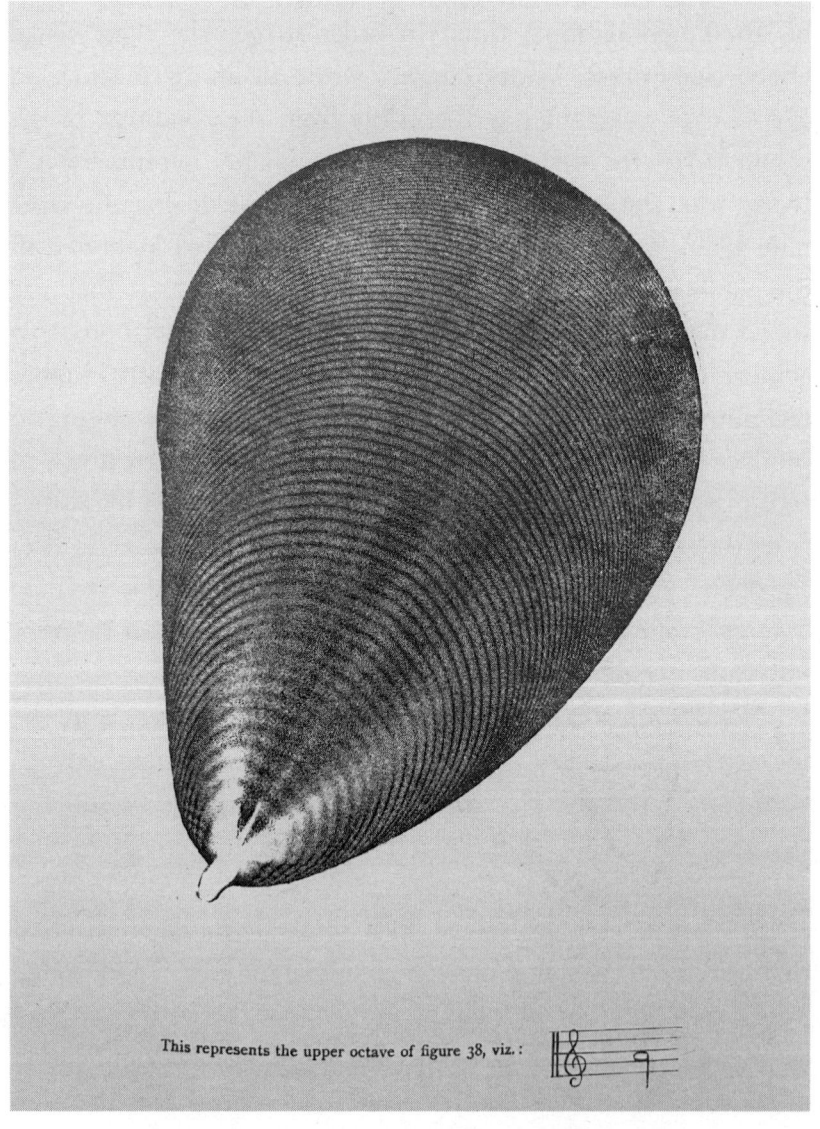

Megan Watts Hughes' voice flower representation of the note A, from *The Eidophone Voice Figures*, 1904.

voice flowers corresponding to each pitch. Let's think deeper, too, about what a musical scale actually is. In the bluntest terms, a musical scale is a graduated system of measurement: an arrangement of notes in descending or ascending order of pitch. Watts Hughes' voice flowers are organised by pitch. She doesn't always name them, because she is more interested in the visual patterns that they take, as 'daisy forms', 'fern forms', 'pansy forms' and 'serpent forms'. Often, though, it's clear that she is thinking about pitch. One depicts three pitches, inscribed along their margins in Watts Hughes' handwriting as 'octave and 5th interval B-flat'. In the example in the plate section, voice flowers combine into what she calls a 'sound impression', and we can see the interaction between the phrasings, twists and turns of her voice as she moves between notes to study their visible interactions.

She tacked these images up in the windows of the orphanage she founded at Mountford House, Barnsbury Square, Islington, bathing the orphan boys in jewelled splashes of illuminated colour: both arresting to look at, and educational.

'Seaweed' or 'Landscape' forms
of Watts Hughes' voice flowers.

People were fascinated by the voice flowers. The novelist Emilie Barrington visited Watts Hughes and her forms at the orphanage in Islington, and observed in a letter to the *Spectator* on 26th October 1889 that '[the Impression Figures] are more like, perhaps, what a dream might make out of the impressions left by nature, perfectly drawn designs of shell-like forms, photographically precise renderings of shapes of which the exact originals were never seen by human eye on sea or land'; such things as '"Alice in Wonderland" might have come upon, had she tumbled down to the bottom of the sea.' They had, Barrington thought, 'a touch of fairy land'. But they are more than images of a chimerical, sub-marine world. They are works of art, and they are also examples of great scientific innovation.

Watts Hughes became one of the first women ever to present an invention to the Royal Society, when she showcased the Eidophone in 1887.[45] In time, her discoveries gave rise to the scientific field of cymatics, the study of modal vibrational phenomena beloved of performers like the avant-garde Icelandic singer Björk, the Californian electro duo the Glitch Mob and the British music producer Aphex Twin. The scientists Robert Hooke, Galileo Galilei, Ernst Chladni and Hans Jenny (who came up with the term 'cymatics') are commonly acknowledged as having done the heavy lifting, but Watts Hughes deserves credit, too. She was the first to use colour to depict the phenomenon of sound waves. It was her invention that was presented at the Royal Society; her work that was published and admired at the time.

The voice flowers are little known today in histories of music, let alone in histories of art. They deserve more attention. I can't help but wonder if they haven't received more notice because they evade easy categorisation – lost in between the gaps of forms and genres and practices.[46] They aren't quite visual art objects – what would we call them? Acoustic monoprints? Sonic engravings? – nor musical diagrams, nor straight-up experimental physics. In mapping the impact of pitched soundwaves to notes on the musical scale, they offer a revisualisation of music; an exciting new way of seeing how music occupies space. Voice flowers also offer an insight into the way that practitioners married art and technology in the nineteenth century.

When that recognition does finally happen, though, it's important that we don't lose sight of one of the most curious aspects of the voice flowers: how close they are to that old, lost mind's eye of music, Guido's hand. Watts Hughes was highly invested in scientific research, but also extremely religious. The two were not contradictions in the nineteenth century. She passionately wanted her experiments to help 'by some slight degree, the revelation of yet another link in the great chain of the organised universe that, we are told in Holy Writ, took its shape in the voice of God'.

So, after all, we are not that far from Guido and his hand; not so far from the cosmic music that infused the worlds of Simon Stevin and Zhu Zaiyu. It's a visualisation of musical space leading, fragment by fragment, note by note, back to the desire for an image of a coherent, sonorous world. Each of these examples – the colour harmony, the odour octave and the voice flowers – hungers for a lost paradise of pitch space.

When I visited China in 2007, my siblings and I went to the ancient Shaolin monastery at Dengfeng where Zhu spent his exile hanging out with the monks, set in the shadow of the towering, phantasmagorical edifice of Mount Song.[47] The temple was a chaotic place – given over to the bustle of tourists, rather than contemplation. No one told us about Zhu. But now, looking back, I can just imagine him contemplating higher things and slowly but surely drifting further and further from princely pursuits, as he wandered through the pine trees and monuments of its pagoda forest. An example of his calligraphy survives, inscribed on the reverse of a monument to an abbot of the monastery: an ode 'To the fusion of the 3 religious sects and 9 philosophical schools', dated 1st April 1565. Below the ode is a circular depiction of a figure combining three faces in one: the clothing of a Confucian scholar, a Buddhist monk and a Daoist priest.[48] Already in this ode, composed a decade before he invented his musical scale, Zhu is intellectually adventurous – unwilling to accept things as they are, looking to push limits, to transcend them.

It's incredible, now, to think of how his idea undertook a similar roundabout journey to the one made by my grandparents: across the ocean from the coastline near Macau, eventually mingling with other similar ideas, and landing in Europe and the United Kingdom. There, my siblings and I would encounter the descendant of his idea, a song built out of 'Do! Re! Mi!', sung by an array of children in clothes made of repurposed floral curtains. And that visualisation of musical space would spark our imaginations, enabling us to create and play with sound, and would entertain us in the doldrums of dead space for many, many years to come.

It doesn't matter that Guido's hand and Zhu's equal temperament are imperfect, that they have to be fudged and manipulated to fit the way we produce musical compositions. They are a visual pattern full of promise and imagined possibility, a cartographical chart mapping out a million ways towards a playground of musical *terra incognita*, all the same. Next time you encounter a musical scale, don't think of it as a fixed thing. Think, instead, of its possibilities – because Here Be Dragons.

4

Sheet Music Scrolled Across the Inside of My Lungs:*
The Music Book

The air is thick with scent: a sweetly cloying aroma of stale frankincense, mixed with slowly decaying paper and ancient stone. Caught in this perfumed web, a shaft of light lances down from the windows. Within it is captured the glimmer of dust motes, gently spiralling down onto the Cinderellas of this chapter as they slumber, dreaming of their past glories.

Rank on rank, they stand by the doorways of churches across the globe: hymn books, possibly the least sexy objects known to humanity. You probably didn't even notice them the last time you visited a church as you toured the sights of a new city. Whether you go to Mass every Sunday or last attended for a wedding or a carol service at Christmas several years ago, though you held one in your hands, your brain barely acknowledged it or registered what it looked like, almost as though it wasn't really there.

One of these papery revenants sits in my little hands, which are still sticky with glitter glue from Sunday school. I am following the words and lines of the music notation and singing along with one of those tumpty-tumpty-tum Victorian hymns like 'Thine

---

*   Andrea Gibson, 'Stay', from *Yellowbird* (2009).

Be the Glory'. I am somewhere between three-and-a-half and four years old. Next to me, my best friend is watching me sing along with the adults with concern and confusion – he is joining in too, but with 'Baa Baa Black Sheep'. He knows what reading is and that he will do it soon, but it's never occurred to him that we could try to do it ourselves, because we haven't yet started school. He is more than capable of reading, but he is interested in other, more practical matters: the mechanics of the dens we build in the garden, in Duplo, in how to set up a run to launch a marble as far as possible.

I, on the other hand, am a relentless, rapacious sponge for any kind of visual information or material, and I demand to be shown how it works. Every week we are taken to Sunday school, and afterwards we are brought into the church to sing with the adults: one hymn during communion and one hymn after. I am a nerdy, restless little child (of, at that time, very unmusical parents), and I have absorbed the basic rudiments of how to read sheet music, using one of those unlovely, battered books.

Most of the books seem to have sat there for a hundred years. They're rubbed soft at the corners of their covers, dog-eared, often taped together and coming loose from their binding. Each sign of wear and tear appears so integral to their appearance that the water stains, ink smudges and ruffled page edges are like decorative embellishments. They have gilded stamps on their covers and spines, faded gold emblems marking the churches they once belonged to and which, more often than not, have now closed.

But looks can be deceiving, and these books are important. They are the direct descendants of the books that were once works of art, fashionable accessories and markers of taste. And they are also part of the dynasty of books that changed the history of music – and the role that music played in everyday life – forever.

They still hold the key to the power that once thrummed through their ancestors' silk and gilded bodies. Take a look at the grass-green ones, my favourites (of course I have a favourite hymn book – I don't get out much). They are the *New English Hymnal* and they lay everything out neatly, they feel nice to hold and, most importantly, they include music for every hymn. There's a line of thought that including music notation in hymn books is elitist – how would you feel, if you didn't know how to read it? – but that conveniently ignores the fact that if you don't ever get to see it, you never *will* learn to read it. In other words, it's another way of shutting people out. In fact, the first version of this book was designed specifically in order to help people learn how to read music.

This is a story that is very close to my heart. It is also a story that is seldom told in the history of music. Despite the fact that the 'notes on the page' are typically taken as the *sine qua non* of music – utterly indispensable – very little attention is paid to their visual appearance, and why they might have come to have these particular forms. Even less attention is paid to the appearance of 'notes on the page' in objects like hymn books.

Compared to the lustrous illuminated manuscripts that are its predecessors, the modern hymn book is mundane. It isn't full of complicated music. Its tunes are so common that they don't feel special any more – quaint little things that belong with your grandparents' sewing kits or antiquated drill bits kept in an old biscuit tin. But this simple elegance, the ability those tunes have to insinuate themselves into your brain, is what lent them such power. It is what made the forerunners of these hymn books so quietly integral to the stories of the artistic and musical cultures of the age. This was a tatty, well-thumbed paper cornerstone in the colossus of the British empire: a brick upon which its foundations were laid, with, as Archbishop Thomas Cranmer had long dreamed, 'for every syllable a note'.

In many ways, the fable of the hymn book is the tale of the English choral tradition – the music-making tradition within which I got the lion's share of my musical education. This tradition is problematic because it is so entwined with ideas about

English exceptionalism, colonialism and chosen races. It would be disingenuous to tell you this story without highlighting these things. But it is also a tradition full of beauty, and one that continues to be quietly, steadily popular across the world even as the chokehold of empire and its legacy gradually subsides. The British-Ghanaian actor, director, screenwriter and poet Michaela Coel noted in 2017 that 'it's quite poetic. There's psalms that tell you things that nobody tells you – that you're fearfully and wonderfully made, that you're beautiful, that you have worth.'[1]

The hymn book was an amazingly neat way of exporting the idea of Englishness. It was portable: you could take it down the road to the next village, or halfway across the world on a ship; its tunes were catchy. You can find music from the English choral tradition sung in spaces from Hong Kong, Nigeria and India to the United States and Australia. Even as the numbers of people identifying as Anglican or Anglican-adjacent have declined in the West, the appetite for its music has continued. Attendees at the service of evensong are just as likely to be atheists or agnostics as believers; something about this kind of music continues to provide a spiritual, calming force, regardless of its original devotional purpose.

'Young people' are typically the psychic dumping ground of the Church of England: every change they make, every strategy they devise is designed to bring in a younger congregation, and so the music of the English choral tradition is often ditched for guitars and worship songs that 'young people prefer'. Recent research demonstrates that, in fact, *more* traditional music and expressions of visual culture (such as vestments, ceremony and stained glass) and services decrease the age of the congregation.[2]

The people strategising to get larger congregations would know this, if they took a closer look at hymn books and their histories. The ideas that went into their making were not so different to what the Church of England wants today; if you take more than a cursory glance, one of its very first hymn books makes this all too clear. I'm talking about *The Whole Booke of Psalmes*, a book that first appeared in 1562 and is still in print today: a quiet little world-breaker-and-remaker, witness to a million marriages, deaths, childhoods, family spats, celebrations, commiserations and battles up and down the tiny island that became Great Britain.

Art historians agree that the arrival of print in the Western world had a huge impact on aesthetic sensibilities. It's rare, though,

Gentile di Fabriano's *Coronation of the Virgin*, with flanking angels holding scrolls of sheet music, 1420.

that they acknowledge that those early, common-or-garden printed books were art objects in their own right. *The Whole Booke of Psalmes* and its offspring illuminate just how passionately normal people embraced the beauty and artistic potential of monochromatic print: not just as a thing to be read, but as something to be looked at, a pattern, a sumptuous surface. The possibilities were endless. It might surprise you to hear me (even me) talking about a hymn book in this way, but it cannot be overstated: that first hymn book changed what music looked like and how it was fantasised, forever.

Yōshū (Hashimoto) Chikanobu, *Concert of European Music*, 1889.

This wasn't the first time that the image of written, notated music had been used as a tool of power, dominance or influence, as we've already seen throughout this book. Plenty of other cultures from ancient Sumeria and Egypt to China had long since discovered how useful written music could be as a means of signalling power, might and longevity even to those who were not – or who were only partly – musically literate, and they had honed the art to perfection.

Sheet Music Scrolled Across the Inside of My Lungs: The Music Book

Music books were visually important in the art of other cultures, too. Medieval European illuminated manuscripts frequently feature them prominently displayed in margins and foliated lettering, and larger panel paintings such as Gentile di Fabriano's *Coronation of the Virgin* (*c.* 1420) use notated music scrolls as a kind of unravelling extension of the frame. In what is now modern-day Iran, musicians of the Safavid court were expected to be skilled in calligraphy and manuscript illumination, alongside musical performance, suggesting that writing, books, music and visual arts were closely associated. Likewise,

Katagawa Shinegobu's *Flower Matching Contest No. 4*, 1835.

Japanese culture held the music book in high esteem as a means of representing accomplishments, narrative devices and decorative surfaces; paintings such as Yōshū Chikanobu's *Concert of European Music* (late nineteenth century) and Katagawa Shinegobu's *Flower Matching Contest No. 4* (1835) show us music books playing a central role in images of music-making.

What marks out the English choral tradition is the global reach of its success – a success aided by the music book. It was so enduring that its impact is nigh-on invisible for us even today, unless we know exactly where to look. These early precursors to hymn books were used by the great political movers and shakers who puppeteered England in the sixteenth century to disseminate the idea of the English as a collective community, after decades of war and conflict.[3] As Thomas Cromwell wrote in 1533, years before England's territories extended much further than its small, wind-swept island: 'Whereby divers sundry old authentic histories and chronicles, it is manifestly declared and expressed, that this realm of England is an empire, and so hath been accepted in the world.'[4]

Before this point, people would have struggled to identify with the nation of England, let alone Cromwell's 'empire'; they were more in tune with belonging to their villages, towns, cities, counties, faiths and trades. Across the sixteenth century, though, the policy-makers of the Tudor monarchs steadily constructed the idea of Englishness. That collective identity, in turn, was necessary to begin the work of constructing an empire that would go on to colonise twenty-five per cent of the world's population and thirty per cent of the world's land at its height. For the next 400 years, it would extract the goods and lands of other cultures until, at its height, 412 million people lived under its rule – people not marked by the glitter of chosen 'Englishness' – and its legacy still reverberates today. All this, facilitated to a substantial extent by the redesign of a humble book.

It might seem odd to dedicate an entire chapter to such a seemingly geographically and culturally limited object, but make no mistake: though diminutive and unassuming, the visual influence of the hymn book seeped into every heart and mind of that twenty-five per cent, even as the books themselves were rewritten and reshaped into new forms. Here's an example from the early settlers of Massachusetts, the *Bay Psalm Book* (1640). The preface lays out the issues, as the founding fathers saw them:

> The singing of the Psalms, though it breath forth nothing but holy harmony and melody: yet such is the subtlety of the enemy, and enmity of our nature against the Lord, and his ways, that our hearts can find matter of discord in this harmony, and crotchets [whimsy] of division in this holy melody.

Unsatisfied with the translations used in England, which they had begrudgingly brought with them, the Massachusetts Bay Colony hired an elite squad of 'thirty pious and learned Ministers' to create new translations. The result was published in 1640, in a print run of 1,700 copies – reasonably large, for the day. Apparently the objections didn't extend to the music, because the translations were designed to be sung to the same tunes until the ninth edition, published in 1698, which was the first to include new music notation.

Even the unimaginable expanse of an ocean away, the early settlers couldn't quite get away from the totemic influence of this little book. They may have left England itself because of religious differences, but some habits were too deeply embedded to root out of their psyche.

Once more to England, then. It is 1562. The young Elizabeth I has been on the throne for four years and the country is tentatively starting to heal from decades of religious turmoil. The discord will continue to rumble on for another hundred years but, for now, there is calm.

A duo of men answering to the names of John Day and John Hopkins are compiling a prayer book, using the translations of the late Thomas Sternhold. It will be called *The Whole Booke of Psalmes, Collected into English Metre*, and it will be the first of its kind. The type has been loaded into the sticks that keep it in line, the sticks into the galley that holds them neatly stacked and inked; the paper is pinned between the tympan and brisket, which will allow it to be clamped down tightly. The type and paper are placed one on top of the other, and pressed. It is an intensely physical endeavour, this early printing process; it requires your full body weight, sinew and muscle. As the handle is unrolled, there, beneath, is revealed a page of music and words. They have chosen a typeface called 'blackletter' – developed from the visual appearance of handwriting, and that resembles, most closely, the decorative blocks called 'printer's flowers' or 'printer's lace' that are used to mark the margins. To us, today, it is almost illegible. To its readers, it will be reminiscent of the fashionable blackwork embroidery that came over from northern Africa via Spain at the beginning of the 1500s; a work of art, yours for just a few pence.

The project had begun many years before under the reign of Elizabeth's father, Henry VIII, and had found its pages stained with blood as the battle raged for England's soul. Henry's split from Rome in 1533 gave his advisors an opportunity to tear up the prayer book and reform it into a better, more 'English' (or so they said) format. Now it would be written in English, not Latin; all the people across the country, from Land's End to Berwick-upon-Tweed, would eventually be able to read it. And *The Whole Booke of Psalmes* would be at the vanguard in this battle. It was designed for normal, everyday people. It included all 150 of the psalms from the Christian/Hebrew Bible, the beautifully poetic series of laments, thanksgivings and songs of praise that, according to legend, were (mostly) composed by King David, he

Edgar Degas, *Dancers, Pink and Green*, c. 1890.

Jan Vermeer, *Girl Interrupted at her Music*, 1658–59.

Eleanor Chan,
If, 2023.

Cave paintings of bison at Marsoulas, c. 16,000 BCE.

Edgar Degas, *Fan Mount of Ballet Dancers from the Wings*, c. 1879.

Anonymous, Alexander on the way to conquer India, in Ferdowsi's *Shahameh*, c. 1411.

Fanny Hensel Mendelssohn, 'Praeludium and Choral' from *Das Jahr*, 1841.

Opposite: Natalia Goncharova, 'Cherub' costume design for *La Liturgie*, 1915.

Aram Gulezyan's 'ancient Egyptian' colour music notation, second or third decade of the twentieth century.

To shew division of colour scale when the spectrum is extended over the whole length of the key-board of the colour organ by spectrum stop.

Alexander Wallace Rimington's diagram of how to map colour frequencies onto sound frequencies to produce a colour octave, from *Colour-Music: The Art of Mobile Colour*, 1912.

George Field's correspondence of colour and octave, from *Chromatics, or, the Analogy, Harmony and Philosophy of Colour*, 1817.

Megan Watts-Hughes, *Sound Impression of Voice Flowers*, pigment on glass, undated, c. 1885–1904.

Opposite: John Piper, *Dungeness*, 1938.

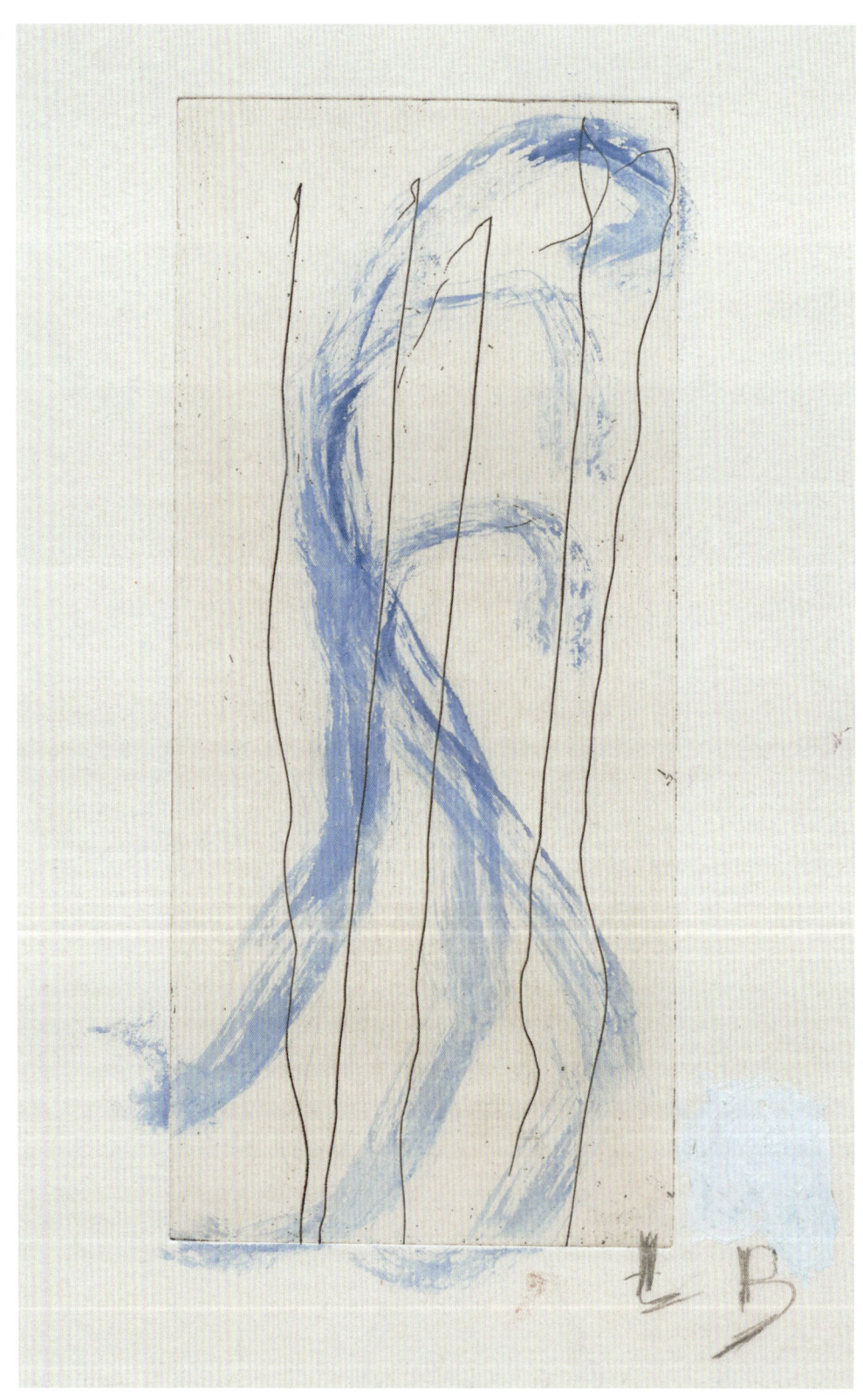
Louise Bourgeois, *La Chanson*, 2009.

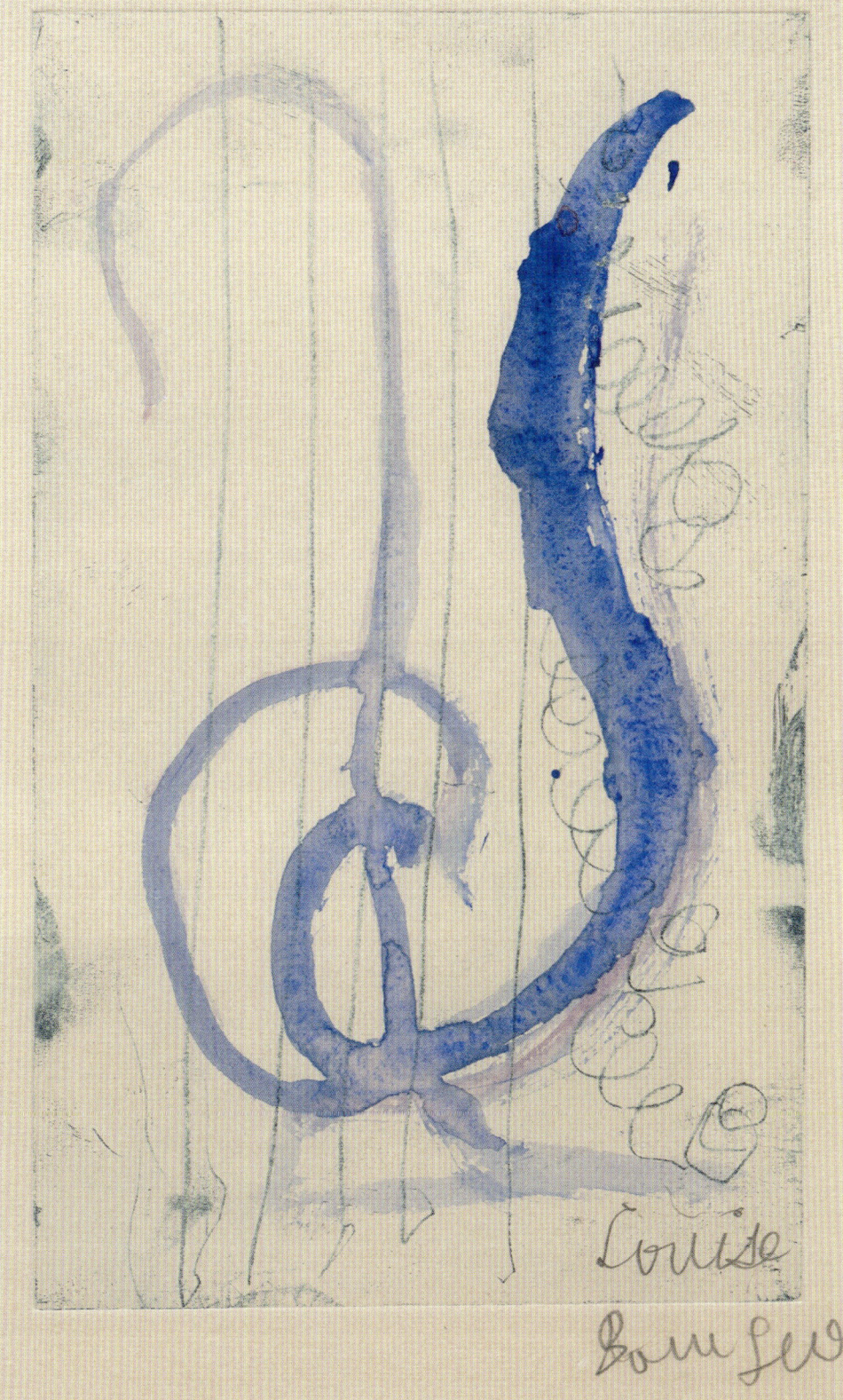

Tin-glazed delftware violin, 1705–10.

Porcelain flute, Jingdezhen, seventeenth century.

Taylor Swift playing her candyfloss pink *Lover* guitar during the Eras Tour, 2024.

Aubrey Williams, *Shostakovich Symphony No. 6*, 1981.

Overleaf: Anna Casparsson, detail from *Sagor (Stories: Little Claus and Big Claus, the Story of Little Rose and the Little Mermaid)*, 1947.

of Goliath-slaying and skilful lyre-playing fame. They were set to music begged, borrowed and stolen from persecuted Protestant composers across Europe, and the notation for their tunes was printed alongside the words. They would be sung in churches, in the home, at work, in the alehouses. Everyone would know the words, and they would bring the people together into a new community known as the Church of England.

It's difficult to fully appreciate just how common this kind of singing would have been. Books of the period are littered with accounts of homely psalm singing. Thomas Morley's *Plaine and Easie Introduction to Practicall Musicke* (1597), the century's most famous music-theory how-to guide, begins with a hapless man named Philomathes searching out a music teacher after being unable to join in with after-dinner singing, which Morley presents as being a matter of course. On the title page of his own 1579 collection of psalm tunes, William Daman advertises them as for 'the use of godly Christians for recreating themselves, in stede of fond and unseemely Ballades'. Margaret Hoby, a rare example of an Elizabethan lady diarist, recorded a typical evening on 6th December 1599: 'I went to supper: after, to publeck praers, then I talked and song a psalm with divers that were with me, and lastly, praied privatly, and so went to bed.' Even the dour Lewis Bayly, in his 1613 guide *The Practice of Pietie*, recommends singing psalms, although with terse rules about how to do it right:

> At Evening, when the due time of repairing to rest approacheth, call together againe all thy Family, Reade a Chapter in the same manner, that was prescribed in the Morning. Then (in holy imitation of our Lord, and in his Disciples) sing a Psalme. But in singing of Psalmes, either after Supper, or at any other time, observe these Rules … Beware of singing divine Psalms for an ordinary recreation; as do men of impure spirts, who sing holy Psalms, intermingled with profane Ballads …

> Behave your selves in comely reverence, as in the sight of God, singing to God, in Gods owne words. But be sure that the *matter* makes more melodie in your *hearts* then the *Musicke* in your *eares*.[5]

The visual evidence is even more telling: wall paintings from middling sorts of homes survive across the country, using lines from the psalms as part of their decorative schemes. Singing psalms was embedded in the fabric of daily life: a way to wind down, to bond, to bring the day to a harmonious close the way we would now watch an episode of, say, *Derry Girls*.

But this project to transform psalms into the pop songs of the day meant that they were not universally popular. Decades later, *The Whole Booke of Psalmes* would still be unsettling people. In his *Church-history of Britain*, published in 1655, Thomas Fuller declared that 'two hammers on a Smith's anvil would make better music'. In the same year, John Phillips condemned it simply as 'Thomas Sternhold's wretched Prick song'. Peter Heylyn described 'that Barbarity, and Botching, which every where occurred in the Translation of Sternhold and Hopkins'. John Wilmot, Earl of Rochester, even made a catchy little poem out of his disgust:

> Sternhold and Hopkins had great qualms
> When they translated David's psalms
> To make the heart full glad;
> But had it been poor David's fate
> To hear thee sing, and them translate,
> By God! 'twould have made him mad.

There's a bit of a theme emerging. For all of these well-to-do gentlemen, psalms had become a little tacky, too vulgar, perhaps too available to the general public. John Wesley, eighteenth-century founder of Methodism, would describe them some 200 years later as 'the miserable, scandalous doggerel of Sternhold and Hopkins'. These weren't innocuous, inoffensive pieces of music. They were divisive; they were upsetting. For all of these people, psalms were worth passionately arguing over.

Given the nerdy, straitlaced aura that choral music now has (none of the throbbing drama of opera, none of the high energy of musical theatre, and no enormous, cool or wacky instruments), it's hard to imagine that in the sixteenth century, English choral music was at the forefront of all that was politically dangerous and radical. The English Reformation was a long drawn-out, fraught thing, but it brought musical opportunities. As it rumbled, it became ever more important to the way that the English imagined themselves: as Protestants, as members of the bright, shining light of the Church of England, freed from the tyranny of Rome. No one knew what this sounded or looked like, in musical terms. All that was certain was that everything written before that point had been for the unreformed, Roman Catholic-style of church service and could be seen as politically dangerous.

Imagine, if you will, that you are a Gentleman of the Chapel Royal, one of Henry VIII's professional church singers who composes a bit of music on the side. Maybe you are Thomas Tallis, or John Sheppard or Robert Parsons – all stellar composers who lived through the first decades of upheaval, and who, in turn, would train the likes of William Byrd in their craft. One day, an announcement comes forth from the throne: you are no longer part of the Roman Catholic Church that has united Christendom against various foes (real or imagined) for as long as anyone can remember. You are now a member of the Church of England, which is more authentic anyway, because you believe it was originally founded by Joseph of Arimathea, a direct disciple of Jesus who supposedly came to England, and so it hasn't been meddled with by generations of Popes. You face a choice. Either you accept this move lying down, watch as the more radical factions of Protestants take over and gradually edge music out of church life, and lose your job. Or you make music integral to Henry's new ('old') church.

You sit there in your cassock. You watch as Thomas Cromwell's men smash the faces from statues of saints, smash the glittering rainbow of stained glass from the windows. You pick up your quill. You write. You write for your life. And in the process you slowly fabricate something astounding: the idea of a tradition of English choral music stretching back into time immemorial, back to King Arthur and his questing knights and dragons, an integral part of the way that Henry and his progeny would mythologise the Tudor dynasty and Englishness for centuries to come – all packaged up in exquisite pieces of music that will still send shivers down spines almost 500 years later.

The Whole Booke of Psalmes sat at the very heart of this effort to construct a mythological inherited English choral tradition. If all went well, almost everyone would be able to read music to an extent, and the Puritan accusations that music in church drowned the Word of God in waves of emotional overwhelm would be baseless – because music and word would be on an equal footing. If all went well, its tunes would be what people hummed to themselves as they went about their daily business, the ear worms of the day, the sixteenth century's answer to 'Despacito'.

This project wasn't just of religious importance: politically, it was vital. We've already encountered the desperate scrabble for a coherent, consistent concept of what being English could and should mean. For Henry VIII's project to be successful, he and his advisors had to ensure that people felt this sense of community far beyond their garden fences, from coast to coast, north to south. People singing the same songs, believing in the same God, worshipping in the same language, would help forge those bonds.

As the desire for colonial expansion burgeoned under Henry's youngest daughter, Elizabeth I, songs like the psalms became even more important. Psalms were a way of enforcing the idea of Us versus Them, the idea of an English Way versus Every

Other Way, that would help Elizabeth and her advisors cast other nations, other communities and their lands as commodities. Thrumming with drama, intrigue, blood, exploitation and aspiration, a Pandora's box waiting to be opened, *The Whole Booke of Psalmes* is a far cry from its dusty heirs. This simple, unassuming book of psalm tunes had a whole lot riding on it, back in 1562.

Esther Inglis' embroidered cover for her *Argumenta psalmorum David's dedicacion*, 1608.

Faced with criticisms like those of Wesley, Rochester, Fuller, Heylyn and Phillips, it's tempting to assume that psalms were met with opposition. We don't have many positive written testimonies, so we need to look for other kinds of evidence. Luckily, it's not necessary to look very far at all.

In a timber-framed building in what is now Edinburgh Old Town, almost forty years after *The Whole Booke of Psalmes* was first published, a woman sits alone at a desk, surrounded by the tools of her trade. Pens and stacks of good paper; inks and lustrous jewel-like pigments made of red ochre, verdigris, vermilion and woad for florey blue; embroidery thread in a rainbow of colours; fine fabrics such as velvet for the covers. Carefully, she has stitched the seed pearls on the cover, embroidered the velvet with silk floss and threads wrapped in gold leaf. The finished manuscript, beautifully calligraphed in her much-coveted handwriting, sits in a stack beside her.

She takes up her pen and begins to draw a sinuous, fluid line.

This is Esther Inglis, and she is a maker of books – every aspect, from start to finish. Over her lifetime, she will produce at least sixty miniature books, combining her exquisite handwriting, painting, embroidery and textile skills.[6] Many surviving copies of psalm books are visually stunning, and Inglis's creations are the best of the best. During her career she would make books of religious texts for all the most influential people: Elizabeth I, the Earl of Essex, Sir Anthony Bacon and Maurice of Nassau, leader of the United Provinces in the Northern Netherlands, England's only neighbouring Protestant ally.[7] These were intensely precious, lauded art objects. The fact that Inglis made a career out of them is testament to their popularity. Although none of the works she calligraphed and decorated included music notation, they were all musical-adjacent, and many could be sung or set to music. Many had psalm texts included in their artfully rendered pages.

And Inglis leaves us in absolutely no doubt as to how important she found music. In twenty-five of her surviving books she included a self-portrait – the first, in fact, by a woman in the British Isles.[8] She depicts herself poised over a blank page, fashionably hatted and coiffed and wearing the loose, belted gown and plain buttoned jacket that mark her as a practical, no-nonsense member of the middle classes. She meets the viewer head-on, eye to eye. On the table beside her fresh sheet of parchment is an open book. In many of her self-portraits, the book itself is full of tiny, legible music notation.

Given the context of what she made, and who she was, we can be pretty sure that she intended this music book to be read as a psalm book. Inglis was a French Protestant refugee – a Huguenot, born as her parents fled the St Bartholomew's Day Massacre. The music she depicts at her hand is more than just a reference to her feminine accomplishments: it's also a strong statement of political and religious allegiance.[9] She doesn't put words to it – but she shows us, quietly, carefully, in her self-portrait, that it is important to her brand as a highly sought-after, devout and entrepreneurial Franco-Scottish artist: an early incarnation of the Protestant work ethic.

Sheet Music Scrolled Across the Inside of My Lungs: The Music Book

Esther Inglis's self-portrait with a music book, 1601.

Even those who didn't have the purchasing power to commission one of Inglis's works, or who didn't have the skill or leisure time to produce their own embroidered covers, have left a trace of their visual engagement with sheet music, and their delight in how it looked. Four hundred and fifty years ago, music notation was available only to the select few. For the most part, music

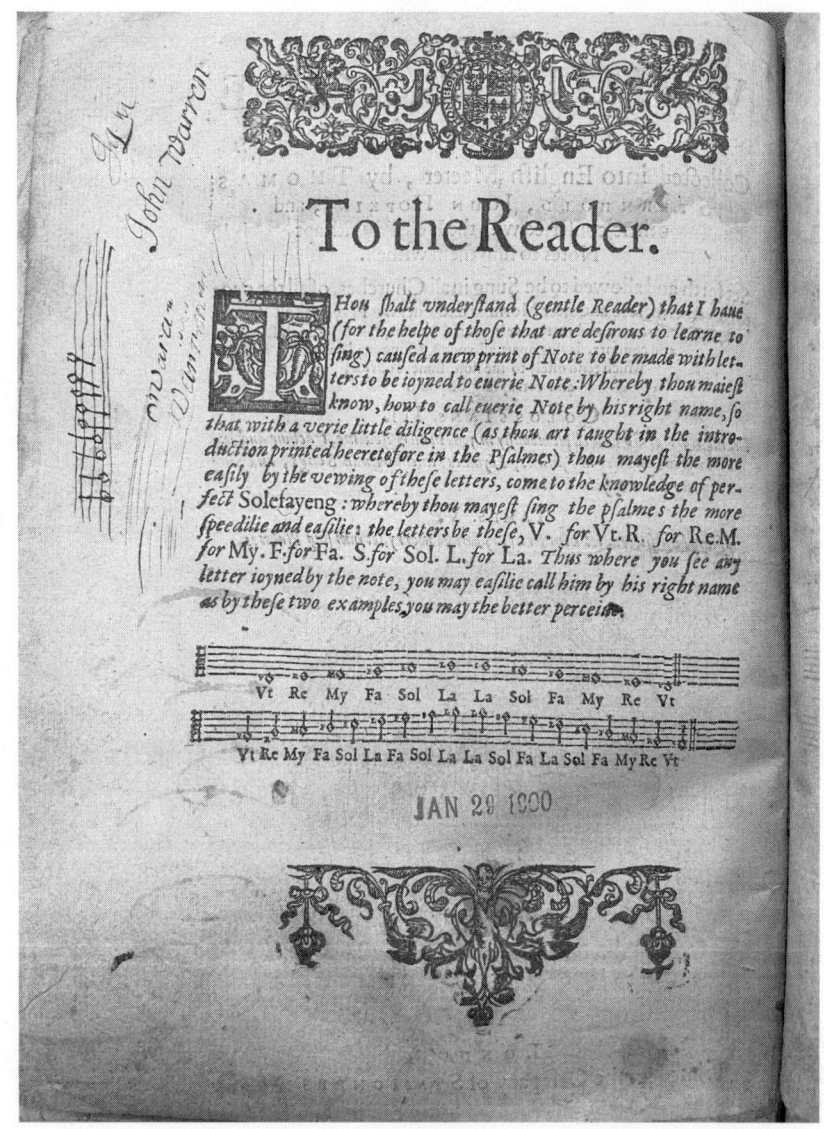

Musical Graffiti in a 'To The Reader', copying the full music.

looked like dancing and jigs; like performers depicted playing musical instruments; like the portrait of the Black court musician John Blanke in the Westminster Tournament Roll (1511), or the group of musicians in the painting now known as *Elizabeth I dances with Leicester* (1580). It was something you learned with your ears, and most certainly not by reading.

Sheet Music Scrolled Across the Inside of My Lungs: The Music Book

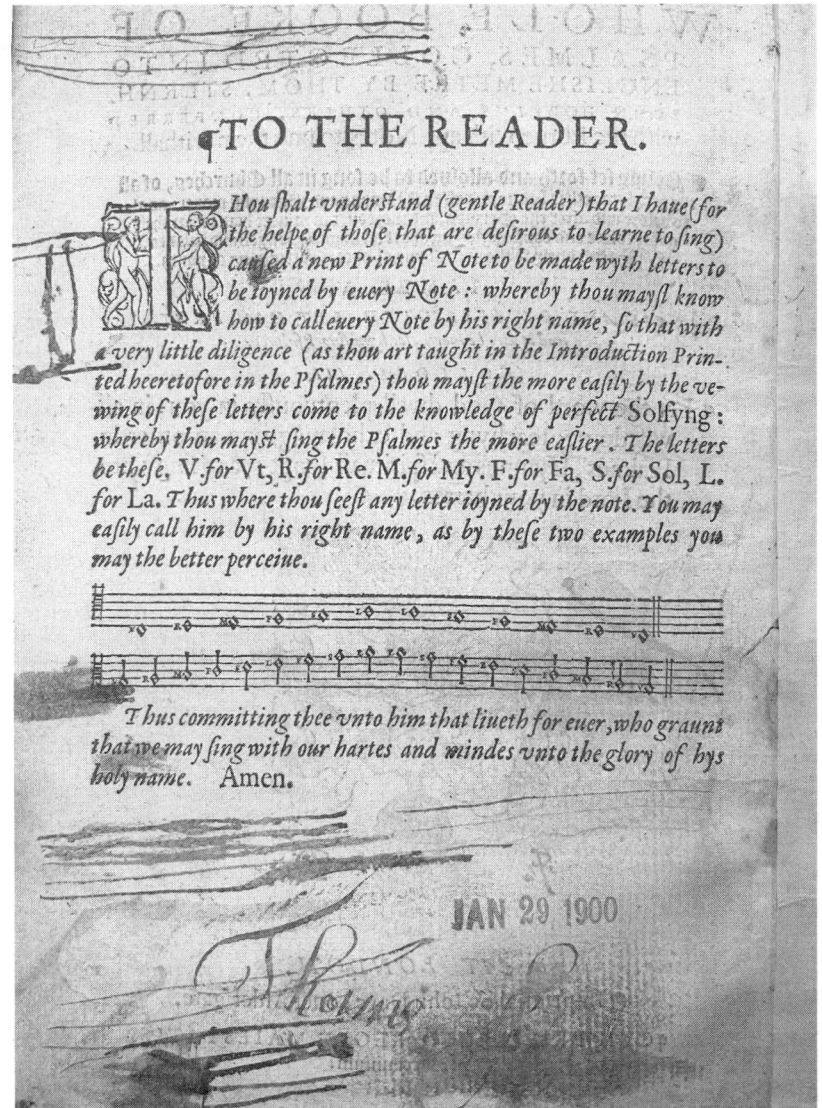

Musical Graffiti in a 'To The Reader', copying the staves.

The Whole Booke of Psalmes changed all of that.[10] Alongside the psalms and the music notation for their tunes, it included a brief introduction to the 'Science of Musicke', later reworked into a one-page 'To The Reader': a how-to guide to help its readers learn how to read music, how to see it. The preface explicitly foregrounds the visual aspects of its idea of music, announcing that 'I have (for

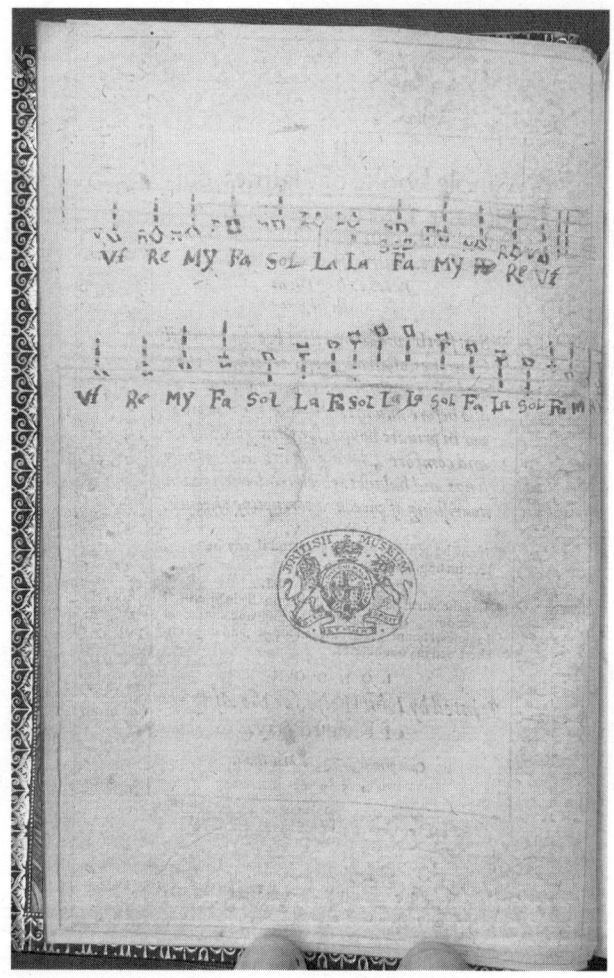

An improvised 'To The Reader' music-reading guide in *The Whole Booke of Psalmes*.

the helpe of those that are desirous to learne to sing) caused a new print of Note to be made with letters to be joined to everie Note ... thou mayest the more easily by the *viewing* of these letters, come to the knowledge of perfect Solefayeng [musical reading] ... Thus where thou *seest* any letter joined by the note, you may easily call him by his right name.'*

---

*   My italics.

Before this point, it wasn't at all usual for prayer books to feature music notation, let alone notation that was intended to help people to learn a tune. Suddenly, all across England – and increasingly across the world, as England's imperial desires grew – music had a whole new look. As a visual form that could be played with and subverted, people *loved* it: early readers doodled in musical notes, musical staves and even the full how-to guide itself, in one especially beautiful example.

I love quiet, understated traces like these. Coming across them in the archive is like someone reaching across the chasm of 400 years, taking you by the hand and giving you the tiniest fragment of their story, even if everything else about them has been lost to the passage of time: Look, of course we could read! We could write! We could read and write music! And what's more, you can watch us at it – making mistakes (look at the top line, the crossings-out), practising, getting to grips, mastering the form of the notes. We are quite literally watching the psalm book in action here, teaching this reader how to read music. What's more, they are doing this by drawing – in other words, by engaging in a visual artistic culture.

These people going about their business are my favourite characters in history. Their graffiti gives us a snapshot of how the everyday person thought about music notation, not just as a way of recording music, but also how it worked as a way of seeing music. Music notation was elegant and attractive and, incredibly, we're still feeling the impact of its introduction to this very day. Glimpses like this give us a fresh way of thinking about how we experience music as something seen, when we look at how luxurious visualising music felt to these quietly enthusiastic musicians and artists.

𝄞

To the rolling hills of the Peak District, where the Midlands of England meet the north. Trudge along this wooded path as it twists upwards and then suddenly reveals the house of one of the most influential women in England. She is known to her friends and admirers, quite simply, as Bess. Her heavily glazed showpiece of a house is Hardwick Hall. And contained within its walls is a music book carefully fashioned not out of paper, but of segments of wood.

For the sake of argument, let us assume it is autumn – so those enormous windows glow with the burnished gold of falling leaves. Passageways glitter in the low equinox light, hung with tapestries and wall hangings made of strips of the old ecclesiastical garments that Bess collected.[11] Follow the turn of the stair, walk through the door, and there, roped off in an enormous bay window that seems tailor-made for its proportions, it still stands: the Eglantine Table. It's a musical source like no other, because incised onto its satiny polished surface is a four-part setting from *The Whole Booke of Psalmes*, written by composer Thomas Tallis only five years after the *Booke* was first published. Every single note, every clef, every accidental is legible.

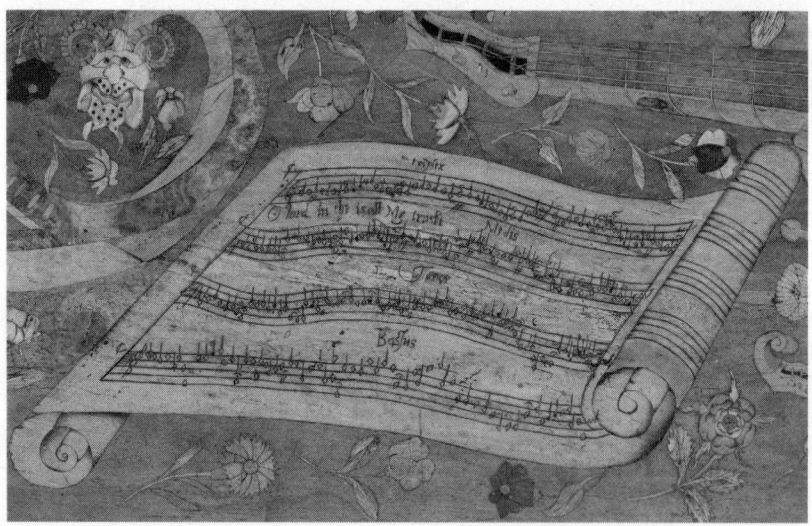

Detail of Thomas Tallis's 'O Lord in Thee is all my Trust' on the Eglantine Table, c. 1567.

The Eglantine Table is a masterclass in intarsia inlay, a technique that takes the principles of your standard thousand-piece jigsaw and buffs it to a surface smooth as silk. Its design is made up of intricately intersecting segments of walnut, limewood and fruitwood, some stained the most delicate flush of pink or the sap green of grass. It shows a whole host of musical instruments, packs of cards, a chess board and a backgammon board: everything you needed for a good Elizabethan night in. The coiling scroll of sheet music, curling at its pseudo-paper edges, embellished with musical notes, is integral to the table's appeal. If you've been lucky enough to see the Eglantine Table with your own eyes, you'll be familiar with its peculiar brand of hypnosis: the moment when this prettily decorated table unexpectedly reveals a closeness to the past; the objects strewn across its surface, abandoned mid-play, as though the owners had just walked out of the room.

The table stands in the High Great Chamber, a room that was possibly designed to hold it. Bess commissioned the table to celebrate her fourth marriage, to George Talbot, Earl of Shrewsbury, and her elevation to the lofty title of Countess of Shrewsbury. For good measure, Bess and George had also arranged the marriage of two sets of their sons and daughters from previous marriages, to ensure that nothing could disrupt this dynastic alliance and the joining of colossal amounts of cash and property (let no man put asunder, indeed…). At the centre of this exclusive, aristocratic celebration of marriage, family and silver-spoon taste, set like a gemstone among the depictions of eglantine, pinks, marigolds, great ox-eye daisies, wall flowers, cherry flowers and cloudberry flowers, is the great incongruity: Tallis's setting of a psalm that anyone could get their hands on.[12]

Closer inspection reveals that it makes a virtue out of the visual form of notation. The staff lines that make Western music notation diagrammatic, rather than a spool of instructions, give us a real sense of the textural sweep of the scroll. If you can read notation, you can read this music, but the image also offers us something else: a satisfying pattern to follow, ending in a coil like the twining foliage that surrounds it. Read it as image, or read it as music. It works either way. It leads us deeper into the image, into the idea of the table and all that a music book could potentially mean.

The Eglantine Table is the most attention-grabbing piece at Hardwick Hall, but it's far from the only object there that celebrates music books as works of art in themselves. Through the Long Gallery and in a back corridor is another example: a piece of fabric around the size of an A4 page. It's one of a set of eight textile panels likely used for interior decoration, for example as cushion covers, that depicted what were then known as the 'Liberal Arts' (Grammar, Logic, Rhetoric, Arithmetic, Astrology, Perspective and Architecture): this one is *Musique*. Each is picked out in embroidered and appliqued taffeta and linen panels on black velvet. The columns, now faded to green, would once have been a jewel-toned turquoise. Each figure, decked out in pseudo-classical dress, is constructed on a linen base, with the flesh parts covered in plain silk and then embroidered in stem and back stitch, and delicately shaded in paint to pick out the details of facial features.

In *Musique*, where convention might dictate that the central figure would hold a musical instrument to represent her 'Art', instead she loosely clutches a book. At her feet, we see what might be the same book lying open. Its tiny silk pages are inked with minuscule musical notation. Bend closer and it is almost legible – a musical clef, a phrase of music notes spreading at a jaunty angle across both pages.

The notes are lilliputian, so it is hard to state for certain. Like the figure of *Arithmetique*, who has a similarly distinctive book laid at her feet, open to the title page of a printed treatise, showing an astrolabe or similar mathematical instrument dimly perceptible in the centre, this music book appears to depict a *printed* musical page; those distinctive blocky, lozenge-shaped note heads cannot quite be captured by a pen. This artwork insists that music is something that can be seen. And by insisting on the visuality of music, it marks a quietly decisive moment in the history of music: it starts to be a matter of taste, of marking people as members of a private community, part of a crew, a tribe. Music starts to be *fashionable* – for people of Bess's circle, as well as for the artisans who made her gorgeous things.

Bess's attitude towards sheet music and music books is in stark contrast to our attitudes today. This elaborate patchwork of fabric assumes that you will try to read it, and that you will expect reading it to be part of its visual appeal; that it will feel like a casual, low-stakes guessing game, the kind you get in a Christmas cracker or at a pub quiz. You can be a hotshot wizard at sightreading, or a beginner. The whole point is participation, joining in, having a go.[13] The idea of sheet music appearing in this jaunty little guise, today, seems preposterous – so presumptuous, so ostracising, so separate from the *enjoyment* of music itself.

Across the Western world, there is a growing tendency to think that we have somehow transcended the need for music notation. There's a fetish for virtuosic performers who are able to perform a long, difficult piece from memory.[14] There's a trend for giving people the words to something and expecting them to sing along without the notes (because apparently not being able to read music is more humiliating than not being able to sing something they're expected to in a large group situation). A lot of people think notation shouldn't be taught to children in school because it's old-fashioned; that it's another hallmark of the elitism of classical music and the way it 'shuts people out' (how can you learn to read music if you never see it?).

Objects like Bess's *Musique* panel insist that music is something we see. It is framed in brocades, velvets and golden thread to seduce the eye as a route to the ear – offering a way into thinking about sheet music and music books that we may have lost. These objects suggest that the problem isn't that music notation is old-fashioned, but the way we think we have to approach it certainly is. Music notation *isn't* just a transcript of a performance that we're expected to slavishly recreate, as the theatre historian Noémie Ndiaye points out in her unpacking of the word 'record': 'recording' music is an invitation to sing *between* the lines, not along them.[15]

All of which is to say that the choice to depict printed music books in beautiful art objects was probably a way of signifying to visitors, friends and to the family themselves that the Shrewsburys were highly sophisticated and eminently fashionable. Even today, when the country houses of England are carefully curated to look just so, it is hard to appreciate what Bess's textile panel might have looked like in its own day. Imagine it. Every wall, every seat, every flat surface is covered with a densely rendered collage of silk, velvet, taffeta or damask. They shimmer in the candlelight, the sheen of their weave and of the gold-thread embroidery catching the glow and rendering it liquid as you shift in your chair. At such close quarters you can see each segment of fabric as a simple chunk of texture among others.

You can allow your eyes to resolve each image into its figurative subjects, as you listen to music and conversation, hear your fellow guests at play or in debate. There is the figure of Perspective. There is the finely worked form of an armillary sphere (the mathematical instrument used to calculate the movement of the heavens). And there, glinting in plain white silk in the dark velvet background, tiny, at your side where you rest your hand, is – lean closer, closer still, catch your breath – yes, it is music! And you can almost, but not quite, make out the tune. Beneath your breath, you hum it as your eyes pass over the exquisite stitches, the dainty paint strokes.

To me, these examples are testament to how far *The Whole Booke of Psalmes* had infused into the culture of Elizabethan England. Bess and her family weren't necessarily the intended readership for the book. They were aristocratic; they could afford music tutors, and the elaborate music manuscripts that were out of reach for the vast majority of normal people. Nevertheless, they chose instead lyrics and a central tune straight from *The Whole Booke of Psalmes*. For Sternhold, Hopkins and Day this was a massive coup. The image of music had changed, and printed sheet music had captured the imagination of the English to become the height of good taste and fashion. This simply wasn't happening anywhere else across the globe.

Compare it to the depictions of music-making from the lavish art of the court of the Mughal emperor Akbar, whom we encountered in Chapter 1. Music was immensely important to Akbar, as it was to Elizabeth I; he had studied painting, actively encouraged developments in the visual arts and was likely heavily involved in the sudden high volume of depictions of music-making. His close friend and chronicler Abu'l-Fazl records in the *A'in-I Akbari* that 'his Majesty pays much attention to music, and is the patron of all who practise this enchanting art.' At the Mughal court there were 'soft-voiced Indian maids', 'light-fingered Chinese musicians [who] produced intoxication with wineless cups', 'singers from the land of Iraq, everlasting capturers of joy', and, Abu'l-Fazl notes, 'both men and women' performers.[16] Musical instruments appear in visual art objects from throughout Akbar's reign, held by fairies, brandished by courtly ensembles serenading lone figures, in mythical, historical and political tales. There is, though, nothing that depicts anything like the *sargam* – the system of syllables used to notate music in India. Surviving depictions of Europeans seem to actively eschew music books: a baffled Jesuit missionary clutches a book that remains resolutely closed, slightly dwarfed by the much larger female figure in Western drapery who holds a *tanpura* or a *sanod*.* The message is clear: music looks like many things but, for Akbar, it doesn't look like a book.

---

*   Both kinds of stringed musical instruments.

Music-making in the wall painting from Thame, Oxfordshire, 1560s.

Some 6,000 miles north-west of Akbar's court in Agra, back in Tudor England, a dinner party is in progress. Welcome to 34 Upper High Street, Thame in Oxfordshire. In the upstairs room we'll eat, talk and make music together by candlelight. As we do so, make sure to lean back and look up as you sip your drink or nibble on your eel pie. It was easier to gaze upwards then than it is today: in the twenty-first century you need to balance precariously on the top rung of a ladder to have a good look (an activity that is not greatly conducive to savouring an eel pie). Still, it is worth it: above wooden panelling, the plaster walls are adorned with a painting that spreads all around us, encompassing three sides of the room.

Our hosts are very à la mode. Wall paintings like this were the stylish way to decorate your middle-class Tudor home. Think of them as like a sixteenth-century equivalent to a feature wall, with jazzy wallpaper. They were far cheaper than tapestries like Bess's and were far less susceptible to decay caused by the damp English climate than textiles and images painted on wooden panels. Most of its fellows have been lost as buildings were demolished and rebuilt; this one has survived only because its plaster was carefully chipped from the walls and carried down the road to the Thame Museum. So, though this wall painting is now rare, we shouldn't assume it was entirely unique. All the same, knowing that it was once in far more crowded company doesn't detract from the painstaking care and craft that went into making it.

The image is designed around a central text, framed in a curly, scrolling ornamental border in the gothic blackletter script – exactly the typeface used for *The Whole Booke of Psalmes*, in fact, and one that was designed to look visually appealing and calligraphic, like a well-trained scribe's handwriting.[17] It reads:

> The First E
> Of Saint Paule for romans
> O the depnes of the aboundant
> Wisdom of God: howe uncerchable
> Are his judgements & his ways paste
> Finding out: for who hathe knwen ye
> minde of ye Lord? Or who was his con
> celoure? Other who hathe given unto
> Him first that he might be recompencyd a
> gayne? For of him, and through him
> And for him are all things
> To him be glory for
> Ever and ever
> Amen.[18]

It's a little elaborate. *Do you perhaps*, you might ask your hosts, *have a bit of sympathy with the old religion?* It's early enough in Elizabeth I's reign that this question of allegiance would have been as fresh and as divisive as Brexit, or the Covid-19 pandemic. *Us?* they cry, laughing, *No! Look, read...* With its reference to the Bible and the New Testament letter of St Paul, this text makes it very clear that, while the wall painting might be a decorously visual form of decoration, this is a pious, Protestant household that knows its scripture, thank you very much. The text is surrounded by figures, all of which lead your eyes up and around it. To the left sit a woman playing or tuning an emphatically outsized lute and two children reading from a book of music; echoing them, on the other side, is a fragment of the neck, nuts, pegbox and scroll of a bass viol (a precursor to the cello), and a fragment of the edge of its body, the remainder having been lost when the wall painting was uncovered. The figures' gazes do not cross or interact, but rather direct the eyes of the viewer to yet more elements of the composition. Look at us, they say. How harmonious we are. What marvellous music we will make.

This riff on sheet music isn't quite as explicit as the examples we saw at Hardwick Hall. The music isn't identifiable. You can't really read the music book that the two children are holding. It has three staff lines, rather than five – not entirely unusual for the time, but there's nothing to indicate what line should correlate to what pitch. Instead, it's the whole aesthetic of sheet music that has been translated onto these walls. The painting is elegantly monochromatic, like the black and white forms of the printed page.

In the twenty-first century it can be hard to imagine, but this was a big departure from how things were before the arrival of print. Before this point, a book (if you could get your hands or eyes on one) was multicoloured; illuminated manuscripts rioted with colour and costly textures like gold leaf. Print blasted onto the scene with a suavely restrained monochromatic pattern that seduced the eyes of the English, and readers across Europe. In the Thame wall painting, it's possible to see a collection of artisans riffing on that visual delight, through its theme of music. Print was a shiny new technology like email in 1997, the iPhone in 2007 or ChatGPT in 2023. Look how cool it is, they cry! It's going to be BIG! The wall painting harnesses that delight in creative novelty by immersing us within a space that feels exactly like the inside of a music book, right down to the knotty ornamental borders that once covered the ceiling. Imagine how proud those original owners must have felt of their fabulous new interior decoration scheme. It was the very height of fashion.

What, then, can approaching sheet music like the hymn book as a visual object, a way of seeing music, tell us about the histories of music and art? Accounts that suppress seeing as an aspect of experiencing music might tell us that it was fashionable, at varying points throughout history, to look as though you were a musical connoisseur – nothing more. But just *how* each of these objects approached music as a visible, visual phenomenon reveals something rather special: there is more than one way of reading a music book. Reading music, too, is a creative act: one that takes the shapes of the notes and makes something new, rather than resurrecting the ossified carcass of an old piece of music that lies languishing, waiting for someone to stitch its parts together and zap it like Frankenstein's monster. Every performance is a new work of art. The life and afterlife of sheet music, and the many ways it can be read, are, in this way, key to what I think are some of the most exciting moments of our collective music-making and artistic expression.

𝄞

We haven't quite lost this earlier, more spellbound way of thinking about sheet music. A closer look shows that this kind of attitude towards notation – one that embraces it as a form that can provide visual enjoyment – endured long beyond the first century of the printing press. It did so with an ancient art form, often overlooked for its status as 'craft': the collage.[19]

Enter John Piper.

Photos suggest he was, first and foremost, a man of thick, woolly jumpers: *no such thing as bad weather, just bad clothing*, his obstinate posture suggests, as he stands ensconced in the windswept landscapes he would depict. His life was steeped in music: his second wife, the painter, art critic and opera librettist Myfanwy Evans provided lyrics for the operas of Benjamin Britten, Malcolm Williamson and Alan Hoddinott.[20] Piper himself was an ardent lover of a huge variety of musical genres, from jazz to classical to the ballet scores that provided the musical element of the Ballets Russes. His other great love, though, was the English landscape – and it is his combination of music and landscape that produces some of the most electrifying musical images of the twentieth century.

Nowadays Piper is mostly known for his architectural drawings – artworks that fit more happily into the arbitrary category of 'fine' art. However, I find his collages, most of which date from the 1930s, utterly fascinating: quietly radical statements on what literary historian Alexandra Harris has referred to as the 'romantic modernism' of the inter-war years in England.[21] Doilies, waste scraps from newspapers, parts of labels from tobacco packets, figurative elements cut from magazines like the bouquet of roses in his *Harbour Scene* (1932) form constitutive elements that grapple against Piper's loose strokes of gouache and ink. Music paper, in ripped fragments, features prominently. Here it is in his *Dungeness* (1938), overprinted to a dense, knotty pattern that captures both the scribbling drift of shingle to the bottom left of the composition and the smudge of the lowering, thunderous clouds in the sky above (see plate section).

In Piper's hands, eyes and ears, collage becomes a thinking tool: a technique of visual curation, collecting and sorting. Each ripped segment of music paper refines his sense of form, of composition, of texture. Its clotted, lacy irregularity amplifies the single shock of rosy pink and scant blocks of air force blue, transforming a muted palette into something stark and punchy; it captures the way that seafoam can wash pebbles and shingle with a luminosity that makes the dull colours of granite and basalt shine with a jewel-like intensity. Just perceptible at the bottom corner of the music paper representing that shingle is a treble clef, a flat sign, and the word *cresc*. Crescendo. The tide, pulling back, seems preparing to oblige.

Piper often compiled his compositions outside, a board on his knees, and with a full, visceral appreciation for the resulting blots and splashes of rain, sea spray smears and paper fragment edges bubbling from unexpected mist or foggy damp. The overprinted music paper in *Dungeness* harnesses this tension between design and fatalism, the impulse to create order and simultaneously relinquish that order to the elements: we can identify it both as sheet music and as the texture, shades and forms that Piper is seeking to capture with it. Piper's intimate sensitivity to all that music might represent or evoke can be found elsewhere, too. His *Still Life* (1933), *Beach at Donegal* (1937) and *Harbour Scene at Newhaven* (1936–7) all harness its textural potential to capture the slab of rock punching out from sand or the towering face of the cliff against the rolling softness of downland.

Hunched over his board on the beach, bundled against the weather that lashes across his face and hands, Piper blinks the rain from his eyes and clutches the flapping shreds of paper that threaten to take flight with the gulls that wheel above. Perhaps you know some of those beaches – Dungeness, Newhaven, Eastbourne, Dymchurch, Angel Bay. Several of them are haunts from my childhood, and the gusts of wind flicker across Piper's collages so evocatively that I can almost taste the briny spindrift. He isn't the only artist to have used collage, or even music paper, to distil his visions and compositions, but the way he harnesses its rhythmic, grainy power to capture landscape is, to me, rather special. His music paper collages lead me straight back to the old medieval idea of cosmic harmony, and the music emitting from everything in the natural world.

It's a fanciful image, but suspend any cynicism you might have for a moment and follow along with me. Look at that lone, huddled figure. Watch as his eyes skim the horizon, then up to the smudge of those lowering clouds; nodding to himself, he reaches to select the paper from his bag of bits and rip it into better shapes. Yes, that lacy braiding of overprinted notation will do it. How it sings against the blue. How it *sings*.

𝄞

The visual afterlife of sheet music continues to exert its influence over minds across the world. Take, for example, the ethereal froth of this striking haute couture gown, designed by Maria Grazia Chiuri and Pierpaolo Piccioli to open the Valentino Spring/Summer 2014 fashion show in Paris, and then worn by Katy Perry at the Grammy Awards the following January. Embroidered across its billowing skirt is what was commonly described in reportage of the event as 'sheet music'.[22] The eagle-eyed among you will adjust your monocles, squint, and note that it is, in fact, the aria *'Dell'invito tracorsa è già l'ora'*, from the first act of Guiseppe Verdi's opera *La traviata*; confusingly, Chiuri and Piccolo named the dress *La Valse de Violetta Valéry* after the aria *'Sempre libera degg'io'*, which occurs later in Act I.

Of course, in terms of the visual effect it doesn't really matter which part of the opera it is named after; unless you get close enough to spot the name 'Violetta' and a few tell-tale phrases, there is no way you'd be able to guess what piece it is, let alone read the notation. Later that summer, it was customised by Valentino for the wedding of the model Marcia Pellegrinelli to singer Eros Ramozzoti, this time embroidered with 'the couple's love song', demonstrating that 'sheet music' could hold this level of aesthetic power regardless of whether it was meaningful or meaningless to the wearer.[23] That same year, Miu Miu (a spin-off sister brand of the fashion house Prada) released music notation stilettos and slingbacks that were entirely illegible, a feature that was praised by fashion enthusiasts as part of the shoe's sartorial appeal. Its monochromatic palette transforms it from a novelty print into an

Sheet Music Scrolled Across the Inside of My Lungs: The Music Book

Sheet Music Notation dress by The Emperor's Old Clothes, 2024.

abstract pattern that catches the eye, appealing precisely because it vacillates between being legible (as musical notes) and illegible (as decorative pattern).

These designers certainly weren't the first to use musical imagery: the couturier Elsa Schiaparelli created her entire Autumn/Winter 1939 collection around the theme of music.[24] The surviving pieces from the collection are exquisite: gloves, an evening gown, a belt. The details are carefully considered – the belt buckle mimics the f-holes of a violin and contains a tiny (and once upon a time, functional) music box. The music they depict is shown as snatches of phrases embroidered in glittering rainbow thread that can be played in fragments, but not as a whole. Unlike the hymn books, these frocks would only have been available to a limited group of people with both the money to purchase them and the glittering events to wear them to. It is probable that they spawned a host of imitations that are either not documented or haven't survived, from women who could not afford the Schiaparelli name tag but who could afford a pattern and the embroidery silks; similar frocks are certainly still being made today. Nevertheless, these objects show us that the taste for sheet music as a source of visual interest lasted well into the current millennium and beyond.

𝄢

For better or worse, once sheet music had become an image of music, it was here to stay. At a distance of over 400 years, all of the bloodshed, ardour and drama of the humble hymn book's genesis might seem like an arcane matter far removed from you and me in the present day. What relevance can it possibly have, this ancient battle of hearts and minds – particularly when, as the 2021 UK census revealed, Anglicanism is no longer the dominant religion in the UK?[25]

Part of our inability to see the relevance of this episode in history is that we are still deeply, inextricably bathed in its shadow. It has inflected our logic, our family pasts, our economy and what we find beautiful. Hundreds of years later, the music book still snags our eyes with its seductive, graceful monochrome. And the places where we find evidence for its popularity are telling, to say the least. Over the centuries, we have transformed music books into beautiful objects. Some objects, though, gain their value and beauty from sentimental, immaterial means: they are carefully stitched, carved or cut and pasted by a loved one, passed down, held or looked at every day. They are often homely, and always highly personal or capable of being personalised. Such objects are decorative, are much mended and much loved, but would never fetch millions at auction in our current art market.

This was the case from the very origin of this image of music. Neither the Thame wall painting nor the Eglantine Table nor the *Musique* furnishing panel were created by a big name. We're unlikely to see them as headline exhibits at national museums. Esther Inglis is the exalted exception, and had a single, solitary object displayed at knee height at the 'Now You See Us' exhibition of female artists at Tate Britain in 2024. But they are vital artistic expressions all the same. They're also a sign that, from the very beginning of sheet music's popular, public life outside of the hallowed rooms of the rich, it was seen as a useful way of decorating a space, showing your sophistication and superior taste, a trend that continues to this day.

I'm going to pause here, because I cannot stress enough that we've now arrived at a pivotal episode in the visual history of music, and in the history of art more generally. And it's important because of the questions it raises: Whose art or artistic responses are considered meaningful? When do their artworks become historical artefacts worthy of study? The examples we just examined are old and rare enough that they are deemed interesting, or, at the very least, suitable objects of study for an art historian like me. But for me, the continued engagement in sheet music and the music book as a visual surface deserves just as much attention because it demonstrates just as fascinating a phenomenon.

We now turn to another kind of artwork that uses the music book. You don't find these objects in art and design museums. I can't give you an example from the V&A or the Met. Instead, we have to turn to online marketplaces like Etsy, and to crafting stores. The market for sheet music art and for vintage sheet music ('gorgeous music ephemera', as one sales description puts it) for craft projects is booming. Collages that create world maps or cityscapes out of the stuff are especially popular, but you can also find plenty of posters, prints and canvases of single pieces of music. Some cut, fold and shape the sheet music into paper roses. Often, the title, composer and any identifying features are cropped out: it's just the staff, notes, clefs, some dynamics.

Other companies will set *your* song, from the first dance at your wedding, or the music that was playing on your first date, birthday or special occasion, and frame it on canvas. There are hundreds of such listings available on the internet, along with plenty of 'how to DIY' hack videos and blog posts.

Finally, there is the furore every time a Keaton Music Typewriter comes up for sale. First patented in 1936 and then made in a minuscule batch in San Francisco in the 1950s, they print sheet music, complete with three different space settings and a handle that allows you to move up and down by 1/24th of an inch per notch, so you can navigate up and down the staff lines. Yours for only $4,000. I'm willing to bet that plenty of these are collected for their own sake, as objects. But perhaps some have been used to create sheet music for interior decoration, for the home, for wedding favours, for Christmas decorations, you name it.

This idea isn't often explored when it comes to music, or indeed to art history. It's not *real* art, a certain type of person (you know them) says. Not if just anyone can make it; not if it's only 'decorative' rather than 'fine', and certainly not if it wasn't made by a tortured genius of an artist with their own anecdotes about how bad-tempered, how competitive or how mad they are or were in life. But the line between decorative and fine art, professional artist and amateur, is as substantial as a cobweb, and fundamentally murky.

Visual responses to sheet music haven't been limited to the exalted few – artists who have received high levels of musical education, or who have devoted years of contemplation of visual forms to arrive at the concept. A huge variety of people, from a huge variety of backgrounds, have revelled in the artistic potential of a page of musical notation. These kinds of visual expressions – those that hang on walls, that decorate cushion covers and clothes, that people can copy and reproduce, that are made by artisans and amateurs – are key to understanding a culture's art, just as much as those works made by lauded individuals. This is an art that is collective: passed around, shared, made together, just as music is.

This episode truly deserves its place in the history of music and of art alike, despite the naysayers. These examples – wallpaper, murals, collages, cards, baubles, shoes, dresses, mugs – aren't separate from the acts of listening and performing just because we encounter them visually first. Such objects are often chosen because they recall a musical memory, regardless of whether their notation depicts a specific piece of music. We shouldn't consider these as *just* visual objects: they are entangled in the experience of listening, of singing along to music, of dancing, of musicking in general. There's a technical term for this: audiation. The literary historian Lucía Martínez Valdivia defines audiation in a particularly useful way: 'like the five senses of the body, the world of the mind has distinct faculties, some easier to engage than others. In a visually biased or based culture such as our own, sighted people can generally "see" with our mind's eyes much more easily than we can "taste" with our mind's tongues or "hear" with our mind's ears.' But there is, she argues, 'a faculty of hearing in the mind that either recollects acoustic experience or, in some cases, can produce an experience of inward hearing that has little or no relation to sensory sound perception [like a] sonic, aural equivalent to imagination'.[26]

That sonic, aural equivalent to imagination is integral to the way that we experience music, and it can be activated by artworks by named, known artists like Piper, like Fabriano, but also by the legions of hobbyist crafters whose work populates Etsy. If we erase these seemingly more commercial objects and the ever-growing hunger for them, we erase crucial parts of our musical history and transform it into nothing but the story of a series of big, virtuosic, untouchable names like Schiaparelli – cool, impressive, but distant and nothing to do with you or me, mere mortals, as we dance across our kitchens, sing in the shower or the car, hum around the supermarkets, or put up posters of our favourite bands.

𝄞

The last stop on our odyssey through the music book brings us to the most crucial question: why? Why sheet music? Why, after hundreds of years, does it continue to ignite so many imaginations? Why is it so visually seductive to so many people regardless of their musical expertise? Why does any of this matter? Some cynical people might argue that it's because music notation has connotations of sophistication and culture, but I think there's something more complex going on. We need to travel back to slightly more traditional art historical ground because, alas, the comments, observations and opinions of all those crafters aren't often written down and preserved for posterity. The advent of the internet means that this may well change in the not-too-distant future, but for now let's turn back to a named artist.

Louise Bourgeois may need no introduction. Brought up in Paris and Choisy-le-Roi (in the Paris banlieue), Bourgeois' life was steeped in music. She had piano lessons, and there was always a record of some sort playing in the apartment, songs that Bourgeois would continue to revisit well into later life during periods of insomnia.[27] From the 1990s onwards, printed sheet music became a key visual surface in her work.

Three of her late series of works, *The Insomnia Drawings* (1994–7), *Fugue* (2002–05) and *Hours of the Day* (2006), use the repetitive lines as a visual rhythm and foil within which Bourgeois can insert herself, react and create contrary forms in thread, ink and paint, typically in cerise and cornflower blue. One is entitled *Change the direction of the music staff* (1997), and flips the lines from horizontal to vertical, interlacing the gaps with cherry-red inked lines. The visual effect is both of subverting the staff lines and of providing a new way of reading them.

Bourgeois' cerise interventions are like a new notation, whether in the form of a handprint (as in *My Hand*, from 2002), a kind of extended, amplified notation (as in her *Untitled*, from *The Insomnia Drawings*, 1994 and *La Chanson* from 2009, pictured in the plate section), floral forms (as in *Petite Pousse I* from 2005), an ovoid clock face (as in her *Self Portrait* collage, from 2009), or a figurative river bank (as in *La Rivière Gentille*, from 2007).

Bourgeois wrote of *The Insomnia Drawings* in particular that 'for the night drawings, it is very peaceful to look at the lines of the staff paper. It gives a rhythm ... a passive direction to the horizontal ... and an active direction to the vertical.' In this way she offers us a striking means of thinking about how sheet music holds our eyes. As Bourgeois herself states, sheet music is visually soothing. It encourages you to read it with a direction in mind and to run your eyes over it, regardless of whether you know how to read it, and whether that direction is 'correct' or not. At the same time, it screams out for intervention. It invites you in. It wants you to put your mark on it – and that's part of what makes it, still, so utterly made for performance, all these centuries later.

You and I will each have our own separate, personal ways to interpret Bourgeois' music paper works, because of how enshrined music paper has become in our collective culture. You might see them as a rejection of the stave lines and the restrictions that they place on visual invention; you might see them as an invitation to explore the stave in different dimensions, from unexpected angles. Or perhaps you see them as Bourgeois' way of experimenting with spirals, the motif with which she had a lifelong obsession: in her music paper works they are emblems of both freedom and control, coils of tension that can be read both inwards and outwards, a rejection of the restrictive form of the musical stave, or route to a new way of engaging with it.

This is the absolute beauty of Western classical notation. Artists (both the professional kind and the anonymous, everyday kind) have loved to play with its capacity for ambiguity, subversion and its potential for reuse. Another of my favourite examples is by the Austrian artist Moritz von Schwind (1804–71). Schwind was a friend of the composer Franz Schubert and was hired to decorate the foyer of the Vienna State Opera.[28] His best contribution to music, though, is a little different.

In 1869 his friend, renowned violinist Joseph Joachim, was appointed founding director of the Royal Academic College for Musical Performance in Berlin.[29] To congratulate Joachim, Schwind created a little drawing – a reimagining of musical notes as cats, leaping and curling across the framework of printed music staves. In addition to its exuberant feline theme, the rumour is that the drawing was a joke at the expense of the composer (and raging antisemite) Richard Wagner, whose music Schwind thought was fundamentally fusty and incomprehensibly elaborate – his music requiring singers to literally caterwaul. Can you imagine a host of silken-furred, triangle-eared, bewhiskered Valkyries descending upon the stage like the helicopter in *Apocalypse Now*, warbling as they go?

So far, so nineteenth-century stylistic feud. But just take a look at *how* Schwind described this joke. He wrote of the drawing:

> I became a musician, a future musician in the second higher degree. Get rid of the old, stiff, dry notation system! Obsolete, overcome, discarded stuff – I need a new, spiritual, lively means of expression for my new, unimagined thoughts – whether they are sounds, images, or the devil knows what – I have achieved the incredible. This sonata dedicated to Joachim is clear proof. He admits that he is unable to play it – that wizard on the violin! Incidentally, it can be noted that Joachim and I belong to the famous Order of the Black Cat and that it was this inconspicuous occasion that brought about this giant leap in music.[30]

In other words, Schwind is getting visual stimulus and inspiration precisely *from* the dryness, the stiffness of the notation system. These comments wouldn't be out of place coming from an artist today, but let's remember: this happened almost 200 years ago. We think our modern attitude towards Western classical notation is a result of having superseded it – why should we need it in hymn books, in schools or in performance? But I think this example demonstrates that all that tension, all that seeming incompleteness and inadequacy, was recognised a long time ago – and it was never enough to make sheet music fall out of use. It should give us pause for thought, and invite us to reflect that perhaps it is precisely the illusory stiffness and dryness of notation that makes it quite so enticing to look at. It is part of how it has evolved as a visual form, as an encapsulation of something we hear as well as see. It is screaming out to be interfered with, to be completed. *Fill me!*, it cries. *Undo me, complete me!*

Schwind has answered that call. And yet, at the same time, he has kept the rigid staff lines and the general concept of the notation and the way it should function. The 'Order of the Black Cat' follows a pattern that evolved across 300 years to reach the music of Schwind, Schubert and Wagner, and another 200 to reach us today.

Sheet music is one of the last socially acceptable things to doodle on. If you have performed in an orchestra, choir or group that uses written music, this will be a familiar experience: being handed a dog-eared copy, taped together and covered with a scrawl of previous performance notes and the (un)helpful observations of earlier performers.

The hilarious X account 'Notes on Copies' documents some of the best instances, and a surprising number are visual as well as verbal. There are copies illustrated with daleks; with mountains; with frogs; a dinosaur; a skull and crossbones; mice; hearts; planes; miscellaneous unidentifiable animals; and most of all, many, *many* eyes and spectacles, a constant shorthand across the years for the performers to look at the conductor at that given

Moritz von Schwind's 'Cat Symphony', 1869.

moment and briefly acknowledge the importance of seeing in the way we make music. If you had music lessons as a child you might remember this practice, too – the teacher leaning over and scrawling directions to play a section *andante* (walking pace) or *piano* (quietly), to not slow down (*no! rall!*).

All over the world, every day, people are encountering music and engaging with it in this way. We don't find these practices talked about in histories of music, but that doesn't mean that they aren't important. Examining the role of marginalia in musical practice even briefly reveals just how important the visual experience of sheet music is for music-making, and in turn, just how collaborative this practice has so often been. Whether we are professional, amateur, complete novice, virtuoso, performer or simple appreciator, we have all played our roles in making this way of seeing music.

For me this is a crucial, and perhaps the most beautiful, part of music: that which links us together, regardless of whether we can sightread, whether we can play an instrument or sing, whether we listen or perform. We have taken the music book and we have mounted it on walls and in frames, stitched it onto gloves, painted on it, painted images of it, scrawled on it and (last but not least) performed from it. All of these acts are part of its meaning, as a musical art object.

So let's dial back to where we began: the unassuming little hymn book. Come back with me to the church, just after the doors have been opened in the morning. Pick up the hymn book. Feel it in your hands. Take a moment, and really *look* at it. Think about all of the things that you could do with it – and this time, recognise that its potential is part of how it is speaking to you and encouraging you to make music. Think of all that is lost when the book you're holding has the lyrics, but not the tune. I doubt that many people today would describe it as a work of art. Nevertheless, it has launched thousands upon thousands of crafting projects, of visual responses that are valuable artworks alongside the famous paintings and sculptures you'd find in a gallery or national museum. It is, ever so quietly, a testament to the visual power of music: the moment when it wormed its way into our eyes as well as our ears.

It is time we acknowledged that the music book is far more dynamic, and offers us far more, than we have been led to believe. It doesn't have to be elitist, if we don't let it; if we recognise its history as an early attempt to democratise music and music notation, and as an image of music that has become totemic and pervasive.

Musical reading comes in many forms, from being able to sightread Western classical notation at first glance to vaguely knowing that it is a map of the sound. Regardless of which end of the spectrum you sit on, you are still able to respond to musical notation, and its omnipresence in our twenty-first-century visual culture demonstrates that you probably already do. Once we embrace the sheer variety of ways that we have engaged with the music book, we can recognise that it isn't the problem: it's the way we've boxed ourselves into thinking about it. Louise Bourgeois knew it. So did Schwind, in his way, and all of those millions of crafters across the centuries who have incorporated its forms into their work.

Slowly but surely, together we can rebuild our way of thinking and begin to appreciate all the things that provocatively 'old, stiff, dry, obsolete, overcome, discarded stuff' brings to our ears, our eyes and our imaginations. Come and join me. Bring your pens, needles, pencils, in black or in a rainbow spectrum of colour. Let them run *wild*.

5

One Sweet Liquorice Stick:
The Instruments

School, at last, is out – for the day.

It's a mizzly, overcast Wednesday in 2004, and that can only mean one thing: orchestra rehearsal.

Forgive me, because it could be a little painful on the ears.*

A collection of teenage misfits traipse into the school hall, wrestling with misshapen music stands, scraping chairs across the scuffed floor into a semi-circle position. The hall has the miasma of English state comprehensive schools everywhere: cleaning fluid, that unidentifiable musk that seeps from neglected 1960s brick, lingering above the smell of the canteen – chips, burgers, luridly glazed doughnuts, secret cigarettes – and the acrid teenage perfumes of choice: Impulse and Lynx.

Heavily eyelinered, in train-track braces, black Doc Martens – 'They're *shoes*, Miss!' – and sweeping emo side-fringes, we shuffle through the pile of battered folders to find our parts. There's mine, Flute I: Desk I. I toss it onto the seat next to my

---

* Incredibly, if you would like to see and hear what our school orchestra and hall looked and sounded like, you can. Earlier that year we were extras in the indie violent crime film *The Great Ecstasy of Robert Carmichael* (2005), in the scene where Robert plays Edward Elgar's famous cello concerto. The music is also us, rehearsing the concerto.

desk partner. Trumpet I: Desk II, Tuba I and the disreputable half of Violin I: Desk I are squawking and riffing off each other, causing a scene and delaying the beginning of rehearsal.* The ringleader, we are guessing, is Trumpet I: II, exhausted from double PE and desperate to waste as much time as possible so we don't have to play the march from Giuseppe Verdi's *Aida* (with its infamously gruelling trumpet duet). We roll our eyes at each other. God, we can't wait to get out of this dump. We're made for bigger and better things.

On top of the pile of sheet music inside is the *Lord of the Rings Suite*, that stalwart of school orchestras everywhere.

Unbeknown to us, a mere fifty miles away, a man clutching a golden flute stands in a concert hall, about to rehearse a version of the same thing. His is a rather different instrument to the standard silver-plated, heavily finger-printed Yamaha version I own. Nevertheless, he's the man that I and my desk partner will be attempting to imitate for our tiny eight bars of equally tiny stardom, come the concert at the end of term.

Nerds like me will know the story of legendary flautist James Galway and his solid gold flute, on which he supposedly played the distinctive 'Shire' theme tune in the 2001–03 *Lord of the Rings* film trilogy. In fact, it's unclear whether this actually happened – Galway has many flutes and flute-adjacent instruments, so it is entirely possible that he used another, less visually arresting flute to accompany the hobbits and Gandalf's bucolic pony-cart progress through the rolling fields of the Shire. I played the flute throughout my teenage years, and have played this particular piece many times, so perhaps I should be able to tell from the timbre – the specific quality of sound that the flute

---

* In the end, Tuba I was the only one of us who became a full-time professional musician. The disreputable fifty per cent of Violin I: I, who had been hot-housed for a conservatoire since we were young children and hailed as the great talent of the school, gave up the violin the moment he turned eighteen and hasn't touched it since.

solo has – which flute was used. A confession: I can't. The point of a solid golden flute isn't necessarily anything to do with the sound quality: it doesn't produce a better resonance because of the material it is made of, but because of the craftsmanship. The solid silver flutes that most professional flautists use will sound just as good. Gold just gives an extra flourish of showmanship, an extra spectacle to the performance.

Unlike the other examples in this book, musical instruments encapsulate the tension that lies at the heart of the dalliance between art and music, the visual and the musical, eyes and ears. In some cases, like Galway's golden flute, it works. But sometimes the balance between forming an instrument as an art object and forming one as a tool for performance that will produce a sound cannot be struck. The instrument remains an image of music – but it does so in a manner that foregrounds the loss of performability and the fragile nature of sound.

But into this vacancy floods something else. Instruments, like almost nothing else, are perfect screens onto which to project our selfhood. We love to personalise them, covering our electric guitars with stickers from bands we like, displaying photos or stacks of ragged sheet music on top of our pianos. We *own* them. When we give them away or sell them, we are giving that little bit of ourselves, too (or how we like to think of ourselves). We love to possess music, and instruments are the ultimate accessory – as every softboi who turns up to a party wielding an acoustic guitar, intent on performing their sensitivity, knows.

Being a flute girl places me in hallowed company. The hip hop artist Lizzo, the fourth president of the United States James Madison, the astronauts Ellen Ochoa and Cady Coleman, the Princess of Wales and the rapper André 3000 all play or played the flute, and together we are part of an extremely venerable lineage of music-making. Flutes are the oldest surviving instruments we have, and incredibly, in some instances, these ancient instruments have survived precisely because they were cherished

Duet

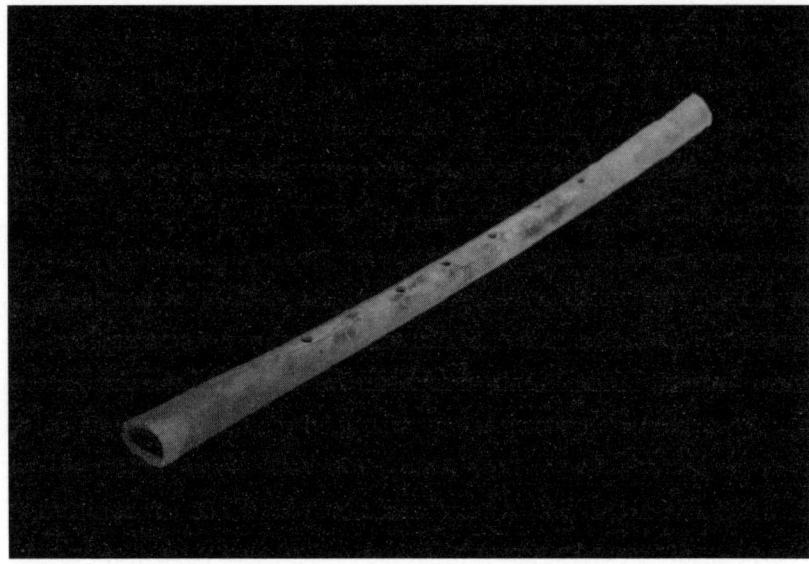

Flute carved from the wing bone of a griffon vulture.

for their visual appearance. At the time of writing, the very oldest musical instrument found is an incredible 43,000 years old, made of the femur of a cave bear; others are made from the wing bones of mute swans and woolly mammoth ivory.

One particularly intriguing example is a whippersnapper at 35,000 years old. A five-hole or 'pentatonic' model, it was carved out of the wing bone of a griffon vulture, a bird with a wingspan of between 2.3m and 2.65m. When it was unearthed in the Hohle Fels Cave in Germany's Ach Valley in 2006, it had been shattered into twelve pieces and buried deep in silt. But here's the odd part. Surrounding it were fragments of three further flutes, made of ivory and slightly less venerable at around 30,000 years old.[1] In other words, it had already served as a vital visual relic to another ancient culture. The cave in which they were found was scattered with tools, all of which were meticulously designed to aid the creation of flutes. This was a workshop. It's also a kind of prehistoric museum: a collection of someone's own history and heritage. The fact that the bone and ivory flutes were kept together, despite the 5,000-year age gap between them, suggests

One Sweet Liquorice Stick: The Instruments

that they were vital for that community's sense of tradition and identity. Researchers universally take such instances as evidence that, at this point in history, humans had developed fully modern behaviour and symbolic communication.[2]

So Galway's golden flute is just one of the most recent in a long, *long* line of flutes that have made space for the visual as well as the aural. Over the tens of thousands of years that have lapsed since the griffon-vulture flute and Galway's, flutes have continued to be central to a huge variety of musical cultures. Because of the nature of how flutes produce sound, and the resonance they rely on, quite a broad variety of materials can be used to make them, which leaves a big margin for beautifying them. However, without doubt, the most audacious examples are the porcelain forms made in East Asia between the twelfth and nineteenth centuries.

One example I'd like to explore here was made in the seventeenth century in Jingdezhen, the great hub of porcelain production in the Jiangxi province of southern China. Its classic cobalt blue decorative imagery pops on pure white porcelain. In the Western world, this type of porcelain was still known at the time as 'white gold' – it would take the remainder of the century before Europeans figured out how to make ceramics with this fickle material; its translucent loveliness understated in contrast to the design, made from cobalt pigment imported from Persia via the Silk Road trade route.[3] The body of the flute is decorated in this cobalt with an imagined landscape typical of the mountains of China. The pointed peak at the centre possibly depicts Mount Huangshan in Anhui province, which recurs in the visual arts and literature of China throughout the ages.[4] But porcelain flutes like this are, generally speaking, quite rare.

If you wanted, you *could* feasibly play this porcelain flute; they have a nice, warm sound that's a little more mellow than their metal counterparts. But it's probable that playing many of these instruments wasn't the main point of them. Unlike with metal and wooden flutes, you can't alter the pitch of a flute made from ceramic: its shape is fixed the moment it is fired in the kiln. As a result, it takes a huge amount of skill to play a porcelain flute tunefully, dependent on how the player breathes and shapes their mouth around the embouchure hole,* and how they allow air to travel down the body of the instrument. Ceramic also makes these flutes much, much heavier, so holding them at the required angles for a sustained amount of time is really tricky. They are far more fragile than their wooden or metal cousins, so travelling with them would have been difficult.

All in all, instruments like these probably weren't made for performance. They were more likely status symbols, something you brought out from your cupboard for special guests or displayed prominently on your mantlepiece. It's a bit like the moment when fictional tech billionaire Miles Bron (played by Edward Norton) brings out 'Paul McCartney's Blackbird Guitar' in the 2022 film *Glass Onion*: *Behold, how very cultured, how very musical I am.*

Instead, they were made to be beautiful, to be decorative objects that could be displayed and admired. That was certainly the case with our next example. It was made in Korea in the early thirteenth century, out of stoneware rather than porcelain. It is glazed in the characteristic celadon colour of the Goryeo dynasty, with its prized satiny grey-green.[5] Gilding, meringue clouds, cranes in flight and tiny chrysanthemum blossoms wind round the body of the flute in a way that draws attention to the uniformity of its glazed surface. You can imagine how satisfying it would feel to hold; how it would sit in your hands.

The Goryeo celadon glaze was probably developed for the way it resembles the colour and consistency of jade, the semi-precious stone highly symbolic across East Asia for its associations with the soul and immortality. And, in case you are wondering, yes,

---

* Mouth hole.

One Sweet Liquorice Stick: The Instruments

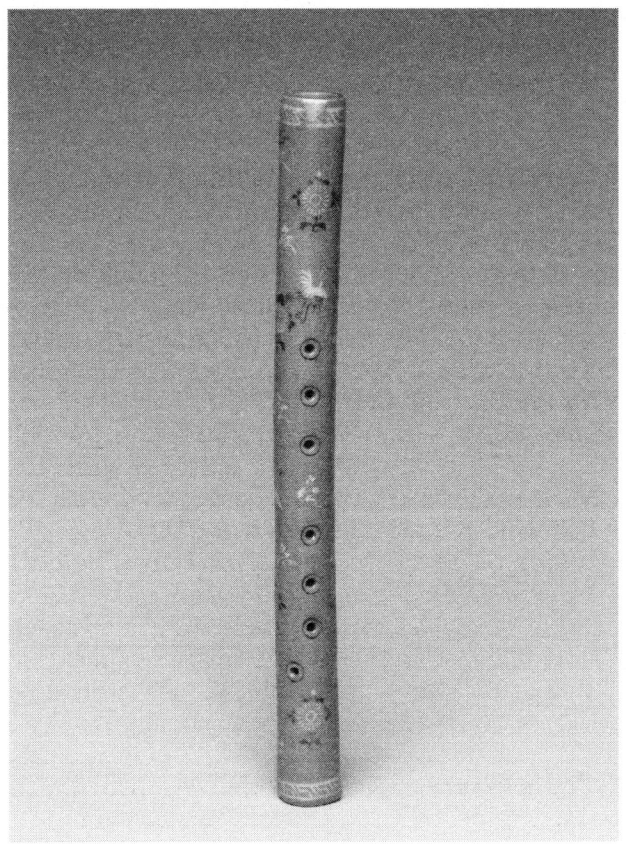

Korean Goryeo celadon flute, stoneware ornamented with gilding, flying cranes, meringue clouds and miniature chrysanthemum blossoms, early thirteenth century.

of course flutes were also made out of jade. I've never heard one myself, so I can't vouch for the quality of the sound, but they should be as playable (if as tricksy) as ceramic flutes.

Why, though, would anyone create a musical instrument that you couldn't really perform on? The answer lies in how heavily symbolic they have been, to a multitude of cultures. It's not incidental that imagery of natural phenomena appear on these flutes. Flutes were key to the East Asian myths about the origins of music. In Chinese mythology, Ling Lun is the founder of music and he was, you guessed it, a flute player. The story goes that Ling

Jade flute with red silk tassel,
eighteenth/nineteenth century.

was so entranced by the song of a quintet of birds that he sought to imitate them. He created five bamboo flutes that made the sound of birdsong, including the song of the mythical phoenix. The ancient Chinese pentatonic – or five-tone – scale was born: *gong, shang, jiao, zhi* and *yu*, equivalent to *do, re, mi, sol, la* in the Western system. The natural world, fed through the forms of a flute, created an entire musical system.[6]

China isn't alone in having a special place for flutes within its mythology. The Persian flute, the *ney*, can be found across Iran as far back as the sixth century BCE; across the Persian empire it was used in all sorts of social contexts, from high

One Sweet Liquorice Stick: The Instruments

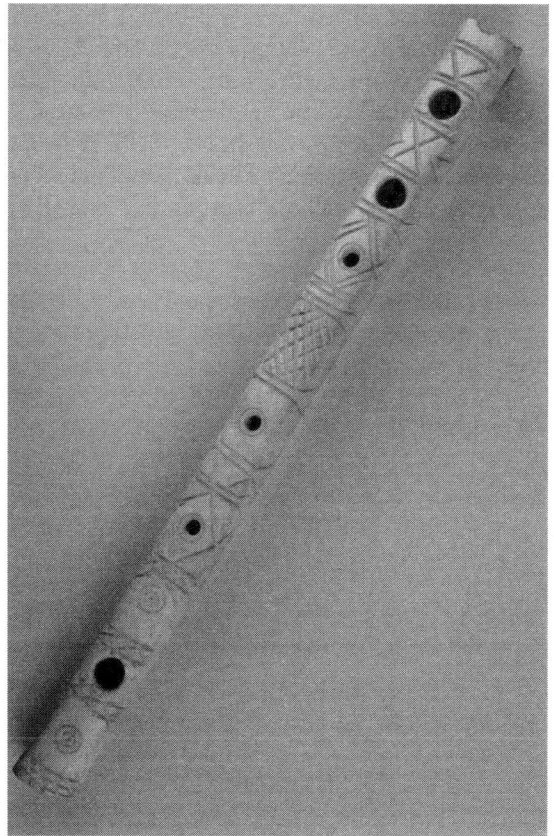

Persian flute or ney, made of
incised bone, ninth century CE.

society entertainment by professional musicians to shepherds herding their sheep in the hills. The example pictured, made of incised bone, was probably owned by a practising Sufi, which adds another, religious context. In Sufi Islam, the ney is said to produce a mournful sound of longing that epitomises the pain of separation from Allah, the beloved, and the preparation and trials of the journey back (in life) towards the joy in reunion with the source of all creation (death, and the return to Allah).

The Persian flute is used to accompany the twirling 'whirling dervishes' dance of the Mevlevi Sema ceremony, named after the thirteenth-century Persian poet, theologian and Sufi mystic Jalāl

Aaad-Dīn Muhammad Rūmī.* The cross-hatching and diamond patterning of this flute frame a dot-in-circle motif associated with magical, apotropaic properties – in other words, this flute is one part musical instrument, one part amulet, protecting against evil.

Across the Atlantic, another flute-playing deity reigned supreme. Kokopelli is a Native American/Mexican fertility deity, typically depicted as a hump-backed flute player. He brings babies, he makes the crops grow, but he is also the origin of music. He appears in petroglyphic art and Hohokam pottery way back to 750 CE, but you might also recognise him from the cerise pink image on the wall of Water White's swimming pool in the TV series *Breaking Bad* (2008–13).** The Hopi tribe believe that Kokopelli can be seen in the full and waning moon; his flute playing chases away the winter and invites in the tender shoots of spring. The Zuni tribe associate him with the rains that allow crops to grow. There it is again: that subtle, quiet connection between the natural world and the flute that summons it, coaxing it back into blossom and lush, verdant life.

All of this is to say that flutes particularly lend themselves to display. They are small, tactile and intimate when compared to, say, a harp or a piano. It's easier to afford a flute made out of costly material, or elaborately decorated, because of this smaller scale. Of course there are bigger, flashier instruments out there, but it is fascinating that these little ones, designed to be held carefully, have so often been decorated so elaborately.

We know that plenty of people have found flute-playing to be grounding. Famously, George III of England was a music lover, and turned to the flute during periods of mental illness (or, as the contemporary records put it, 'incessant loquacity'). Being able to play music, and particularly the flute, was said to bring him great

---

*   Alias Mevlânâ or 'our Master'.
**   Kokopelli is a trickster and not entirely to be trusted – so we could argue that he's one of the reasons for White's descent from plodding chemistry teacher to violent producer and dealer of blue crystal meth.

One Sweet Liquorice Stick: The Instruments

Pueblo petroglyph of Kokopelli, c. 1300 CE.

solace while he was in recovery at Kew Palace. Incredibly, what appears to have been one of his own instruments survives.

Another 'china flute', also formed of much-coveted porcelain, it was made in around 1760 at the Meissen porcelain factory near Dresden, Germany. Its origins are quite murky. A handwritten label in the box it is now stored in announces proudly that it formerly belonged to Charles II. We know that can't be true because the flute is transverse, meaning it is blown sideways or horizontally, a fashion that didn't reach Europe until the eighteenth century; likewise the fact that it is made of four parts to enable different pitches, another eighteenth-century innovation. Instead, it is possible that its royal origins became muddled somewhere in its history. Whoever it was intended for, it has been in the Royal Collection since the early nineteenth century, and its dates certainly suggest that George was the monarch who owned it.

Regardless of who possessed it, this porcelain flute gives us a poignant insight into how musical instruments can have a

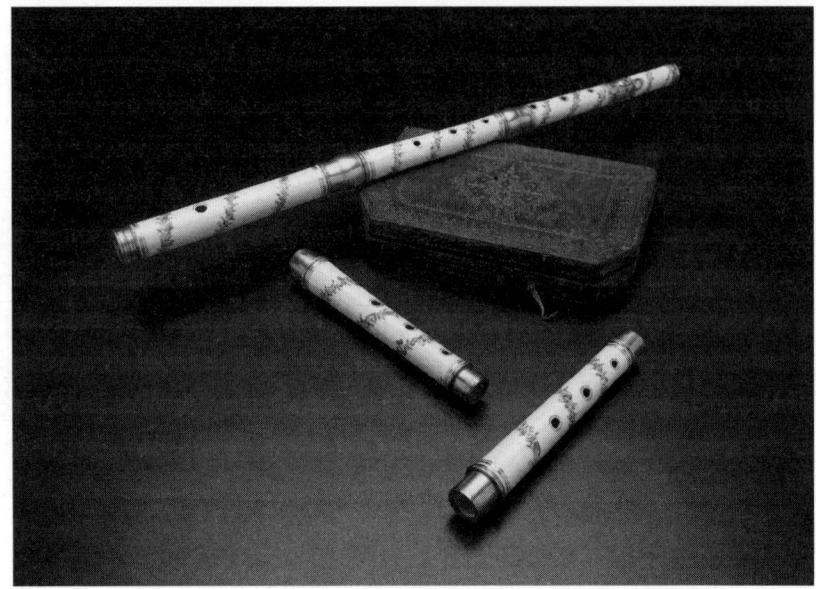

Porcelain and gilt copper flute, c. 1760.

transformative impact on the sense of self. It now seems probable that George III had bipolar disorder.[7] Reports describe him losing control both of his body and of his mind. He foamed at the mouth, overturned his dinner table, had moments of psychosis when he kept 'imaginary company' (conversing with members of his family who had died, including his favourite daughter Amelia, to whom he described her own funeral). Heartbreakingly, he seems intermittently to have been aware of his illness. A letter from his daughter Princess Mary to her brother the Prince Regent in 1813, during another bout of illness, reports that he had moments of lucidity when he was 'sensible of his own deplorable situation'.

Nowadays we are moving towards better ways of thinking about illness. Chronic, recurring ill-health, or even one deep bout of mental or physical illness can be part of us, but we are coming to see all the ways that it doesn't have to define us. For George, though, his 'incessant loquacity' was a loss of self and his sense of who he was. Playing the flute, even for the briefest, most fleeting moment, brought back a sense of himself, a treasured part of his own identity. A kind of magic, in tiny, hand-held porcelain form.

I knew, not long after that afternoon in 2004, that the flute wasn't the instrument for me. That's the strange thing about musical instruments: sometimes they empathise with you and your body and sit well in your hands, or your arms, or beneath your fingers, beloved objects like the American clarinettist Benny Goodman's instrument, which he referred to affectionately as 'one sweet liquorice stick'; or they don't, and it takes a while to work out which one suits you. But I am glad of the time I spent as part of this ancient group of musicians – from James Galway and his golden flute to the owners of the porcelain, Goryeo celadon, talismanic and ceramic flutes, to the cultures where Kokopelli governed all music. It is a musical instrument that, time and again, has been about binding the self into the cosmos and the earth that brings life-giving rain.

𝄞

The next instrument on our journey was also associated with a king. Rather than recreational in purpose, it had a considerably more triumphal role to play. It wasn't a matter of soft power, but cold, hard military dominance.

It's a hand-held clapper in the form of a bird of prophecy or *ahianmwen-oro*, beautifully fashioned out of brass and iron. Idiophones* in this form became popular under the reign of the Edo king (or Oba) Esigie, who ruled the kingdom of Benin in the early sixteenth century (c. 1504–50) and was hugely influential across the Niger Delta. The clappers in this particular form commemorate his victory over the Igala kingdom.

---

* The general term for all self-sounding instruments like rattles, chimes or bells.

Esigie's father, the Oba Ozolua, had nominally converted to Christianity in order to develop an amicable trading relationship with the Portuguese empire. He had thoroughly militarised Benin during his reign. His burgeoning friendship with the Portuguese explorer John Alfonso d'Aveiro raised the intriguing possibility of access to a brand-new technology: firearms, which would give Benin a significant advantage over its neighbours. D'Aveiro, like any good pal, offered some advice. Portugal, mate, doesn't do trade in firearms except with its *Christian* allies. You really do need to convert. A clutch of Ozolua's nobles were very unimpressed with this turn of events, and betrayed him for Igala. The Oba wasn't simply a political leadership position: Ozolua and his descendants were religious leaders, expected to serve as chief priests as well as military leaders. The dissatisfaction of these defected courtiers fermented even after Esigie came to the throne, and in 1515 the Igala attacked.

Legend has it that on the way to battle, Esigie's army met the bird of prophecy (the ahianmwen-oro). In the ultimate party-pooper act, the bird predicted that Benin would lose the battle – so, like any wise ruler, Esigie ordered the bird killed, and went on to defeat the Igala. Esigie rather cannily declared that the sound of clappers during the Ugie Oro court ceremonies celebrating his victory was a sign that the kings of Benin were endowed with the power to alter history.[8]

Elaborately decorated musical instruments were key to Benin culture and performances of kingship in general. One of the oldest surviving African ivory sculptures is a double bell, or *egogo*, which dates from Esigie's reign and was probably used by him. Egogos were used by the Oba during the Emobo ceremony to drive away evil spirits; the central figure depicted is probably Esigie himself. However, the idiophone is something special. As a musical instrument, it epitomises the harnessing of the spiritual, the ineffable transmuted into material form so for a fleeting moment, as the clapper is played, we are able to *see* music as the manifestation of Esigie's power and his success in the Benin–Igala or Idah War.

Anonymous, bird of prophecy idiophone,
sixteenth to nineteenth century.

Morally speaking, Esigie was a bit of a mixed bag. Under his reign, the title of Iyoba or queen mother was instituted.[9] Previously, a king's mother would be executed on his accession, presumably to smooth the new king's path to power. Queen Idia, Esigie's mother, had been instrumental in the strategy of the Benin–Igala War, and so really it was the least he could do. But by allying with the Portuguese, Esigie's reign offered one of the decisive steps towards the transatlantic slave trade: his kingdom sold prisoners of war as slaves to Portugal and other European merchants, bolstering Benin's economy and enabling its eastward expansion.[10]

Those beautiful bronzes that form the most distinctive objects of Benin's visual culture, used to commemorate the culture's history and to consolidate its rituals,[11] were made of ingots derived from the Rhineland in Germany.[12] These ingots, cast into ring shapes and known as 'manillas', were brought over by the Portuguese and used as currency in exchange for slaves, ivory, pepper and palm oil. They sparked huge creativity in the kingdom of Benin, and huge wealth. They were also, however tiny, a structural cog in a machine that would cause several hundred years of unimaginable suffering and exploitation. The bird of prophecy casts a long, distorted shadow.

Esigie's bird of prophecy had a troubled afterlife that extended long after his death. Clappers like it are used in the Ugie Oro ceremony that continues to this day. But not Esigie's clapper, not any more. The British invaded Benin City in 1897, after a prolonged campaign to bring the territory now known as the country Nigeria under British rule. In the Benin Royal Palace, altars dedicated to all the Obas had existed stretching back into the 1300s. The invading army unceremoniously dismantled these and looted all of their priceless artefacts.[13] To the eyes of the looters, they were just beautiful things to display, emptied of any cultural, sacred, political or even practical usage.

Two hundred objects went directly to the British Museum; innumerable others were sold on the international art market, which is probably how this clapper eventually ended up in the Metropolitan Museum of Art in New York. Countless others have been lost track of, because soldiers and administrators took their pick and never had to account for their lootings. We don't even know how many objects there originally were. When the

Oba was reinstated (in name, at least) in 1914, the objects were not returned to Benin.

Anonymous, an egogo or double bell, ivory, early sixteenth century.

The clapper and others like it are dated vaguely as having been made between the sixteenth and nineteenth centuries, because when they were ripped from their original context no one made a note of when they were made, nor who made them. They are stained with the blood of cultural as well as corporeal massacre, and we cannot separate this history from their role as musical art objects. As curator Dan Hicks has observed, 'the silence and stillness are not natural conditions for the displaced objects on display here. They are the effect of a stilling, as when detention interrupts transit, and of a fracturing, as when a shrapnel shell explodes its target, and of a silencing, as when a gun is silenced.'[14]

For the past 130 years, the clapper has not been shaken joyfully at the Ugie Oro to celebrate Esigie's victory; instead it has lain silent, displayed out of its musical context. It is dislocated from the kings of Benin and their ability to alter the course of history.

𝄞

Some instruments succeed in forging connections between people, allowing them to rally around communities and places and ideas; and some, on the other hand, fail to create a bond and end up ultimately as nothing but curiosities, useless but beautiful gifts that no one knows what to do with.

Drowning out the birdsong, the wheeling cries of gulls, the tinkle of fountains and the distant swash of the sea against the harbour, hammering, sawing, screwing and drilling are disturbing the peace of the Royal Privy Garden of the Topkapı Palace, Constantinople. A squad of engineers swarm over an array of oddly shaped pieces of metal and wood. They are hastily reconstructing an object that was supposed to be presented as soon as their boat landed in this year of our Lord 1599, but which, after weeks at sea, has slowly started warping in the damp sea air, coming apart at its seams.

Eagerly awaiting the result of these proceedings is Mehmed III, sultan of the Ottoman empire. He doesn't care that, technically, this object was supposed to be a gift for his father (who had conveniently died some four years earlier, leaving Mehmed free to execute all nineteen of his brothers and ascend the throne). The gift has been sent by Elizabeth I of England, with whom he has struck a tentative alliance in order to combat their common enemy, Spain. But on the global stage, Elizabeth is small fry compared to the might of Mehmed's empire. She needs him more than he needs her – so she has, pardon the pun, pulled out all the stops.

This gift is a large clockwork organ – not too dissimilar from ye olde barrel organs once found on the street, or fairground organs on traditional funfair rides. Nothing like it has ever been witnessed on these shores before.[15] The Ottoman court has a vast array of musical instruments, from the *tanbur* (a kind of lute) to the ney (a flute, as we have seen), the *kanun* (a kind of zither) and the *keman* (a kind of violin). But nothing like the organ, with its sounding system of keys and strings that are hit, rather than plucked. Its bejewelled case is topped with dancing sculptures, among them a flock of blackbirds and thrushes that sing and shake their wings when the music draws to a close. The organ has been designed, in fact, by one of the industrious engineers currently hard at work, one Thomas Dallam.

Dallam kept a meticulous account of his time in Istanbul, rather decorously titled *A Brefe Relation of my Travell from the Royall Cittie of London towards The Straite of Mariemediterranum and what happened by the waye*. And, luckily for us, this manuscript, along with his account of how the organ worked – and what Mehmed thought of it – was rediscovered by the collector Henry Rhodes in 1848.[16] Here's Dallam's description of the first performance:

> The presente [the organ] began to salute the grand sinyor [the sultan]; for when I lefte it I did alow a quarter of an houre for his cominge thether. Firste the clocke strouke 22; than The chime of 16 bels went of, & played a songe of 4 partes. That beinge done, tow personagis which stood upon to cornders of the seconde storie houldinge tow silver trumpetes in there hands did lifte them to theire heads, & sounded a tantara. Than the musicke went of, and the orgon played a song of 5 partes twyse

over. In the tope of the orgon, being 16 foute hie did stande a holly bushe full of blacke birds & thrushis, which at the end of the musick did singe & shake theire wynges. Divers other motions thare was which the grand sinyor wondered at.[17]

Mehmed was *thrilled*. So thrilled, in fact, that he tried very hard indeed to keep Dallam along with the organ. Dallam had to invent a fictional wife – who was very, *very* angry and really needed him to come home now – in order to be allowed to leave. The success of the organ is more significant than it might now appear. Though the Ottoman empire had links with England, and Mehmed had met plenty of English-speakers before, it is possible that this is the first time he had heard an instrument playing music structured around English, and more broadly European, ideas about harmony. Ottoman music was composed around *makam*, the system of Arabic melodic modes that bore very little resemblance to their European equivalents when it came to which notes were appropriate to use where, and in which combination. There was no guarantee that Mehmed would find the European style of music pleasant. Sending a musical instrument to express esteem and respect, no matter how decorative, was rather a gamble.

We don't know what the four- or five-part song was. Dallam's record is also the closest we can get to knowing what the instrument looked like. His instruments survive only in fragments – a lonely embossed organ pipe that was mysteriously kept and handed down, until it found its way into the Victoria & Albert Museum in London, and some larger pipes and pieces thought to be still part of the organ in King's College Chapel, Cambridge.

In fact, the singing blackbird organ didn't survive much longer than Mehmed himself. His son Ahmed took a far more rigid view of the rules of Islam, and, because figurative visual representations and automatons were strictly speaking an affront to Allah, he had the organ uncermoniously dismantled.[18] No one was particularly concerned. Elizabeth was dead, Spain was

One Sweet Liquorice Stick: The Instruments

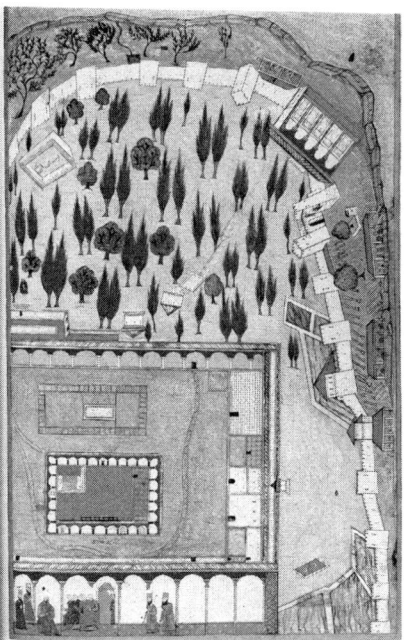

The Royal Privy Garden of the Topkapi Palace, where Dallam's blackbird organ stood, from the Hunername, 1584.

no longer a huge worry to the Ottoman empire, and England was busily attempting to make friends (and 'friends') with other, further-flung cultures by this point.

You and I, though, can mourn this as the tragedy that it is. All the things that were lost with the organ, and the questions that it could answer. What did it sound like? Precisely when did the blackbirds open their wings? What gems were used? Did Dallam make any effort to decorate it with Ottoman-appropriate embellishments – with the familiar, knotty Islamic strapwork patterns that were all the rage in England? The blackbirds might suggest not, but we'll never know.

But one thing is clear: the visual appearance of the organ – its decoration – was key to its meaning, because it is that which ultimately resulted in its untimely destruction.

There are musical instruments whose visual decoration interferes with their meaning, transforming them, for better or worse, into something that can become politically or religiously suspect. And then there are musical instruments for which visual appearance is the whole point. The next step on this odyssey takes us to what, for me, is surely one of the most unusual musical instruments ever created.

A man strides down the streets of The Hague in the Netherlands on a balmy evening in 1876. Suited, booted and frock-coated, his name is John F. Loudon, and he is the second most prolific collector of delftware ceramics in the world. He is on his way to see the collection of his rival W.G.F. van Romondt, who has pipped Loudon to first place, and is exhibiting his treasures.[19] The glowing light hits the canal – everything, everything a luminous still life. Here, suddenly, as though lit by a spotlight, that single, unassuming cobble is the main character – now this apple, on a market stall, now this person hanging out sheets. And, catching the shimmer off the canal, there is a glint in Loudon's eye. He has a plan. There's something very particular that he wants to purchase today.

He will pay 1,500 guilders for it – an almost unheard-of price for the time. He comes from a family that made its fortune by trading sugar and indigo in the Dutch East Indies, and he followed suit by building up that fortune through the same trades. He is fanatical about delftware, and he has an unlimited budget.[20] Nevertheless, it's quite a price to pay for a curiosity.

And, truth be told, we have no idea why it was made.

It was constructed c. 1705–10 out of tin-glazed delftware, the ceramic that rose to prominence as the cost of porcelain from East Asia spiralled further and further.[21] European potters simply couldn't figure out how to mix or fire a clay to produce such fine pieces of ceramics. As more and more people clamoured for porcelain arriving on East India Trading Company ships, the potters of the Netherlands developed a workaround. They would apply a thin layer of pearly white tin glaze over the standard stoneware that most European ceramics were made of, and so achieve the superficial appearance of oriental porcelain. Delftware was born. Along with its rough equivalent ceramic forms Italian maiolica and Portuguese azulejos, it would be one of the most desired decorative art forms for centuries. Even after European potters mastered the art of throwing and firing porcelain ceramics, the pots of Delft continued to be highly prized, as Loudon's little frenzy demonstrates.

This violin follows the general style of East Asian porcelain by depicting a harmonious scene. A cluster of men and women in fashionable eighteenth-century dress are standing in genteel conversation, sharing a ewer of wine, some perhaps dancing. Overhead, a pair of musicians play a bass viol and violin, serenading this conviviality. The fingerboard is decorated with a pattern known as strapwork, leading our eyes up to the grotesque head of a leering court jester-like figure at the top of the scroll, made out of marble and possibly added later.

There's a peculiar irony to Loudon's decision to collect delftware in general, let alone this violin. The trading goods with which he and his family made their fortunes, indigo and sugar, are both material products of the transatlantic slave trade.[22] Both were extracted from plants grown in in South-East Asia and the Indian subcontinent, areas that Europe had colonised and economically suffocated with oppressive trading restrictions.[23] More shockingly, the material forms of these goods, when fully processed by enslaved labour, mirrored the deep-blue-on-white appearance of Loudon's beloved delftware. In the case of sugar, the white colour was achieved by a refining process that involved passing the sugar through a material known as bone char – quite literally, the incinerated skeletons of animals and possibly even of dead enslaved workers.[24] Delftware was a visual marriage of these materials, both in terms of how Loudon funded his habit, and in their actual physical appearance.

There's every chance that this was a deliberate choice, or it may have been a complete coincidence. Nevertheless, it is odd. It transforms all that hurt, all that exploitative labour and plundering of resources, into a beautiful object: if you will pardon my language, a polished turd. At the same time the violin is a visual reminder of that labour and plundered resources, there in indigo blue and white. Loudon didn't commission this violin, but he is the one who gave it such an astronomical value. It's yet another reminder that there is no such thing as art for art's sake, divided from the world in which it was made. Every beautiful object requires material to make it, and that material has to come from somewhere. Every object requires money to purchase that material and, we would hope, to pay for the labour that will make it. Every object is designed for a customer, and a context.

This violin troubles me – and not just for the reasons listed above. Unlike a flute, it really does matter what material you make a violin out of. String instruments are typically made out of wood because it has the best sonorities and produces the broadest range of pitches. The German artist, composer and instrument builder Robert Rutman created what he called a steel cello in the late 1960s, but in order to make it sound he needed to radically rethink the shape – it resembles a sail, rather than the hourglass form associated with string instruments. You can make the strings themselves out of many different materials, from silk to metal to pig gut, but the body, in this shape, only works with wood.

For this reason there aren't many surviving examples of ceramic violins. Other ceramic violins make this plain; one, now in the National Museum of American History, was made in Europe in the nineteenth century, so is a little younger than our delftware friend. The body is still violin-shaped and violin-sized, yes, but there are no strings or spaces for strings, no peg box, no finger board. This violin was never intended to be played; in fact, it cannot physically be played, even if you tried.

One Sweet Liquorice Stick: The Instruments

Porcelain delftware mandolin, 1800–1825.

Another close relative is a porcelain mandolin, also made of delftware but around a century later than our violin, c. 1800–25. It has turnable pegs and a fretboard patterned all over with a beautiful strapwork pattern, but no place to attach strings at the bottom. You could hold it, the way you'd hold a mandolin. You could mime playing it. But you can't perform music on it.

Our little delftware violin pal, on the other hand, was cast with holes in its pegbox at the top of the neck, designed to allow pegs to be inserted. They are angled, as though to demonstrate that, yes, of course they can be adjusted to allow for tuning. At the bottom of the body, it also has the part known as the tailpiece, with the 'fine tuners' where the strings are attached and that also enable tuning. Should the mood take you, you could literally pick up a bow and play this violin – even if the sound it produced might leave a little to be desired.

The delftware violin tells us something crucial about how we experience music, and most of all about what musical instruments are actually *for*. As we've already seen from the exquisite parade of jade, ceramic and porcelain flutes, it's pretty clear that instruments don't need to function as performable instruments in order to evoke music itself. The violin takes us one step further. It functions as a visual joke. *Trompe l'oeil* – literally, trick the eye – is a painting and sculpture technique that had been around since Roman times, but gained huge popularity across the seventeenth and eighteenth centuries, particularly in Dutch still life paintings. You see it everywhere, from sheaves of creased paper seemingly exploding from canvases, to painted columns in perspective to illusionistically extend the height of a ceiling, to minutely observed reflections in glass or pewter goblets, reflecting the painter seemingly lingering behind us, peering over our shoulders.

In this context, the delftware violin begins to make sense. It is a performance of a musical instrument, masquerading in the role. You think this is what a violin looks like, and that's all there is to it? Think again, and see how easily your eyes are fooled.

This subversion of our expectation takes the visual clout of a musical instrument – how beautiful it is, how carefully made, the craft that makes it so covetable – and turns it on its head, transforming the instrument into an emblem of its uselessness. It is as though this masterful ceramicist is smirking slightly, throwing up their arms in simultaneous acknowledgement and refutation of their own exquisite craftsmanship. *I tried*, they say. *Look, I even included the pegs and the tailpiece and I strung it, but no, nothing doing. It doesn't work. See how foolish we are for wanting beautiful things.*

But here's the thing: it does work. It is still recognisably a musical object, and thus a comment on how the people of the early eighteenth-century Netherlands thought about music. Another way we can think about the delftware violin is as a memento mori: a warning against earthly vanity. Dutch still life is littered with broken or unused musical instruments, iconographical reminders of how short life is, how quickly it can be snatched away.[25] Other cultures and other periods were interested in using visual art in this way, but it was an especial preoccupation of the Netherlands during this period. So there's another layer of meaning to the delftware violin: music is brief, and in its brevity it is a reminder of how short a human life is, too. Where the other instruments in this chapter were about celebrations of, or displays of, individual or collective selfhood, this violin is a refutation of selfhood.

This is how music was conceptualised when the delftware violin was made. Loudon splurged his 1,500 guilders on it some 150 years later. Maybe it held some of this moral meaning for him, too; maybe it was his way of demonstrating (however cynically or sincerely) his piety and his recognition that his earthly goods and his life were ultimately meaningless. Maybe he thought the epitome of piety was throwing an enormous sum of his blue-and-white fortune at a beautiful but 'useless' blue-and-white musical instrument.

Of course, we know that it isn't useless – indeed, far from it. We know this from the simple fact that, unlike Dallam's blackbird organ, it was never destroyed. The people who preserved it knew that beauty itself is useful. Highlighting the visual aspects of a musical instrument, at the complete expense of its capacity to produce a sound, is useful. It gives us a moral story about music. And 300 years after it was made and 150 years after it was bought for such an astronomical price, it gives you and me an insight into how people once thought about music. It tells us about the people who made it, the people who collected it, and about *ourselves*, the people who continue to be fascinated by it now.

These objects, which are designed to be collectible, allow us to self-fashion. *Yes, I understand this*, our brains say, or *No, I do not understand. I know about physics, so I am aware that it probably sounds strange. I know about violins, so I can see that it is playable. I know about ceramics, and recognise this as delftware.* These thoughts are all ways that we define ourselves to ourselves, and to everyone around us. Musical instruments are an integral part of this.

𝄞

There is, of course, one instrument that has existed the longest of all, though for much of its history it has seldom left any kind of material trace: the voice. One person made the combination of visual and voice the linchpin of her career. Elaborately coiffed, with blonde hair that bears more than a passing resemblance to that of Marilyn Monroe, she stands before the camera. She's dressed in a floor-length floral dress over a mermaid-turquoise button-down shirt. With great theatrical ceremony, she stretches her left hand high and emits a Tarzan-style yodelling bellow. *AAAAiAiAiAAAAiAiAiAiAAAAAA!!!!!!*

Her name is Cathy Berberian, alias Catherine Berio, alias the 'Bette Midler of Modernism'. Berberian first exploded onto the musical stage as a classically-trained singer – but not, like many of her contemporaries, through a conservatoire. Private lessons with renowned singers eventually culminated in the Fulbright scholarship that brought her to Milan. Obsessed with the Armenian music of her parents, she identified her passion early – by her own account at the tender age of seven, when she found a pile of her parents' 78rpm records in their unused Victrola record player, and 'fell down the long rabbit hole into the wonderland of music'. Her impressive three-and-a-half octave range, and her musical adventurousness, captured the ears of many of the emerging figures of Europe's post-war experimental scene. These included John Cage who, in 1958, wrote and dedicated his graphic score *Aria* to Berberian, who would in turn perform its world premiere. The impact of *Aria* extended far beyond what it enabled Berberian to do with her voice, though. It sowed seeds that would eventually come to fruition in the Pop Art score that Berberian would create with cartoonist Roberto Zamarin in 1966: *Stripsody*.

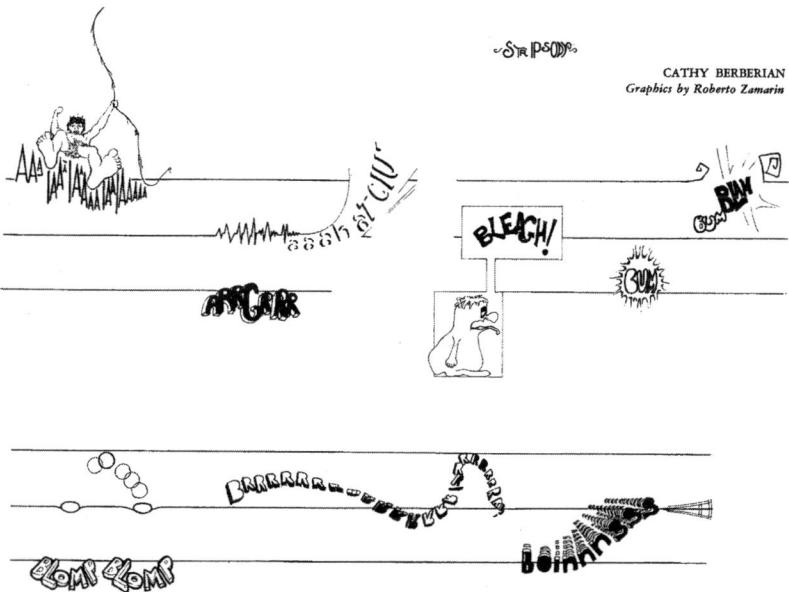

Section of Cathy Berberian's *Stripsody*, 1966.

Stripsody could only have been conceived by a singer, intimately conscious of the frustrations (and potential, almost euphoric liberations) of fitting a voice to a visual, graphic representation. It takes a three-line staff, each roughly representing low, medium and high pitch, and uses the graphic cartoon script of word, image and vocal exclamation as its notation. It encapsulates that push and pull; it's also a madly virtuosic expression of what Berberian knew she could do with her own voice. She was an incredible vocal mimic, and could perform the trickiest of the classical opera repertoire in the style of Marilyn Monroe, Marlene Dietrich, baby talk, bird calls and *Sprechstimme*.*

Stripsody takes her vocal acrobatics and showcases them. One inspiration seems to be the gloriously campy *Batman* TV series with Adam West as Bruce Wayne/Batman, Burt Ward as Robin and Eartha Kitt as Catwoman.[26] First broadcast in January 1966, *Batman* featured many hilarious sound effects that would later be parodied to excellent effect in *The Simpsons* (ZUFF! PAN! SNUH! BORT! POOO! NEWT! MINT! ZAK!). Charles Schulz's *Peanuts* cartoon strip and the 1966 TV series *Tarzan*, of course, are also huge influences. Superman, via the Broadway musical *It's a Bird... it's a Plane... it's Superman* (also first shown in 1966), gets a look-in too. *Stripsody* is an amalgam of popular culture and sound art, all that was cutting-edge in the mid-1960s art of sound recording. As Berberian writes in the preface to the printed score:

> The score should be performed as if by a radio sound man, without any props, who must provide all the sound effects with his voice. The three lines represent the different pitch levels: low, medium and high.
>
> The lines enclosed by bars are to be performed as 'scenes' in contrast to the basic material which is a glossary of onomatopoeias used in comic strips.
>
> Wherever possible, gestures and body movements should be simultaneous with the vocal gestures.

---

* Speak-singing, used in The Kinks' 'The Village Green Preservation Society' and Lou Reed's 'Walk on the Wild Side'.

On page 10 is a child's figure which represents a silence in which the performer places her thumb in her mouth and cups the other hand to her ear.

Basically, the spacing of the 'sound words' indicates the timing. In performance, the entire work generally takes 6 minutes.

This work was comissioned by Hans Otte on behalf of the Bremen Radio for the Festival of Contemporary Music of May 1966 and was first performed on that occasion.[27]

Where other creators of graphic scores were happy to make use of their own graphic skills (however developed they were), the visual appearance of *Stripsody* was clearly of paramount importance to Berberian. She sought out the comic book artist Zamarin in order to ensure that her 'sound words' evoked the aesthetics of a cartoon, as well as the sound effects. It had to look right.[28] As well as the age of *Tarzan* and *Batman*, this was also the era of Roy Lichtenstein, whose distinctive paintings had transformed the perception of the comic strip from a medium seen only in children's magazines to one that had the potential to be 'high art'. What's more, Berberian's graphic score had to be experienced as a read entity as much as a performed entity: a considerable part of its information about how to transform it into a piece of music was contained in the visual appearance.

Twenty years earlier, sound sampling had been a big feature of the *musique concrète* experimental composition style, taking natural sonic elements and recordings and splicing them together on magnetic tape. In 1963 the Mellotron was invented – an electromechanical keyboard that connected the magnetic tape to keys, allowing pre-recorded tape loops of orchestral instruments to be played whenever you compressed a given key. The sound sample captured the zeitgeist. You can hear it in many of the distinctive tracks of the 1960s, from the Beatles' 'Strawberry Fields Forever' to the Rolling Stones' 'She's a Rainbow'. But in *Stripsody* Berberian takes it one step further. She recognised that many of the distinctive sounds – sounds from pop culture, made possible by newly widely-available media like television and film – were inseparable from their visual representation. And so the forms of cartoon pigs, cats, fizzes, knock-knocks and chomps parade across her score.

Berberian's need for the visual on her score is matched by her need for the visual in performance. She was, by all accounts, frustrated by the conventions of modern recitals of arias from opera: walk on, sing, take a bow, leave. Why not exploit the flamboyant possibilities of inhabiting a *body*, she wondered? Why not let it become larger than life, part of the music itself? Her other work is all part of her effort to establish the integral role that theatricality and the human body as instrument could play in music – recording humorous operatic versions of the Beatles' songs as *Beatles Arias for Special Fans* in 1967, or ushering in the comeback of the music of sixteenth-century composers like Monteverdi as part of the early music revival in the twentieth century.[29]

Stripsody is a reinvention of the opera genre and what it means to be an opera singer. To many it sounds like a jazz improvisation, rather than something that follows a specified order of sounds and gestures. But it's also a reclamation of what it means to be a woman in music, to inhabit a femme-presenting body in the same way that we saw Alice Prin, Man Ray's 'violon', earlier in this book. In 1983, Berberian stated:

> Little by little, music gave me an identity, all mine, not just somebody's daughter, sister or niece. Music gave me a profession. It brought me a great love and, when it ended, it filled the void with an incentive to live more fully as a person, not an appendix. It liberated me as a woman, it forged my independence of mind and spirit. Music stimulated my creativity and gave me a sense of confidence and inner serenity.

> Music is the air I breathe and the planet I inhabit. The only way I can pay my debt to music is by bringing it to others, with all my love.[30]

Stripsody offers us a fresh, smart way of thinking about music. The presence of its composer and original performer is inextricably enmeshed in the way that it was conceived, and in its demands upon any aspiring performer. Even fifty years after Berberian's untimely death, *Stripsody* is still highly accessible for anyone to perform, regardless of how much they know about music notation and how it works: you can *see* exactly how Berberian wants you to follow it. Plenty of graphic scores are still based on the idea that you understand the mechanics of Western classical notation – in other words, that you know what the visual forms are pushing against and rejecting. This isn't a condition of Berberian's *Stripsody*. It's all about vocalisation: about visualising things that can be done with your voice. All you need is the cultural associations of Tarzan, Superman et al. – associations that, given how globalised these influences have become over the past half-century, aren't hard to get hold of. Berberian is still there, 'bringing [music] to others, with all [her] love', in that opening Tarzan bellow.

This kind of music requires a huge amount of virtuosic skill to really pull off – but almost none at all to try, and to experience its account of what music can be. It's playful, and a bit silly. But what it offers is also deadly serious: music as game, music as deconstruction, music as inherently democratic and hospitable, no matter how tricky its vocal acrobatics are. You try offering *Stripsody* to a child, and you'll see this in action as they navigate the corners of their voice and how they can manipulate it into a performance. It's an entry-level snatched glance into all that music can offer.

We have a tendency to see all 'high' art forms – visual arts like painting and sculpture, performance genres like opera – as needing to be deciphered. *Stripsody* completely and utterly eschews the concept that there is but one answer, and that it should be puzzled out. It offers a different way of thinking about music, based on an idea of performance that we have seen resurface time and again in this book. Join in, take part, experiment with it, make it your own. This music thing is yours.

𝄞

Kings, queens, leaders and business magnates have scrapped over musical instruments; they have used them to announce their dominance, to display their mastery and taste and generosity. But, as Berberian shows us, the supercharged potency of these objects is not simply confined to history. Musical instruments continue to be of enormous importance for self-fashioning right up to the present day. In fact, they take a central role in one of the biggest disputes over copyright and music ownership of our times.

In 2005, a girl from a Christmas tree farm in the state of Pennsylvania signed a record deal. Her music was country and wholesomely young; her voice, winsome but raw as though audibly untrained. She liked and was influenced by Shania Twain, LeAnn Rimes and The Chicks. It's tempting to think there was no way of knowing that in just over a decade's time, this girl would have become one of the great phenomena of twenty-first-century pop music. But that would be to overlook the grit and determination she had already displayed. Earlier visits to Nashville, Tennessee saw her pitching herself to every record label going, determined to become a country singer, but no one was interested. She recognised the need to transform herself into something a little different, to find a unique selling point – and so she spent the three years leading up to her deal focusing on learning to play guitar, and on cultivating her songwriting.[31]

In time, she'd come to categorise her songwriting in three different types. There are 'quill lyrics', which 'sound like a letter written by Emily Dickinson's great-grandmother while sewing a lace curtain'. Then there are 'fountain pen lyrics', which offer modern storylines with poetic twists and 'try to paint a vivid picture of a situation, down to the chipped paint on the door frame and incense dust on the vinyl shelf … like confessions scribbled and sealed in an envelope, but too brutally honest to send'. And then there are 'glitter gel pen lyrics', which are frivolous and syncopated perfectly to the beat, like 'the drunk girl at the party who tells you that you look like an angel in the bathroom'.[32]

Her name was Taylor Swift. And songwriting would be the key theme of one of her most distinctive musical instruments. Some fourteen years later, now an award-winning, platinum-selling artist, Swift was invited to perform at the 2019 American Music Awards (AMAs). For the majority of her set, she played on a customised grand piano emblazoned with the names of her albums, from *Taylor Swift* and *Fearless* to *Lover*, with song titles and lyrics included among the coiling strapwork decoration. Each of these elements looked as though they'd been piped on with glittered pale pink frosting. It looked like an old-school iced wedding cake. *Eat me*, you almost expect it to declare, *and I will magnify you to the size of a house, or shrink you to the size of a mouse.*

This sugary confection of a piano might look like a bit of canny self-promotion (*'Do you like this? Then try my entire back catalogue!'*), but it's more than that: it's a powerful statement of artist's rights and what it means to be a musician. Up until her seventh album *Lover* (2019), the master recordings for Swift's entire back catalogue were owned by Big Machine Records, the label she had signed with all those years ago, rather than by the artist herself.[33] This was far more restrictive than it might first sound. Decisions about what could be performed, where, and how, were in the hands of the record label, all because of a contract she had signed before she had even reached adulthood. Crucially, Big Machine Records claimed ownership of those songs: quill, fountain pen, glitter gel pen lyrics and all.

The AMA performance marked the beginning of her reclamation of her own music; soon after, she would begin re-recording her old albums to regain ownership of her own voice, words and songs. At this pivotal moment in our recent history of music, her sugar-frosted candyfloss grand piano was at the heart of her message. It was an externalisation of her music, her work, her life striving to take back her voice. In her 2023–4 Eras Tour, she referenced this moment again, playing the *Lover* portion of the set on a guitar in the same candy floss-toned shade as that iconic piano.

Music can feel so close to us, so deeply entangled in our pulse and our breath, so integral to our essential being. Musical instruments are the most tangible manifestation of this. Sometimes, as I carted my flute case from class to class, accidentally leaving it in biology, or having it unceremoniously dumped onto my desk by a classmate in textiles, it felt like an imaginary friend that had somehow taken physical form. Later, I realised the relationship was more like that between a parent and child (with the exception, we hope, of constantly leaving it behind). What was this thing that I had somehow opted to care for and play with and cultivate?

Instruments are visual extensions of our musical tastes and identities; they leave their impacts on our bodies, from the calloused fingertips of a guitarist to the angle of my chin, which is permanently moulded from my flute's lip plate. Like Taylor Swift's confection of a grand piano, Thomas Dallam's ill-fated blackbird organ at the court of Mehmed III, and every teenager who lugs their sticker-clad guitar wherever they go, musical instruments are extensions of our selves. The instruments we play are always with us, like a phantom limb made flesh, wood, porcelain, brass, eternally on the cusp of having been silenced, and waiting to sound again.

6

Watching Paint Sing:
Abstracting Music

Some pieces of music chime with you at particular moments in your life; some seem unremarkable the first time you hear them, and then grow on you; some you adore instantly, but gradually they lose their lustre, becoming as irritating as a persistent fly. And then there are some that grow alongside you throughout your life, that transport you, and that sound as fresh and spine-tingling as the first time you heard them, as though they know the secret words and harmonies inscribed on your heart.

At the tail end of 1945, as the world began to patch itself back together in the wake of the Second World War, the British composer Herbert Howells composed a set of canticles for the evensong service, to be sung by the choir of Gloucester Cathedral. They're now known as the *Gloucester Service*, or Howells' *Gloucester*.

It's the 'Nunc Dimittis' or 'Song of Simeon', the second half of the set, that has embedded itself in my brain; and it's the 'Nunc Dimittis' that is now drifting out of the radio like an unfurling billow of perfume.

As it ebbs and flows across the room, I am seized by an irresistible urge to understand it: to get deep within its mechanics. I know it's a reimagining of the musical figure named the 'English cadence'.[1]

Twentieth-century music theorists thought this cadence was invented by Tudor musicians, and were so obviously enthralled by its resemblance to the blue seventh of contemporary jazz.[2] Howells riffs on the nostalgia for something that never was, making it somehow mournful, mysterious and ebullient at the same time. But this is a way of dissecting the piece with music theory, and I want to get at something more intangible. Languishing at the back of a cupboard somewhere is a large canvas, scrawled with a painting I'd never been happy with. I wrestle it out, size it up. A quick wash of opaque white, and it's ready. I take up a fat, tapered brush, and begin.

Howells' *Gloucester* is an incredibly evocative piece of music that seems, on the one hand, to look back on the losses and hard-won peace of the Second World War, and on the other, to look back further, more murkily, into the mists of something lost. Coupled with this are lyrics that have captured the minds of writers for centuries. They are taken from the Biblical story of Simeon, who, almost as though under a fairytale enchantment, had been visited by the Holy Spirit and told that he 'would not see death' until he saw the Messiah. When the infant Jesus was presented at the Temple, according to Jewish custom, for the redemption of the first-born son or הבן פדיון, the Holy Spirit brought Simeon there too. These are the words he was reported to have spoken when he laid eyes on Jesus. They speak of a lifetime of hope and waiting, a longing that chimes with our modern life just as it did then, at the height of the Roman empire. They appear as a recitation by Merlin in T.H. White's Arthurian romp *The Once and Future King* (1958), in no fewer than three separate novels by John le Carré, and in David Mitchell's *Cloud Atlas* (2004). Howells' braiding together of words and music is something extraordinary.

The soprano melody line soars like a gull, buffeted by the ferocious sea breeze. Underneath it, the unison alto-tenor-bass is the beat of a wave, somehow both densely, powerfully textured, and completely immaterial. *Lord. Now. Lettest Thou. Thy Ser-vant.*

Dep-a-a-a-art i-in peace. Howells sets that word 'depart' to a slow-motion downward freefall, like nothing so much as an evening reply to the lazy, yawning launch of the opening clarinet line in George Gershwin's jazz concerto *Rhapsody in Blue*. The swoop of the melodic line it describes is out of this world, a cat-eye flick of eyeliner that only ever happens by accident with a sigh, an almost throwaway movement. Listening to it, you can feel the grinding of tectonic plates deep fathoms beneath you. The earth moves. The full churning force of the undertow beneath the surface of the waves resounds against the floating, fragile, drifting soprano timbre.

There is incredible drama, but it drifts beneath a haze that seems to smudge and bloom beyond the edges of the notes themselves. The sinuous melodic line hovers, half caught and carried away by the buffeting wind. This drama infuses its way throughout the image of the music I had, beyond its use of line to the kind of coloration it demanded: the muted, ice-lolly vintage shades you see in old-school railway destination posters, undercut with a moody, murky darkness.

Unspooling this image takes fastidiously close, slow work, in a way I'm simply not used to – my handling of paint is typically loose, the time poured into planning but the marks themselves quickly committed to canvas or paper. For the duration of this finicky process, I hear snatches of the music as a three-dimensional, dense Thing; where lines and motifs pass between voices, where one voice part rests upon or supports another. The way it asks me to listen is similar, but subtly different, to how I need to listen when I sing it. Every cumulative texture bears witness to this oblique form of attention, as though I am attending with the periphery of my hearing, rather than a pinpointed centre.

Many artists over the years have sought to do what I am attempting: to capture a piece of music, or a musical performance, in purely visual form. But many of these artworks also go far beyond a simple illustration. They offer complex statements on the nature of listening, of making music, and of experiencing music, often from visual artists who were highly trained musicians themselves. As we shall see, each one proposes a challenge to rethink the way we conceptualise music.

𝄞

A new queen has come to the throne. Her sister, who reigned before her for only five years, has left a bloody trail in her wake. Briefly, freed from the intense violence, there is an aura of optimism, of hope. Perhaps this will be a new era of tolerance. Perhaps this tiny country might begin to flourish again, after the damage wrought by this queen's father.

You served her father, and her brother and sister before her. Now, she is all that is left of the audacious Tudor dynasty.

At New Year, it is customary to give elaborate gifts in the Tudor court.[3] As one of the court artists, yours typically takes a painted form. Your name is Levina Teerlinc, and you have been at the Tudor court for almost twenty years, since you arrived from Bruges in around 1546. You are from quite a dynasty yourself. You are one of five daughters of the renowned miniaturist Simon Bening, and you are related via your mother to the Flemish painter Hugo van der Goes.[4] You earn the hefty sum of £40* a year for your services to the crown, way more than your colleague, Hans Holbein.[5]

And this year, you want to create something quite special.

Your miniature for the young Elizabeth will be a depiction of the Maundy ceremony – a service conducted every year on Maundy Thursday, the week before Easter, where the monarch traditionally gives alms to the poor for clothing, and washes their feet.[6]

It's not the first time you've created such an image for a queen. For her sister, Mary, you illuminated a full manuscript

---

*   £30,000 in today's money.

Levina Teerlinc, *An Elizabethan Maundy*, 1560s.

with images of the queen curing scrofula, ominously known as 'the king's evil', on Good Friday; that book has survived in the collection of Westminster Cathedral in London as *The Manual of Blessing of Cramp Rings and Touching for Evil*.[7] But for Elizabeth, you've gone for something rather more atmospheric.

The result is the miniature now known as *An Elizabethan Maundy*, painted somewhere between 1560 and 1564. It fits, nestled, in the palm of your hand. The way it asks you to look at it, to appreciate its visual effect, is intimate. You need to lean in. It is shared, quietly, between people – passed hand to hand, or seen by heads bent together, like a polaroid or a photo on a smartphone screen.

Although the painting has definitely been trimmed, Elizabeth stands at the bottom left, rather than at the centre of the image. Instead, our eyes are ensnared by the scarlet gown of a woman in the foreground, with her back to us. The visual strategies of Italian paintings of the same period allow the eye to rest upon the focal point, but Teerlinc aims for something else. She adopts the classic English strategy of drawing the eye continually to new, complementary or competing points of focus.

The miniature depicts the crowds gathered round during the Maundy, their faces nothing but tiny, eloquent daubs of paint. These swirl around an open space, an ovoid of absence, skewed to lead the eye around the form of the painting. Our eyes are drawn to the other nodes of colour dispersed throughout the scheme of the miniature: to the golden yellow of the lady to the right of the composition, the scarlet gown of the lady in the foreground, the paten, a plate used in the Mass and held by a lady next to her who briefly catches the viewer's gaze, and from there to the scarlet and gold flashes of costume dispersed throughout the crowd to the right, the red cassocks and copes of the choristers at the top, and the sleeves and glint of underskirt in the crowd on the left-hand side.

The trajectory is not one of fixed-point perspective, one directed line of sight, but of a spiral, drawing the gaze of the viewer into the gathering. Our sightlines are pulled obliquely down to the figure of the queen, Elizabeth herself, right at the heart of the performance of the Maundy ceremony. At the top are the forms of the Gentlemen and Choristers of the Chapel Royal: the musicians. The whole visual dynamic of the miniature, that swirling spiral of direction, is driven by these musical figures at the top of the composition.

This painting is a world away from the focused solitude of Teerlinc's depiction of Mary's Touching for Evil ceremony. In that image, Mary is the focal point. Elizabeth's Maundy is about the moment; the sights, the smells, the sounds. It thrums with people, with voices, with music.

Incredibly, this would have been even more the case for the original (tiny) intended viewership of this miniature. Elizabeth, Teerlinc and those of Elizabeth's inner circle whom she deemed worthy of seeing the painting were all there at the ceremony. And so they would have been able to identify the people depicted, and remember the music performed by the Gentlemen and Choristers of the Chapel Royal. The visual experience was thus entwined with and amplified the sonic memory, the mind's eye and the mind's ear implicated equally.

This isn't an abstract representation of music, but it approaches music in a similar way to some of the abstract examples we'll see later in this chapter. It assumes that the movement and forms of music are important, and that the viewer would like to see them. It offers us a sense of the reverberation around the performance space (in this instance, probably somewhere like St George's Chapel in Windsor, Westminster Abbey or the Chapel Royal at Hampton Court). Music fills the image, binding the queen, the choristers, the poor and the court together into one community. Colour, shape and form are all part of this image of music, just as in an abstract painting.

Teerlinc's *Elizabethan Maundy* gives us an insight into an idea about music that we have broadly lost. Music is entangled at the very heart of this ceremony. It was central to how the ritual functioned, and crucial to its meaning. Even today, we have a rough sense of which pieces of music would have been performed (although we can't be sure of the exact piece chosen for this year). We know the names of the choristers, garbed in red and white at the top of the image, though we can't pinpoint precisely who is who. Our old friend Thomas Tallis was appointed to the prestigious post of Gentleman of the Chapel Royal in 1543; in the 1560s his peers in this post were the composers Richard Farrant (appointed in c. 1550 and made Master of the Choristers in 1569), Robert Parsons (appointed in 1563) and William Mundy (appointed in 1564). All would have written music suitable for the Maundy.

John Sheppard, a Gentleman of the Chapel Royal who had died in 1558, probably composed *Deus Misereatur Nostri* specifically for Mary I's Maundy ceremonies in the earlier 1550s; it sets the exact text that was sung during the foot-washing in the rite used at Mary's court, and so was also likely used in Elizabeth's ceremonies. The *Lamentations of Jeremiah I* and *II* were composed by Tallis in the 1560s, and are liturgically appropriate for a ceremony performed on Maundy Thursday. All are densely woven, interlacing works, conceived around the idea of multiple lines twining around and over each other – much like the visual composition of the *Elizabethan Maundy*.

This is an artist painting 450 years ago, for eyes and ears long since returned to earth. That's why, for me, this is one of the most powerful images in the artful history of music. Despite the sprawl of years in between, so close in the general scope of known history and yet so far, Teerlinc's interpretation of that most ephemeral of forms, music, still speaks in a visual language we can understand.

This is also a language that has a clear relationship to the lines and forms and compositional strategies of abstract art. All strive towards the same end: to visualise a thing that is just beyond the reach of our eyes. Once you lean back from the *Elizabethan Maundy* and let it return to its tiny, hand-held proportions, it becomes a pointillist swirl of colour, like work by impressionist painters Georges Seurat or Camille Pissarro. Out of its time, out of its place, Teerlinc's minuscule masterpiece offers us more than just a scene of music-making. It gives us a sense of how Elizabethans recorded music for posterity; how they could relive a musical experience; and how they believed it was possible to do this through the eyes as well as the ears.

𝄞

Three centuries later, it had become rather harder for a woman to follow her creative calling. But still, Teerlinc's successors found a way.

Saltsjöbaden, 1905, a few miles from Stockholm on the edge of the Baltic Sea. The landscape beyond the windows of your house is straight from a fairytale: clusters of silver birches and moss-bound granite. According to Swedish folklore, these mossy boulders are trolls, waiting to spring to life at any moment. You watch as small fingers stumble up and down the piano keys; over and over, gradually, hesitantly smoothing the same mistake. On the third repetition, your eyes glaze over and you allow your mind to wander to the piano cover that you are in the middle of embroidering. You think of the lustrous threads and the tiny seed pearls you will use, and another piece of music insinuates itself between the gaps of the scales.

Your name is Anna Casparsson and, strictly speaking, you are a piano teacher. Like your mother, you are a very, *very* good performer. You could have been a concert pianist, but most of the men in your life – your father and husband chief among them – don't see performance as a respectable career for a woman. One of your great cheerleaders, the Swedish painter Ernst Josephson, sent you a drawing after hearing you playing Beethoven sonatas: Beethoven cutting his own heart out because hearing you play was so soulful, as though the composer were wrenching the notes from the depths of his body.

But you have more tricks up your sleeve. Day in, day out, you fill your time with the piano – and with your own textile artworks: patchworks, appliqué and embroidery that you use to embellish cushions and throws and your piano. Exquisitely bejewelled, glimmering with gold and silver thread, sequins, seashells, fragments of mirror, buttons and glass, they are focused on narratives from Hans Christian Andersen's fairytales, and from the music

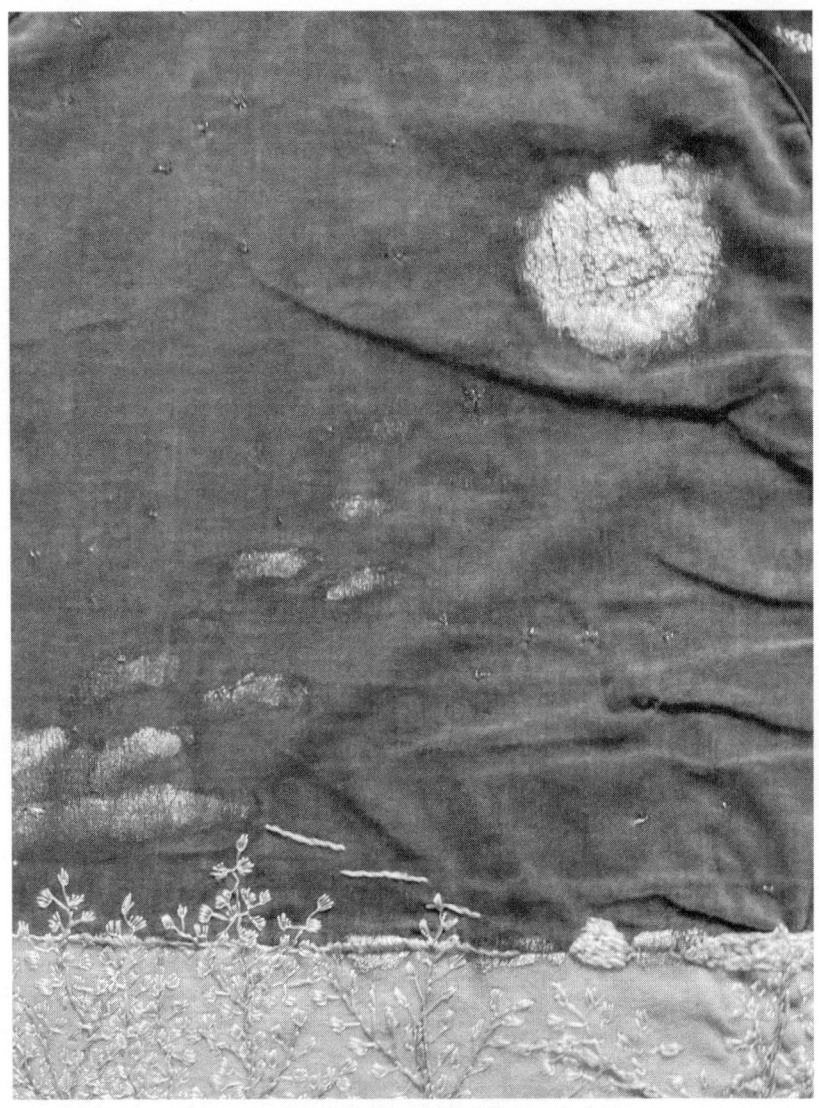

Anna Casparsson, detail of *Life Saga from Blue Fairy Tales by Laboulaye*, 1930.

that you adore. To some, both then and in the twenty-first century, they look strikingly like East and Central Asian textiles, which isn't as surprising as it might sound: Scandinavia has a long-established trading relationship with Persia and the territories that make up modern-day India and China, along the Silk Road. Only a year

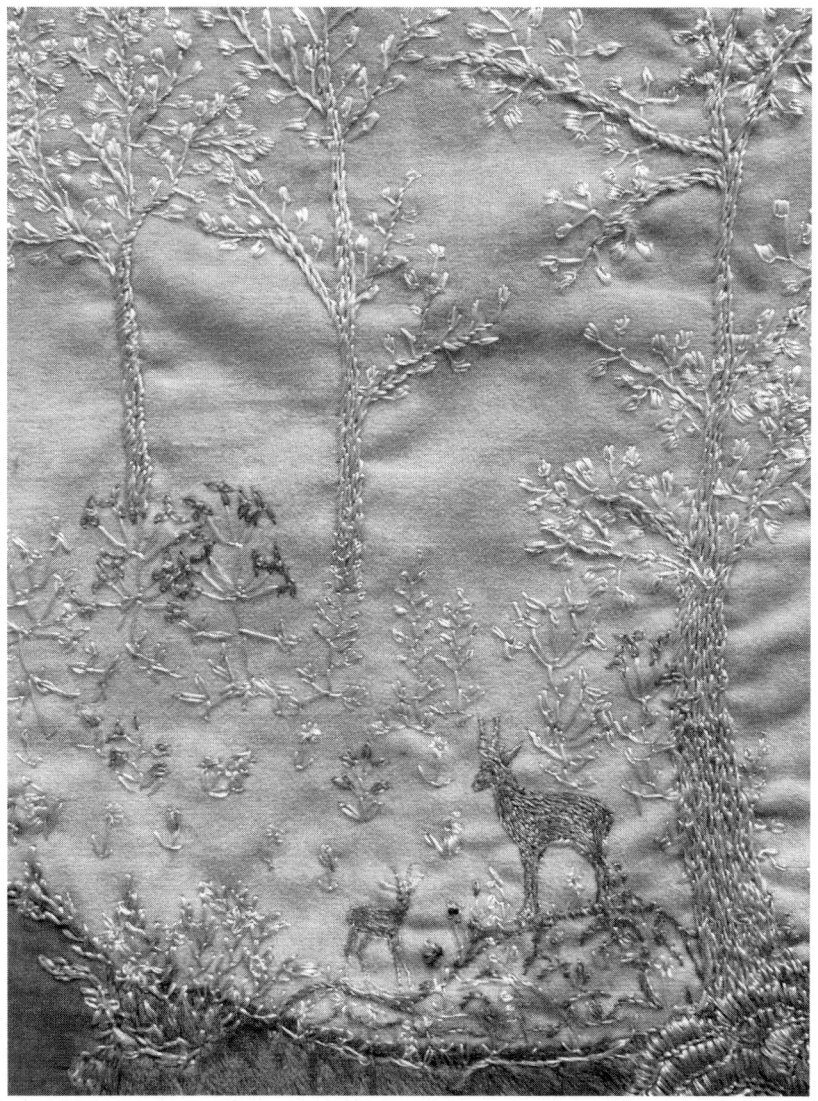

Anna Casparsson, detail of *Life Saga*
from Blue Fairy Tales by Laboulaye, 1930

previously in 1904, a ninth-century ship burial was uncovered at Vestbold in the neighbouring country of Norway, filled with over a hundred scraps of silk fabric, some embroidered with golden and silver thread like your own works, with symbols that had travelled thousands of miles.[8]

Opulent though your works are, they are quaintly, almost naively old-fashioned. It wouldn't be surprising to find a textile artist producing work like this in 2025 or in 1625. They are unnerving engagements with artistic modernism, playing with form, proportion and mark-making. They aren't deliberately representational reactions to the abstractions of cubism or impressionism, but rather other ways of thinking about what abstraction can mean. You represent objects with a focus on breaking down form similar to the techniques of artists like Pablo Picasso, Joan Miró and Henri Matisse. You are friends not just with Josephson, but with a whole coterie of cutting-edge artists including the Swedish-Jewish expressionist painter Isaac Grünewald, so you know your stuff.

Anna Casparsson had to wait until she was in her sixties, and the death of her husband and son, before she was able finally to burst onto the artistic scene of Swedish modernism.[9] In 1944, aged eighty-three, she was hailed as a 'newly discovered artist', the latest hot talent. In 1959, she was exhibited in the Museé National d'Art Moderne in Paris. And aged ninety-nine, in 1960, she was the subject of an enormous retrospective at the newly opened Moderna Museet in Stockholm. And yet as I write this, eighty years after her 'discovery', her name is obscure – alongside her musical talent that was once enough to make an imagined Ludwig van B rip his heart out.

I first met Casparsson in the Moderna Museet, where she hangs alongside her rough contemporary Hilma Af Klint; there is absolutely no incongruity between her quaint, lustrous embroideries and Klint's stark geometric abstractions. The two are in a duet that makes perfect sense, between form and colour, as though they are two different voices or instruments riffing on the same theme. As a nonagenarian artistic-cum-musical superstar, Casparsson offers an insight into some complex subjects: the way societies think about older women; attitudes towards textile art techniques as somehow lesser forms of visual expression; what modern art looks like; and the relationship between visual art and music.

Teaching a piece of music, as well as playing it yourself, gives you an intricate, intimate sense of its textures and forms. This deep, particularised consciousness has translated into Casparsson's artworks: in her *Livets Saga* (or *Life Saga*) *from Blue Fairy Tales by Laboulaye* (1930) or her *Sagor* (*Stories: Little Claus and Big Claus, the Story of Little Rose and the Little Mermaid*) (1947). The repetitive act of forming an image through stitch – chain, braid, stem, scallop – is like the repetition of refrains in a musical composition, and of the hand shapes needed to form chords and phrases. Pale blue silk over lace, over velvet, is topped with gold, silver or fuchsia thread, working the minute form of a tree in blossom, a castle or a boat. Each added layer is like the lines of melody in the musical technique of counterpoint, which weaves different 'tunes' or versions of the tune together into one whole. Both piano and embroideries are worked with the hands, with memory in the movements of both needles and keys. We might not be able to hear Casparsson's music, but we can almost see it.

Casparsson is a rare example in our artful history of music. Her musical expression was almost entirely suppressed. All we have, instead, is her visual art and what it tells us about how she thought about music, about repetition and timbre and counterpoint. Plenty of other artists, though, were also trained musicians and avid music lovers – but in those cases, we have far more records of their musical expression, and how they saw art and music relating to each other. Their surviving artworks can give us insight into how these artists thought about music, how they performed and how they listened. Their artworks, in other words, are shared musical experiences.

Ukrainian-American Janet Sobel and the African-American Alma Thomas, both abstract expressionist painters, were also famous lovers of music. Like Casparsson, Sobel and Thomas became recognised artists later in life, Sobel after she had finished raising her five children and Thomas on retirement, after thirty-five years as a high school art teacher. Listening to music was a core part of their painting practice. Sobel is on record as having announced that: 'I love music ... I don't think ever I would paint a picture without music to listen to. All humans must have something like that, that warms them inside.' Nevertheless, when we examine her work – for example, my favourite of hers, her delicious jewel-like *Milky Way* (1945), roughly contemporaneous with Casparsson's *Sagor* – it's not always clear precisely how the music left its mark.

It would be wonderful to be able to say that Sobel's ears were filled with Gustav Holst's 'Planets Suite' (1914–17) while she painted; we could attribute those intersecting forms to that notorious moment in the 'Neptune' movement where the sopranos sing a top G for a frankly insane thirty-plus bars (over ninety seconds), giving the piece an otherworldly quality that closely fits Sobel's painting. But we have no way of knowing exactly what Sobel listened to as she created *Milky Way*.

And yet. Looking at Sobel's painting, those unravelling coils of pale pink enamel paint, where they bleed almost into translucence over the dense layering of deep, murky, earthy colours, it is easy to see how we might begin to move towards reconstructing the music that she listened to as she painted. A similar dynamic is at play in Alma Thomas's works, which have far more explicitly musical names: *Cherry Blossom Symphony* (1972), *Grassy Melodic Chant* (1976), *Wind and Crepe Myrtle Concerto* (1973), *Red Rose Cantata* (1973), *White Daisies Rhapsody* (1973). All of these artworks are captured in Thomas's signature mosaic-like compositions of the forms she referred to as 'Alma's stripes', arranged in irregular, thrumming patterns that echo Teerlinc's, and held together by a masterful use of colour: the movements of a symphony, a chant, a cantata, a rhapsody that might have guided the gestures of her brush, still there for all to see and enticing us to get swept up in their textures, in their undertow.

This is important, because it tells us something significant about the way that we collectively imagine music. No matter how detached an artwork becomes from the music that inspired it or

Watching Paint Sing: Abstracting Music

that accompanied its making, knowing that it was painted or sculpted or embroidered to music gives us a fundamental way to understand that artwork. It gives us an interpretive structure: a way to read it, and a way to find ourselves in it.

An interpretive structure, such as music, is particularly useful when it comes to abstract art; even the most abstract of artists have been fascinated by the idea of capturing something seemingly so ephemeral. It's all too tempting to fall for the old 'my four-year-old could have painted that' argument.* Art has nothing to do with 'looking like' something, precisely because it's about challenging and changing the *way* we look at things. Bringing music into the picture can invigorate some of these more perplexing artworks. They can be interpreted as being in dialogue with music, as visualisations of the music itself, or even as subversions of the seeming invisibility of music.

One dialogue between art and music began with a parcel, received a handful of days after midsummer in 1950. Inside its paper wrappings was a musical score. Along with it came a gushing letter, describing it as 'this miracle of architecture in sound'.[10] The recipient was the artist Barbara Hepworth, and the writer was Ivy Priaulx Rainier, the British-South African composer and Hepworth's dear friend and partner-in-creation, who was coming to stay later in the summer. Together they would work in the lush, windswept garden beside Hepworth's Trewyn studio in the fishing town of St Ives in Cornwall, and see what they could create.

Hepworth was a trained pianist and had won music prizes at school, but visual art had been the centre of her life since the age of seventeen when she was admitted to the Leeds School of Art,

---

* An argument only ever expressed by people who have never noticed how good a four-year-old's art can be.

moving on to the Royal College of Art in London the following year.[11] Thirty years later she still drew, but she was primarily a sculptor – a creator of curved edges and rugged surfaces. Now, though, she had set herself a formidable task: translating the dense lines of sheet music into copper, bronze and stone.

Rainier arrived a few weeks later. It was an incredibly fruitful period of cohabitation. In a letter written in July 1950, Hepworth gushed to another friend: '[Rainier] is a very beautiful person with a rare intelligence & astonishing creative power. She has been composing in a corner of Trewyn garden – somewhat disturbed perhaps by the odd rhythms of hammers.'[12] Nevertheless, Rainier managed to write music in that leafy, noisy space: on 20th July 1950, she composed 'Rhythms of the Stones', transforming the sound of Hepworth and her assistants carving her Festival of Britain commission, *Contrapuntal Forms*, into music notation.[13]

The score that Rainier had sent along in June, however, was not one of her own: it was the Tudor composer Thomas Tallis's *Spem in Alium*, a forty-part motet, a short(ish) sacred vocal composition designed to stand alone. 'I'm determined,' wrote Hepworth, 'to understand something about the construction. I must unravel its simplicity and understand its complexity.'[14] In this little garden, music collapsed into visual art, into music, then into visual art again, in an unbroken circle of creation and inspiration: Rainier's music translating Hepworth's sculpture translating Rainier's music.

Contrapuntal Forms was one of the earliest of Hepworth's explicitly musically-inspired works. She would go on to create the set and costumes for a production of Sophocles' *Electra* at the Old Vic (1951) and the composer Michael Tippett's opera *The Midsummer Marriage* at the Royal Opera House (1955).[15] In *Electra*, one of her sculptures 'played' the role of Apollo: a curving wire that delineated several profiles which, when lit, casted shifting shadows, creating the illusion that Apollo was in multiple places at once.[16] *Motet* (1951) was the sculpture that appears to have been inspired by Tallis's *Spem in Alium*; Hepworth consulted Rainier on alternative full titles – *Motet (contrapuntal forms in blue limestone)* or *Motet (praising) blue stone figures?*[17] – which gives us a beautiful insight into how she grappled with defining her musical meaning. At the end of a monograph published in 1952, she observed how very subconscious the centrality of music was to her work:

> [I]n these very brief notes I seem to have omitted everything that goes to make up my usual working day. These things are immensely important to me; perhaps more important than the things about which I have written. My home and my children; listening to music, and thinking about its relation to the life of forms, the need for dancing as recreation, and where dancing links with the actual physical rhythm of carving; the intense pleasure derived from tools and craftsmanship – all these things are daily expressions of the whole.[18]

Some of Hepworth's most striking music-inspired works are *Forms in Movement (Galliard)* (1956), four of which survive in looping, copper forms, and their twins, *Forms in Movement (Pavan)* (1955).[19] The pavan and the galliard are dances that would have had very strong musical associations for Hepworth. At school she had been trained in the Dalcroze method, a form of dance or 'eurhythmics' designed specifically for Western classical musical education by Émile Jaques-Dalcroze, Professor of Harmony at the University of Geneva in the late nineteenth century.

The Dalcroze method is built around a simple premise that is recognisable even today: he wanted his students to learn to listen to music with their bodies as well as their minds, and to be conscious of *how* they were doing so. Musical concepts would be introduced through movement first, before a student learned their visual representation in sheet music. Physical awareness of rhythm laid a solid foundation for musical understanding, and enhanced

Barbara Hepworth at work on
Contrapuntal Forms in her garden.

the students' interpretative performance abilities. Techniques included polyrhythms, where one rhythm would be performed in the hands and one in the feet at the same time; cross-rhythms, where students would perform a rhythm in the hands and a different one in the feet, and then switch on the teacher's cue; and swings, where the teacher would improvise music in a given musical pattern, and then the students would use prescribed body motions to determine the pattern.[20] Given her crop of performance prizes from school, it clearly worked for Hepworth.

The galliard dance is a highly athletic dance in triple time, popular across Europe in the sixteenth century and possibly danced by Tallis himself. Rhythmic movement is marked by leaps, hops and jumps across the dance floor, in an intricate choreography not dissimilar to the Dalcroze method. Three years before Hepworth embarked upon her musical sculptures, galliards by Tallis's business partner and protégé, William Byrd, had appeared in the programme of the St Ives Festival, which was organised by Hepworth, Rainier and Tippett; evidently the dance had been playing upon her mind for a while.

Forms in Movement (Galliard) revels in the pattern of the dance, bending paper-thin copper sheets into three vaulting curls, ribboning and coiling and echoing its jumps and twists. The copper sheets, by turns dense and thin as you walk around the sculpture, suggest the line-driven texture of much of the music of the sixteenth century, not least Tallis's *Spem in Alium*, the piece of music that so captured Hepworth's imagination. She described how she made this work: 'experimenting with sheet metal, I bent and twisted the sheets under tension until I found out the nature of its construction and forced it to express what I wanted *by* its nature and not against its nature.'[21] It was a duet between sculptor and sculpture – even, we might say, a contrapuntal song, a weaving of two lines together, as in the favourite Tudor technique of composition.

The delight is exuberant, almost infectious. Hepworth would later donate one of the editions of the sculpture to her old school, Wakefield Girls' High School, intended specifically for the new gymnasium: a commemoration of the music and dancing that had formed such important building blocks in her early education.[22] Where the light catches the sheen of the copper, other shimmering loops appear; in *Galliard*, Hepworth is showing us her listening by *dancing* it in copper sheets. Her love of the 'construction' of sixteenth-century music, and her unravelling of its simplicity and complexity, are all laid bare in this sculpture. It really does allow us to *see* the way that she listened.

And these traces of music can be found in works even without an explicit musical theme or inspiration. Later, when her works were too large for the garden and outbuildings at Trewyn, Hepworth headed across the street to the St Ives Palais de Danse, the village dance hall that she bought in 1961. This is where she created some of her most famous works: *Memorial*,

Duet

Barbara Hepworth, *Forms in Movement (Galliard)*, copper, 1956.

which stands outside the United Nations building in New York, and the *Winged Figure* on the side of the John Lewis store in Oxford Street, London. At the Palais de Danse, her sculptures were mounted on plinths with rubberised wheels so she could move them about, choreographing them against and among each other and the colossal space of the dance hall. As the art critic Charles Darwent has noted: 'she danced them, danced with them.'[23]

Hepworth's artworks take us deep into the intricacies of how she thought and felt about music, from the early association forged by her music teachers between sound and bodily movement, to her taste for sixteenth-century music throughout the 1950s. Unlike her fellow female artists Casparsson, Thomas and Sobel, Hepworth didn't fade abruptly in and out of obscurity. Though all three lived and worked at the same time, fate dealt her recognition during her life and after her death. As a result, much of her musical education and taste was documented. Even so, there's a sense that part of Hepworth's story hasn't really been told yet. She was at the heart of the British classical avant-garde scene, showing her art to composers, discussing form, structure and rhythm with them. And yet she's rarely more than a sideline figure in histories of music. If Casparsson is the greatest performer we have never heard, perhaps Hepworth is the greatest composer whose music we have always been able to see.

𝄞

Casparsson and Hepworth were working at a watershed moment in the history of art. Abstraction was at the fore, and though of course not everybody was looking to push the abstract card, it drove much of the conversation about what it meant to represent a subject during this period. Exactly how far could visual representation stretch? Would we recognise something from just its shape; just its texture; just its essence?

It is no wonder that music became such an inspirational force during the first half of the twentieth century, because of the sheer potential that it offers. The romance between art and music is like an unsolvable riddle – drawing potential answers like moths to a flame. Each work, each attempt in paint or ink or marble or copper or silk floss, was an opportunity to bridge

Duet

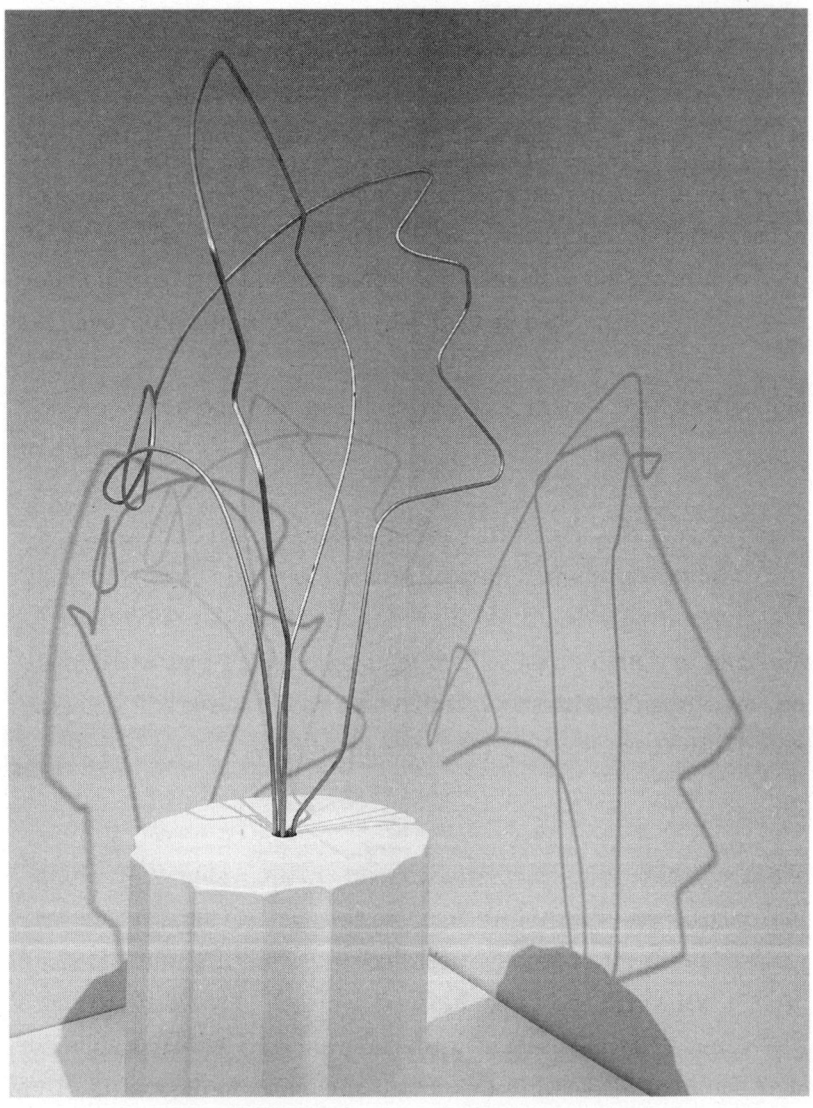

Barbara Hepworth, *Apollo*, 1951.

the gap between those long-parted lovers, art and music, and for someone – maybe it could be you, as you sit there leafing through this book – it might finally slot into place.

As the 1920s turned to the 1930s, Aubrey Williams was sitting on the front steps of his house in Bourda Street, Georgetown, in the British colony of Guiana. Three years old, he didn't yet know what he wanted to be. But he did know that the world was full of beauty, and that anyone could be responsible for constructing it, with craft and care. He later recalled:

> I was born into a world in which there was a natural appreciation of [artistic] excellence, and this permeated the whole society. It went down to the grassroot peasants in the country. An Indian farmer would make his rice-paddies in certain ways what we call today 'artistic'. His mud fireplace would be like a piece of sculpture. It's only now with the coming of modern technology and so on that these art forms or making of art have become part of a professional activity. ... I must explain here that by 'Indian' I mean East Indian people who were brought to Guyana from the Indian Subcontinent as indentured labour to work on sugar plantations. They have their own profound concepts and behaviour patterns and iconography which give them a tremendous insight for handling the environment beautifully.[24]

That day, a turkey vulture caught his eye: it was devouring a dead rat, perched on a white tombstone in the early colonial cemetery that stood opposite his house. The image was so captivating that his little three-year-old hands had to draw it. When his parents found the drawing, they sent for a Mr de Winter – a skilful restorer of church paintings, and the first white man little Aubrey had ever seen – who served as his first art tutor until he enrolled in the Working People's Art Class at the age of twelve.[25] But Guiana was not a place to make your name as a painter in those days, nor a place to earn your living by painting. Sugar was what made that economy turn, and so Williams trained as an agronomist – an expert in the management of soil health and crop rotation. Here, while serving as an apprentice in sugar production at a governmental college in Georgetown, he first heard the music of the Russian composer Dmitri Shostakovich. He was in his mid-teens, and he was gobsmacked. It would be another three decades before he found that music flowing out of his paintbrush into a series of thirty increasingly enormous paintings on the theme – but I'm getting ahead of myself.

Williams's route to the Shostakovich series was a meandering one by sheer dint of the number of obstacles he needed to traverse. He took up a post as Agricultural Field Officer on a sugar plantation on the coast of British Guiana in 1944, setting up more Working People's Art Classes as he went. It didn't go well, and not because he wasn't good at it. *Why*, he wondered, *should these farmers accept such poor terms?* He encouraged them to protest against their exploitation and claim greater rights.

The colonial administration took one look at what he was up to and banished him, paint, easel and all, to the remote rainforest settlement of Hosororo, close to the border with Venezuela. This little sojourn did very little to temper his politics. He socialised with the indigenous Warrau* Amerindians who lived in and around Hosororo, absorbing their culture and history into his art like a sponge. The forms of their pictorial language would surface again and again in his art, repurposed, echoing, for decades after he left the Warrau world.

Meanwhile, back in Georgetown, the government had marked him out as a political agitator for his work with the sugar farmers – not a category anyone wanted to be in, as the campaign for Guyanese independence grew hotter and hotter. Williams applied for, and was awarded, a scholarship in Agricultural Engineering at the University of Leicester in 1952 – a safe, if rather enormous, 4,500 miles from harm. Unsurprisingly, the course had very little to offer someone who had been practising soil management and crop rotation for the past eight years in a completely different climate to that of the soggy United Kingdom.

He dropped out and went travelling across Europe, encountering the writer Albert Camus, who, in turn, introduced him to

---

* Literally, 'boat people'.

Pablo Picasso. Picasso was very taken with him, but more as a potential subject than as a fellow painter. But you don't fight for the rights of your countrymen, get yourself marked as a dangerous political activist, and travel halfway across the world if you're the kind of person who will simply give up their dream because of the lack of approval of a notoriously unpleasant man. Williams was going to be a professional painter, and that was that. He enrolled at Saint Martin's School of Art, and immersed himself in the London art world.[26]

The London art world did not know what to make of him. He was bewitched by a couple of exhibitions at the Tate Gallery, first 'Modern Art in the United States' (1956) and then 'New American Painting' (1959), declaring Jackson Pollock 'our God!'; in a sense, his work should be seen as being in dialogue with the American abstract expressionists he was so taken with.[27] But what Williams does with abstraction, how he approaches mark-making and figuration and gesture, is of a completely different quality. The abstract and the figurative are not separate entities in his work.

The Russian painter Wassily Kandinsky was another huge influence. Kandinsky saw music as colour, and even went as far as recording his theory in his effusive 1910 monograph *Concerning the Spiritual in Art*:

> Colour is the keyboard. The eyes are the harmonies, the soul is the piano with many strings. The artist is the hand which plays, touching one key or another, to cause vibrations in the soul …
> A painter, who finds no satisfaction in mere representation, however artistic, in his longing to express his inner life, cannot but envy the ease with which music, the most non-material of the arts today, achieves this end. He naturally seeks to apply the methods of music to his art. … The sound of colours is so definite that it would be hard to find anyone who would express bright yellow with bass notes or dark lake with the treble.[28]

Kandinsky was convinced of the universality of colour, that this would translate and finally help reunite art and music. But of course, there are plenty of things he didn't think of: people who are colourblind; people who are blind or partially sighted and therefore have a completely different concept of colour; the age-old debate between people who see turquoise as green and people who see turquoise as blue. And that's not even to mention the fields of aural perception which, if the sense of sight is anything to go by, probably has its own spectrums and varieties of deafness that we just haven't discovered yet.

But Williams was convinced that 'not even Kandinsky got it right'. He began a mammoth project to capture how he saw the interrelationship between music and paint. Between 1979 and 1981, he painted a series inspired by Shostakovich's fifteen symphonies and fifteen string quartets. 'This music,' he said, 'hit me really hard – I was hearing for the first time a sort of total sound ... it had profound visual connotations – I could feel colour ... The music of Shostakovich is humanity in sound.'[29] The image in the plate section titled *Shostakovich Symphony No. 6* is from right at the end of the project in 1981, and encapsulates that thrumming feel of colour. The Shostakovich series was originally intended as a new kind of notation (through colour), but Williams ultimately abandoned that aim in favour of embracing each composition as a unique visual manifestation in itself.

Nowadays the main characteristic associated with Williams's art is primitivism. Racially demeaning connotations aside, when you see his paintings yourself it's clear that highlighting this one aspect is completely reductive. He was interested in the limits and possibilities of his form; he was interested in translating the deep affinity he felt with the music of Shostakovich, and the composer's own struggles to exist and work within the confines of the Soviet regime. He was interested in the limits of abstraction, and we can feel it particularly in images such as *Shostakovich Symphony No. 6*. It almost, but not quite, suggests a figurative landscape, as though we were squinting or briefly dazzled by sunlight. These fleeting resemblances matter – they aren't just coincidences, but part of how Williams wanted us to *feel* the way he listened to Shostakovich.

Williams isn't as well-known as he should be. Kandinsky on the other hand is a well-established trailblazer in the development of abstraction. Yet this musical aspect of both artists' work is not given the credence it deserves. Their engagement with sound is often mentioned as an incidental aspect, or as a matter of personal taste. It's always presented as the beginning and end of a cutesy, if generally insignificant, episode in their stories.

Looking at their work together, alongside so many of the other artists working during the late nineteenth and twentieth centuries and across continents, it's clear that something more monumental – something more ubiquitous – is at play. There it is, again and again: music. More music. Music advocating for abstraction, infecting the minds of these painters and sculptors and embroiderers, pulsating, rippling beneath the surface, striving to burst out: *TADAAA, it's me!* The development of art movements concerned with abstraction – from surrealism to cubism to Dadaism to Fauvism – can be considered a collective demand to rethink the way that we listen, and how we think about the relationship between the eyes and the ears.

𝄞

The impact of abstract art's striving towards music can still be felt in works made today. A stone's throw from the clog of London traffic, the blast of horns, is a door leading to a quiet space cushioned by glossy wooden bookshelves that run from the floor to the base of the lofty, vaulted ceiling: the British Museum Prints and Drawings Room. The wonders here would leave even the most seasoned art-lover salivating: tiny Rembrandt drawings, extravagant Michelangelos, exquisite Paula Regos and doodles by Andy Warhol. Today, though, we are here to see something extra-special: a piece by an artist who worked for over seventy years, pushing the boundaries of abstract art. Before us on the desk is Japanese artist Tōkō Shinoda's *Symphony* (1985). Slashes of deep black cross the surface of the paper, intersected with gauzy swipes of pale grey. The left-hand side of the composition is accentuated with Shinoda's trademark sinuous lines. As an assemblage it resonates with texture and the dialogue, sometimes overlapping, sometimes separate, between Shinoda's forms.

Shinoda (1913–2021) wasn't interested in creating abstract representations. 'If I have a definite idea,' she stated, 'why paint it? Mount Fuji is more striking than any possible imitation.'[30] Rather, she was interested in representing the abstract; those slippery or evanescent things that evade visualisation. Subjects, in other words, like music.

Her practice is grounded in the very traditional discipline of calligraphy. Students of Japanese calligraphy are taught to develop their craft through the process of *shuhari* – *shu* meaning to obey, *ha* to digress, and *ri* to separate. In other words, calligraphic craft has three distinct parts: firstly, one must master time-honoured techniques; one then experiments with the possibilities offered by those techniques; finally, one abandons the rigidity of those processes to create something new and highly personal, using the instincts honed over years of systematically practising one's craft, and the Buddhist principles of imperfection and impermanence. 'While abstract painting opens up myriad endless spaces depending on the person who sees it,' Shinoda observed, 'calligraphy is different, being enjoyed within one space, one realm. Within me, you see, lie not one but two things.'[31] She felt she was both an abstract artist and a traditional calligrapher.

Working in sumi ink, cinnabar ink, silver and platinum leaf and swoops of gold, teal blue and red, the phantasm of what is heard often takes centre stage in Shinoda's work. 'I sometimes,' she stated, 'work thinking of converting sound into form. I depict sound using sumi ink. I always try to listen for good sounds so that they can come to my mind when I am ready.'[32]

Shinoda's back catalogue is a treasure trove of these representations of abstract sound. In addition to *Symphony* there's *S o u n d* (1950–54), *Duet* (1955), *Pause* (1972), *Listen* (1973), *Song of Wood* (1988), *Nocturne* (1990), *Intermezzo* (1993), *Cadenza* (1998), *Legato* (1998), *Chord* (1999), *Interval* (1999), *Sonority* (1999), *Choral* (2000), and *Silence* (2002) – as well as many undated works and many returns to the concept of 'hymn' and 'song'. The rhythm of brush strokes, the balance between delicate and robust line and between forms and blank space, all constitute Shinoda's vocabulary of visualised music.

All in all, these are gracefully noisy works of art. Take her *Interval*. Shinoda's slashes of black sumi ink and deep turquoise hover over chiffony, broad cubes of black, layered from translucent to opaque to a final swipe of pearly grey. In between is a starkly profound blank space of unmarked paper. It is an almost literal illustration of an interval – the tonal gap between musical notes. The composition suggests it might be a large one that leaves the impression of a lot of air between pitches, such as a fifth (that leap in the main *Star Wars* theme), a minor seventh ('The Winner Takes it All' by ABBA), or an octave ('Somewhere Over the Rainbow' from *The Wizard of Oz*). Another version, created in 1997, shows the same forms rearranged, the lines intersecting the chunkier blocks of brush strokes, which have been laid side by side horizontally across the surface of the paper, rather than layered – another interval, perhaps closer, a dissonant second (the *Jaws* theme interval) or a diminished fourth (*The Simpsons* theme tune). Shinoda shows us how she experiences movement through musical sound, as she listens to a performance.

Interval isn't the only one of her works that offers us a peek into her musical imagination. Again and again, technical terminology from the field of Western classical music appears in her work. There's *Nocturne* – named after the kind of musical

Tōkō Shinoda, *Interval*, 1999.

composition typically written for evening parties and intended to atmospherically evoke the night, beloved of composers Frédéric Chopin, Francis Poulenc and Lili Boulanger, and latterly pop musicians Billy Joel and Kate Bush. Shinoda's version shows a diffuse sweep of black that covers almost the entire left-hand side of the composition, peppered here and there with whiteness that evokes the stars. There's *Cadenza* – inspired by the improvised section played by the solo instrument at the end of a concerto – which shows a dense, extravagant flourish of brush strokes.

Finally, there's one of my favourites, *Legato*. In Western classical music, the performance instruction 'legato' denotes that a string of notes are to be performed with a lyrical smoothness, leaving minimal gaps between; it literally means 'bound together', and has some etymological connection to the ancient Greek *legein*, *legare*, also the root of the English 'word' via *logos*. Shinoda depicts a flowing transition between forms as each brush stroke bleeds into the next, capturing the creamy effect of the legato timbre that joins musical notes as though in a continuous line of sound. At the top of the composition, she has left just a breath of a gap between the two forms, an unbelievably poignant reminder of the performer behind that sound – an inevitable failure of human breath or fingers to smooth over every join between notes. Shinoda's work is full of tiny, beautiful observations like this one: a close, deeply intimate kind of listening made visual.

By her sheer longevity – she was 107 when she died in 2021 – Shinoda offers us a unique window into the artful history of music. She began practising calligraphy at the age of six, and by her teens was already frustrated with the forms of the *kanji* (Chinese characters, adapted for the Japanese language) that she was supposed to be practising. She experimented with their forms, attempting to elaborate the simple shapes into deeper nuances. The restrictive expectations of her parents and her teachers eventually became too much and she ran away from home in 1936, earning her living by teaching calligraphy.

Slowly but surely her work shifted towards the abstract. Shinoda herself attributed it to the fall of imperial Japan in the Second World War: 'The air of freedom after the war suddenly nurtured the seeds of a desire within me to express the shape of my heart visually. I was suddenly emancipated from the oppressions of my twenties, and my brush moved like an outpour. Like a spur,

Tōkō Shinoda, *Cadenza*, 1998.

[this new feeling] pushed me outside the constraints of characters, and it became my exciting job with limitless scope.'[33] Garnering attention with an exhibition of her work at MoMA in 1954, she moved to New York.[34] The abstract expressionist scene she found there was exciting, and provided an artistic world where Shinoda flourished, but ultimately the climate was too dry for her working process, desiccating the inks before she could form her shapes. Back to Japan she went, and there she remained for the rest of her life.

Even at 100 she was still working, producing a 194cm-long piece to celebrate her birthday. She lived through two world wars and was old enough to consciously remember both; she lived through the Cold War and the creation of the borders of Pakistan, Bangladesh and India; Mauritania, Senegal, Mali, Guinea, Côte d'Ivoire, Burkina Faso and Benin; North and South Korea; Israel and Palestine; she lived through the advent of the washing machine and the computer, the internet and the smartphone. If, like me, you are still slightly bewildered by the loss and/or haunting memory of the dial-up sound when logging on to 'surf the world wide web', all of this is pretty eye-watering.

But her offering goes beyond the breadth of changes that she witnessed. She once confessed to a journalist that she had never studied Western art.[35] So, though many assume she was heavily influenced by the American abstract expressionists like Jackson Pollock and his famous drip paintings, Shinoda's work in fact came from a very different angle and a very different place. It gives us the view of the East, looking west; a Japanese artist, taking in Western classical music and its concepts and language and effects and norms. It's a long way from the episode we looked at briefly in Chapter 4, the sixteenth-century Jesuit missionaries dismayed by the Japanese lack of enthusiasm for harmony and polyphony. Through the medium of a very traditional, ancient art form, Shinoda distils the essence of musical concepts into strikingly fresh, modern visual images.

But of course they aren't the zingy, sap-fresh images that they appear to Western eyes. Each line, as sparsely elegant as it might seem, is the result of an accumulation of hundreds, thousands of years of inherited practice. In this way Shinoda offers a lesson on abstract art, and a new way of thinking about abstraction.

Shinoda's aims with her art were the same as those of her predecessors, stretching back millennia – and she knew it. Every mark she made was loaded with – and freed by – the burden of history.

When art objects are detached from what they represent, or when they represent abstract phenomena, it is all too tempting to interpret them as pretentiously lofty. So much more impressive to achieve those photorealistic paintings of the sort that Jan Vermeer churned out, goes the thought. Shinoda's work reveals the fallacy of that logic. The camera has only existed in the sense we understand it since the mid-nineteenth century. It has skewed our concept of reality, and what representation is: 'realistic' paintings become profoundly static, viewed only from a single, fixed perspective, staged, and with none of those incidental sights you get when you are actually looking through your own eyes (glare; the flicker of a bird's shadow wings cast on the ground as they cross the sun; the ways that objects briefly mirror each other or amplify each other as you move).

Abstract art techniques are just rediscoveries of the multiplicity of different ways that we have seen and continue to see. The subject matter of music – so ephemeral, so intangible – offers a perfect opportunity for exploring the possibilities of abstract representation. Next time you are in an art gallery or museum, find yourself a musically-inspired artwork (and given the volume of works that I've just skimmed, I'm willing to bet that it won't be too hard). Wander the halls of the Tate Modern, MoMA, the Pompidou, the Louvre Abu Dhabi, and look around. Ask yourself: how does this *sound*? How does that sound feel? Perhaps, after all, the 'my four-year-old could have done that' cliché is the trace of another secret that everyone has been in on all along: we remember what it was like to try to represent things as children, how limiting our hands were, and how desperately we wanted to find some sort of essence of a thing, as we drew, painted, carved, shaped, sewed.

𝄞

The twenty-first century dawned, and art forms grew into new media, new approaches, new technologies, but in so many cases, music remained its muse, partner and co-conspirator. This work of art, in particular, remains an icon almost twenty-five years after it first graced our screens.

A ship has been wrecked.

Helicopter blades thud. The sun blares down. 'Somewhere in the South Pacific...', announces lime green text in a typeface straight from a 1980s video game.

Waves crash on the shore and a woman lies on the white sands of a desert island, the froth of the ocean washing around her. She is dressed only in an egg-yolk yellow smear of a ragged dress or bikini. She is part bewildered, shipwrecked mariner, part mermaid, about to stride ashore out of her native watery element to take over the landlubbing world. What country, friends, is this?

It's 2001, and another queen has come to the throne. This is the music video for 'Survivor' by the girlband Destiny's Child, a holy trinity of Kelly Rowland, Michelle Williams and Beyoncé Knowles-Carter.

The influence of Beyoncé Knowles-Carter upon twenty-first-century global culture is difficult to overestimate – if you've been living under a rock for the past quarter of a century, it's possible, just, that you've never seen an item of clothing inspired by her, heard a song inspired by her, or indeed never seen the woman herself. But since she crawled out of the sea in the music video to 'Survivor', Beyoncé has been fixed in the firmament. For those who came of age between the 1990s and 2010s, she is foundational. My friend Christine plays the following game: would you trade the existence of Destiny's Child/Queen Bey – childhood, teenage and young adult memories and all – for a million pounds? For a billion? For a house, and an end to the relentless trials of renting? For your dream job? The answer is always, always, no. Sacrificing those birthday parties, graduation balls, nights out, nights in, road trips long and short, to which Beyoncé and Destiny's Child were the soundtrack, is a no-brainer. She and they are too deeply ingrained in what it meant to be a child, teenager or young adult, for so many people.

At the very heart of her success is her recognition that image and sound are indivisible. 'I see music,' she proclaimed, at the beginning of her announcement of her self-titled audio-visual album in 2013. 'It's more than what I just hear.'[36] In a very real sense, Beyoncé has turned herself into an image: the musician as artist as artwork.

The icons and images that she has adopted are numerous, so I'm going to talk about just one: the one that graced the stage of the Staples Center (alias the House that Kobe Built and now renamed the Crypto.com Arena) in downtown Los Angeles, for the Grammy Awards in 2017. Beyoncé's performance is about to begin; she has been nominated for nine awards, more than any other artist in attendance.

A flash of golden yellow.

Beyoncé stands on stage in a golden diadem reminiscent of the Virgin Mary, visibly heavily pregnant. Yellow fabric billows around her shoulders, held out by her hands, across the enormous screen behind her, engulfing her, cradling her, concealing and revealing her. The air surrounding her seems to have been transformed into a watery substance in which she floats, weightless. Her voice permeates through, reciting lines by the Somali-British poet Warsan Shire, whose reworked lines feature heavily throughout Beyoncé's *Lemonade* album. The lines she speaks are from Chapter 8 of the album, titled 'Forgiveness', and focus on the pain and beauty of maternal lineage.

The water, the yellow, that golden diadem, are all elements that fashion her as the Yorùbá *orisha*, or spirit, of fresh, sweet or running water, Oshún (associated with fertility, beauty and love), and Yemaya, Yorùbá goddess of the ocean, mother of all the orishas and protector of pregnant women.[37] Both figures are more than simple folklore; they are sacred in the Yorùbá religion and culture. The Yorùbá diaspora originated in modern-day Nigeria, but spread through West Africa and across the Atlantic to Cuba and Brazil. Oshún's legend travelled with the enslaved people forcibly stolen to work in plantations across the American continent, and evolved. She is known as Oxum in Brazil and

A reimagination of the goddess variously known as Oshún, Oxum and Ochún.

Ochún in Cuba, but still has the same key characteristics of motherhood, divination and healing, and the ability to bring about cleansing change to all life. Her physical manifestation is the River Òṣun in Nigeria, which flows directly into the Atlantic; for the Yorùbá diaspora she is a key linking figure, a marker of a collective heritage and identity.[38]

She's also the manifestation of something strikingly universal: the sacred dimensions of water that can also be found in the Abrahamic religions in Islamic ablutions, the Jewish *mikvah* and Christian baptism, and in Hindu ritual bathing.

Oshún has been central to Beyoncé's personal mythology for a long time. The orisha was a reference in her 2017 pregnancy announcement, in a Botticelli-esque series of photographs masterminded by the Ethiopian-American sculptor, painter and musician Awol Erizku. Her appearance at *The Lion King* UK premiere in London in 2019, and her costume in 'Brown Skin Girl' from her visual album *Black is King* (2020) channelled the imagery, too. There are flashes of that spicy, mustardy shade everywhere in Beyoncé's back catalogue: yellow swirls underwater and the flounces of her outfit in 2016's 'Hold Up' from her second visual album *Lemonade*; the image of yellow threads through in 2012's 'Run the World (Girls)'. It reaches the whole way back to that moment in 'Survivor' and the yellow bikini she wears as she emerges from the waves. It is, on the one hand, an excellent example of the Afrofuturist aesthetic – the art, literary and musical sci-fi movement that imagines the African diaspora at the vanguard of innovation and technology; on the other hand, a reclamation of Black identity; and in total, protest at its musical-visual finest.[39]

In comparison to the other examples we've looked at in this chapter, this is a different way of visualising music and embracing the way it feeds the eyes. Beyoncé's career began after the initial rise of the music video as an art form, from avant-garde origins in the 1970s to the 1990s artist-in-white, slo-mo smashed-glass-and-rain-trope to the absurdist offerings of 2020s bands like Wet Leg.

Watching Paint Sing: Abstracting Music

Ancient shrine to Oshún, in the Òṣun-Osogbo Grove, Nigeria.

Arguably, many music videos should be enshrined as masterpieces, deserving of the same amount of respect as a sculpture, a painting or any object of what we once called 'fine' art. Their creation takes huge amounts of work and skill, and many have ceased to be simply incidental to the music and have become central to how we remember a song. Think of (either of!) Kate Bush's 'Wuthering Heights' videos (1978), or Michael Jackson's 'Thriller' (1982): the songs themselves are inseparable from the images of the dances, the costumes, even the sets.

But Beyoncé's visualisation of music is different from the examples we've explored in this chapter in yet another way. She recognises the ability of music and image, interwoven together and separately in themselves, to carry an inheritance, to tell a story of who we are and where we are from. It can be hard for those from countries that weren't colonised to fully appreciate the ease with which these threads can be cut. Tools like family trees and ancestry.com don't work when your ancestors were uprooted because of violence, famine, revolution or ethnic cleansing, or to be used as enslaved labour.

Although I am descended from a long line of labourers, I can trace one of my English ancestors back to the eleventh century. On the Chinese side of my family, by contrast, there is nothing but fractures: everything stunted with the horrible fate that my great-grandparents met in the wake of the Cultural Revolution (1941–9). For reasons that remain unclear, my great-grandfather was beaten to death, and my great-grandmother was made to kneel in broken glass for three days until she died of either exposure, dehydration, sepsis or a combination of all three. We know this because my father's cousin, then a small child, was made to watch. It's likely that my height comes from this side, because my Chinese grandfather was six feet tall (some six inches taller than the national average for his sex, just like me), but there is no one to ask or check with. Such incidental pieces of information have been lost. It's not a matter of being rootless, more of having been transplanted and truncated and made to grow in a different shape.

I'm by no means alone in having heritage like this. These stories recur in families from Sudan and Sri Lanka and Syria and Cambodia and too many other territories to name, forced to seek refuge across the globe, moved on from country to country, city to city. Narratives, images and songs of deities like Oshún are vital ways of understanding selfhood where individual family memories have been truncated.

Of all the images that Beyoncé has adopted over the years, this is one of the most powerful. All of the visual art examples that I've shown you in this chapter, from Anna Casparsson's embroideries to Aubrey Williams's splashes of colour to Tōkō Shinoda's restrained calligraphic forms, were designed to show us how these artists listened to music. Beyoncé's Oshún iconography lets us in on another way of listening. It is a kind of song and sound that insists on its continuity, on the traditions it rewrites, and it is built by communal memory and it flows through people like blood, one generation to the next. *We* make the music, because it is part of our human inheritance: it is in our veins.

𝄞

Music has thrummed throughout the visual arts of humanity across continents and millennia, a constant, recurring reminiscence of that old romance between sound and vision. But for some artists music has also been an integral part of their practice: how they make their art, how they see (and hear) the world and how they interrogate the limits of their vision. These artworks, where they are well-known, have fed how people have thought about music. Where they aren't well-known, they show us how important the act of sharing music was. *Listen!* they cry, *can you hear what I hear? How do you feel when you hear this? Does it feel a little like this?*

When I look at the visual work that Beyoncé has created with set designers and artists and costumiers, at the embroideries of Anna Casparsson and the delicate abstractions of Aubrey Williams, the exquisite miniatures of Levina Teerlinc and the calligraphic forms of Tōkō Shinoda, I see a chorus of difference. It doesn't matter how virtuosic any of these artists were, how great or small their musical skill. Though we do know that many of them *were* very good performers, by putting their musicality into paint and ink and silk and film, it is as though they were eschewing any idea of who is good enough or important enough to be allowed on stage, and whose music *matters*.

All too often we can feel like our performances shouldn't be heard, or that they are not 'real'; that music should be left to the professionals. We can feel, too, as though there is a right and a wrong way of listening to music – dancing a certain way, not dancing at all, moshing, standing up, clapping, not clapping too much except in special circumstances that no one ever fully articulates (always clap if you are listening specifically to Johann Strauss's 'Radetsky March' on New Year's Day in Vienna, and especially if it is the Vienna Philharmonic Orchestra playing, *obviously*). These art objects invite us into a different way of thinking about music. This is music enshrined in sharing. They want you to join in and bring your own reaction and interpretation. Each of these artworks was created as an act of listening or performing, and the simple act of making them visible is an invitation to join in that creative process. That dreamed-of collective listening offers us a history of music that is full of the people in the stalls, in the mosh pit, on the dance floor: *We were here too, you and me*, these paintings and drawings and embroideries and sculptures argue, *and we, too, made the music.*

Music has the capacity to forge new worlds; to bring us together, breaking down the boundaries between our bodies to allow us to see just what a community of music-makers can do. We may not always be in perfect harmony, but there remains a constant, ever-evolving, ever-experimental dialogue, striving towards a flawless, yet-to-be-achieved musical moment that is forever just – *just* – out of reach. Ultimately, visual responses to music – from the cave paintings of our earliest history, to Beyoncé's yellow reimagining of an ancient goddess – offer ways to build a new artful history of music. This history of music accounts for the contribution that all of us can make to music-making and dispels, once and for all, the myth of the invisible, disembodied ear, and the unhearing eye.

Cadenza

Fields of Gold

Sound persists.

It sticks, winding its threads

    through
        one
            ear and
                out
                    the other,

weaving over and over again throughout our brains.

                It is inherently nostalgic. It is
                a resurrector.

It leads us straight into that liminal zone where things hover between the visible and the invisible; an ethereal space populated by the spectres of things, people and places that we have loved, loathed and found unutterably beautiful. The potent ephemerality of these ghosts is all driven by music, the way it hooks and embeds within our brains.

Eleanor Chan, *Fields of Gold*, 2017.

This is an emotive truth that most of us will be familiar with; the way that songs, lyrics and entire symphonies can lodge themselves in our consciousness. The composer Edward Elgar supposedly said on his deathbed, of the 'Moderato' section of his 'Cello Concerto in E Minor' (1919), that 'if you ever hear someone whistling this melody around the Malvern Hills, that will be me.' It had wormed its way so deep into his psyche that he imagined it living on after his death, long after his corporeal body was gone, drifting over a landscape he had loved. To quote another well-known ghost: remember me, remember me.

I adore these moments more than almost anything else. They encapsulate such exquisite power *and* powerlessness: you are filled with the music, made big by it, and yet at the same time you have no choice but to submit to it.

Cadenza: Fields of Gold

May 2017. Back in that scrappy kitchen. My PhD is done; my voice is back and almost (almost) as good as it has ever been. I'm at a crossroads, and need to make a big decision. Do I, now, go back to where I left off? Find a singing teacher, do the last of the exams that will qualify me to audition for the Royal College of Music or Guildhall, and do a postgraduate diploma in vocal performance? Do I buy back in, wholesale, to that world, even though I've seen how ruthless, heartbreaking and fickle it truly is? How dependent it is on sheer, cruel luck? Do I really believe that is the only way for me to be a 'real' musician?

Things are changing for everyone around me too. The people I have sung with in the chapel choir – some of them for seven years, which, when you're in your mid-twenties, is basically your entire adult life – are graduating, moving away for new jobs, new courses, new lives. We have scrapped, lost our tempers, been *intensely* frustrated, fallen out and made up with each other over the years. But there's something about making music with someone. Scientists have shown that singing together brings your heartbeats in sync: add that up to twenty hours a week for seven years and you have a deep, profound kind of intimacy. We want to mark this occasion: to commemorate what we had. Over a couple of months, two of our members compose a four-part harmony of a song we all loved: 'Fields of Gold'. And, as we sing through fragments of drafts, reworking, learning its twists and turns, I paint the process.

The original working title of this painting was the extremely catchy *Places that May or May not Exist: An homage to the cassette tape that got stuck in the tape player of our ancient Toyota Space Cruiser for four years, and so provided the de facto soundtrack for many, many childhood adventures through the wilds of the West Country, aka 'The Very Best of Sting and the Police' (1997)*. How I loved that car. It was shaped like a biscuit tin so it *bounced* over potholes; it could only manage some steep Cornish lanes at a maximum of 3mph with no passengers, so we walked slowly alongside it laughing, throwing our meagre child-size weight against it to 'push it' and cheering it on while my mother desperately ground the accelerator to the floor. It had the most enormous 1980s of 1980s moon roof that slid the whole way open, so if you were feeling especially reckless you could stand up as the car bumbled along. You could climb right up onto the roof through it, and frequently we did.

And no matter how much we complained about the jammed tape player – how much we wanted to listen to the Red Hot Chili Peppers, to Good Charlotte, to Avril Lavigne, to *anything* but Sting – how lucky we were that it *was* that album. It has so many bangers: 'Roxanne'; 'Every Breath You Take' (whose guitar riff, incidentally, somehow precisely captures the way that the Space Cruiser bounced); 'Englishman in New York'; 'If I Ever Lose My Faith in You'. And, of course, 'Fields of Gold'.

𝄞

This painting was already loaded with memories, ready to receive a palimpsest of more, one laid over the other. It is so important to understand that there is almost nothing new in this world, apart from *your* way of experiencing it – and in that light, when I look at the painting now it still strikes me as so profoundly, miraculously odd that I chose to interpret those fields of gold literally. I remember the golden yellow causing endless trouble: always a shade too sickly, never quite luminous, light and glowing enough to capture the harmonic texture the composers were going for, to catch the lowering stormy grey of the sky and lift it back up. Some versions of 'Fields of Gold' can be a little saccharine, a little sentimental: this, categorically, was not what any of us wanted.

We sang it at a college dinner at the end of June to a not-so-intimate audience of 150.

Felt the tears prick in our eyes.

Drank to its health.

There is no recording of that performance, but there is one from after the end of that dinner. I won't share it with you, because that is a vulnerability frontier too far even for me – but I will try to describe it for you. The phone camera wobbles a little. We are clustered around the antechapel of our college, a space we had sung in many, many times, and we are visibly the worse for wear for drink. You cannot quite see due to the pixelation, but there are tears running down a few of our faces. We are entirely lost in the music. Absolutely no one is watching, apart from the person filming. The tuning is absolutely terrible, but the passion is there. Even now, watching it is incredibly painful. I feel the goosebumps shiver down my spine as a thing that is lost turns in its grave and reaches back for me: a world where I rediscovered a voice the universe had taken from me, a thing that I thought had gone forever; a singing experience so comfortable, so loveworn and lovelorn, so intimate, so irrecoverable, all inscribed onto a landscape of rolling fields of gold beneath an unsettled sky.

Somewhere in the process of learning the arrangement, singing it, performing it, painting it, I realised: I wasn't going to do it. I wasn't going to go back to music exams, to the conservatoire route, to grafting the professional circuit. Not because I couldn't, but because now, at last, I knew. There was more than one way to be a musician, and that one wasn't mine.

Throughout this book I have tried to capture for you the briefest impression of just how much visual information goes into the experience of music-making. This is what I want to leave you with: a painting of what it is like to come of age and find your own singing voice so deep within a musical ensemble that you can barely tell where your breath ends and another's begins. To embrace the image of music is to record it; to rehearse it; to perform in counterpoint to its ephemeral form, a nostalgic art of remembering and recreating and resurrecting. It is not rigid and fixed, it is endlessly fluid and malleable; the way that it allows us as humans to bend and shape it is inherent in its enduring beauty. It is a dance at the very lip of the void between the visible and the invisible, the audible and inaudible, the known and familiar and the great wide somewhere, yet to be discovered.

And in the end, perhaps this is what music asks us to visualise: the evanescent feeling of home – of a dilapidated 1989 Toyota Space Cruiser as the hedgerows whisk past, of singing with a group of people with your eyes closed because you know the timbre of their voices so intimately that you feel the pulse together, inside your bodies. Nostalgia comes from the Greek *nostos*: a homecoming. The concept crops up in many other languages across the world, all inflected with slightly different meanings but clustering around that same deep ache of incompleteness that, for the space of a heartbeat, is made whole. There is the Portuguese *saudade*, the Romanian *dor*, the Turkish *hüzün*, the Welsh *hiraeth* and perhaps most poignantly, the Ethiopian Amharic *tizita* (ትዝታ), which refers not only to bittersweet longing, but to an entire musical mode and style designed to evoke these feelings.

Knowing and loving (or even hating) a piece of music is a homecoming of sorts. It's a heartbreaking place, taunting our eyes with images that evanesce like smoke the minute you look hard at them, but filling our ears in a way that constantly goads our eyes into seeing. It's a push and pull against the limits of our bodies and what they can know and experience. Ultimately for me that is a crucial part of what music is, for better or worse: a way of seeing through your ears, your hands, your tongue, your breath that ever so fleetingly, ever so spellbindingly reanimates the pictures that we cherish in our minds, and that washes over us as a balm of forgetting its loss.

In the meantime, come and sing with me. You can read from sheet music, from lyrics, or learn it by ear. It doesn't matter. It doesn't matter what your voice sounds like. Embrace the way it tantalises your eyes, and let those pictures in. This is my gift to you. And in music, let's commemorate the things, people, places, feelings, moments we have lost: tell the sun, in his jealous sky, about those glorious times when we walked in fields of gold.

Notes

Prelude: Noisy Pictures and Music for the Eyes

1 John Levack Drever and Andrew Hugill (eds.), *Aural Diversity* (London and New York: Routledge, 2023); Zhou, Kyrie Zhixuan et al., 'Exploring the Diversity of Music Experiences for Deaf and Hard of Hearing People', in *arXiv* (2024); Sylvain Brétéché and Christine Esclapez, 'Music(s), Musicology and Science: Towards an Interscience Network. The Example of Deaf Musical Experience', in *Music Technology with Swing* (2018), 637–657.
2 Peter Brook, *The Empty Space* (first published 1968, this edition New York: Scribner, 2019), 16.
3 Henkan Honing, *The Origins of Musicality* (Cambridge, MA: Massachusetts Institute of Technology, 2019); Iain Morley, *The Prehistory of Music: Human Evolution, Archaeology, and the Origins of Musicality* (Oxford: Oxford University Press, 2013), 177–200.
4 Lynda Nead, *The Female Nude: Art, Obscenity and Sexuality* (London: Routledge, 1992); Kenneth Clark, *The Nude: A Study of Ideal Art* (London: Penguin, 1983).
5 Billy Klüver and Julie Martin, *Kiki's Paris: Artists and Lovers 1900–1930* (New York: Abrams, 1989); Kiki, *The Education of a French Model: Kiki's Memoirs* (introduced by Ernest Hemingway), (New York: [Black Manikin Press], 1962).
6 Michael R. Taylor, *Man Ray: The Paris Years* (New Haven, CT: Yale University Press, 2022).
7 Richard Kendall, *Degas Backstage* (London: Thames & Hudson, 1996).
8 Benjamin Roberts, *Sex, Drugs and Rock 'n' Roll in the Dutch Golden Age* (Amsterdam: Amsterdam University Press, 2017), 139–158; Jan W.J. Burgers, *The Lute in the Dutch Golden Age: Musical Culture in the Netherlands, c. 1580–1670* (Amsterdam: Amsterdam University Press, 2013).
9 Marjorie E. Wieseman, *Vermeer and Music: The Art and Love of Leisure* (London: National Gallery, 2013); Roger Harmon, '"Musica Laetitiae Comes" and Vermeer's Music Lesson', in *Oud Holland*, 113:3 (1999), 161–168.
10 Robert D. Huerta, *Giants of Delft: Johannes Vermeer and the Natural Philosophers. The Parallel Search for Knowledge during the Age of Discovery*

(Lewisburg, PA: Bucknell University Press, 2003); Rozemarijn Landsman, *Vermeer's Maps* (New York: The Frick Collection, 2022); Laura J. Snyder, *Eye of the Beholder: Johannes Vermeer, Anthoni van Leeuwenhoek, and the reinvention of seeing* (London: Head of Zeus, 2015).

11 I've written a lot about this in my academic work. Eleanor Chan, *Syrene Soundes: False Relations in the English Renaissance* (Oxford: Oxford University Press, 2024). For an account that focuses on how a single figure weathered the Reformation, see Kerry McCarthy, *Tallis* (Oxford: Oxford University Press, 2020).

12 Bernhard Warner describes the heavy lifting wonderfully, if slightly anatomically vaguely. See Bernhard Warner, 'Why Do Stars Like Adele Keep Losing Their Voice?' in the *Guardian*, 10th August 2017.

13 Larry Sherman and Dennis Plies, *Every Brain Needs Music: The Neuroscience of Making and Listening to Music* (New York: Columbia University Press, 2023). See, for example, the 'Mozart Effect', where neuroscientists record improved cognitive function when subjects listened to Mozart's 'Sonata for Two Pianos in D Major, K 448'.

14 Muriel T. Zaatar, Kenda Alhakim, Mohammed Enayeh and Ribal Tamer, 'The Transformative Power of Music: Insights into Neuroplasticity, Health, and Disease', in *Brain, Behaviour, & Immunity – Health*, 35 (February 2024), 1–11; Laura Chaddock-Heyman, Psyche Loui, Timothy B. Weng, Robert Weisshappel, Edward McAuley and Arthur F. Kramer, 'Musical Training and Brain Volume in Older Adults', *Brain Sciences*, 11:1 (50) (January 2021); Ana Carolina Rodrigues et al., 'Musical training, neuroplasticity and cognition', *Dementia & Neuropsychologia*, 4:4 (2010), 277–286.

15 Chiara Cantiani, Chiara Dondena, Massimo Molteni, Valentina Riva and Maria Luisa Lorusso, 'Intergenerational longitudinal associations between parental reading/musical traits, infants' auditory processing, and later phonological awareness', in *Frontiers in Neuroscience*, 17 (July 2023).

16 Jo Yee Cheung, 'The Day the Music Dies? Why time is running out to tackle the decline in UK music education', Royal Northern College of Music website, 11th March 2024, https://www.rncm.ac.uk/news/the-day-the-music-dies-why-time-is-running-out-to-tackle-the-decline-in-uk-music-education/#:~:text=Despite%20the%20bold%20ambitions%20of,in%20GCSE%20level%20pupil%20numbers; Diane Johnson and Andrew Percy, 'Music Education: State of the Nation' report, Incorporated Society of Musicians (ISM), (2019), https://www.ism.org/images/images/State-of-the-Nation-Music-Education-WEB.pdf.

Chapter 1: Curtain Up

1 We have only the most fragmentary ways of knowing which sex shamans tended to be. We do know, however, that the Magdalenian culture revered the female form (see, for example, the so-called 'Vénus de Vibraye' found near Les Eyzies in 1864). There's also a strong tradition

of female and gender-fluid spiritual leaders in a broad variety of ancient cultures. See Serinity Young, *Women Who Fly: Goddesses, Witches, Mystics, and other Airborne Females* (Oxford: Oxford University Press, 2017), 172–188; Fuzuli Bayat, 'Women Shamans from the Gender Aspect', in *The Journal of International Social Research*, 3:13 (2010), 44–51; Barbara Tedlock, *The Woman in the Shaman's Body* (New York: Random House for Bantam Dell, 2005).

2 Andreas Maier, *The Central European Magdalenian: Regional Diversity and Internal Variability* (Dordrecht: Springer, 2015); Martin Francis Hemingway, *The Initial Magdalenian in France* (Oxford: Oxford University Press, 1980).

3 Andy Needham, Izzy Wisher, Andrew Landley, Matthew Amy, Aimée Little, 'Art by Firelight? Using Experimental and Digital Techniques to Explore Magdalenian Engraved Plaquette Use at Montastruc', in *PloS One*, 17:4 (April 2022).

4 Christine Desdemaines-Hugon, *Stepping Stones: A Journey through the Ice Age Caves of the Dordogne* (New Haven, CT and London: Yale University Press, 2010), Chapter 2.

5 Elena Paillet, 'Pour être utile à la science: Denis Peyrony et l'art préhistorique, de la découverte à la protection', *Paléo*, 29 (2018), 151–178; 'Denis Peyrony, Prehistorian and Precursor', on Lascaux-Dordogne website, https://www.lascaux-dordogne.com/en/partager/les-personnalites-du-perigord/denis-peyrony/ (accessed 4th November 2024).

6 Denis Peyrony, *Denis Peyrony: Journal d'un Préhistorien 1912–1948* (Les Eyzies: Musée du Préhistoire, 2017).

7 Louis Capitan, Henri Breuil and Denis Peyrony, *La caverne de Font-de-Gaume aux Eyzies (Dordogne)* (Monaco: A. Chêne, 1910); Louis Capitan, Henri Breuil and Denis Peyrony, *Les Combarelles aux Eyzies (Dordogne)* (Paris: Masson, 1924).

8 Carole Fritz et al., 'First Record of the Sound Produced by the Oldest Upper Palaeolithic Seashell Horn', in *Science Advances*, 7:7 (10th February 2021); Karina Shah, 'Listen to the Oldest Known Conch Shell Horn from 18,000 Years Ago', in *New Scientist*, 11th February 2021; Jonathan Amos, 'Ancient Hunter-Gatherer Seashell Resonates after 17,000 Years', *BBC News*, 10th February 2021.

9 I am both exasperated and filled with terror at the prospect of what a historian would make of my own research next century, should any of it survive the passage of time and the ravages of climate, particularly if no one sees fit to preserve it.

10 Carole Fritz, Mark D. Willis and Gilles Tosello, 'Reconstructing Palaeolithic Cave Art: The Example of Marsoulas Cave (France)', in *Journal of Archaeological Science*, 10 (December 2016), 910–916.

11 Carole Fritz et al., 'First Record of the Sound Produced by the Oldest Upper Palaeolithic Seashell Horn', in *Science Advances*, 7:7 (10th February 2021); Karina Shah, 'Listen to the Oldest Known Conch Shell Horn

from 18,000 Years Ago', in *New Scientist*, 11th February 2021; Jonathan Amos, 'Ancient Hunter-Gatherer Seashell Resonates after 17,000 Years', *BBC News*, 10th February 2021.

12 Miriam A. Kolar, 'Acoustics in Music Archaeology: Re-Sounding the Marsoulas Conch and Its Cave', in *Acoustics Today*, 18:2 (2022), 52–61.

13 Daniel E. Commins, Yves Coppens and Takayuki Hidaka, 'Acoustics of the Lascaux Cave and its Facsimile Lascaux IV', in *Journal of the Acoustical Society of America*, 148 (2020), 918–924.

14 Ibid.

15 Ibid.

16 Ìegor Reznikoff, 'Prehistoric paintings, sound and rocks', in *Studien zur Musikarchäologie III. The Archaeology of Sound: Origin and Organisation*, edited by A.D. Kilmer and R. Eichmann, Papers from the 2nd Symposium of the International Study Group on Music Archaeology at Monastery Michaelstein (17th–23rd September) (Verlag Marie Leidorf GmbH, Rahden/Westf., 2002).

17 Bruno Fazenda et al., 'Cave acoustics in prehistory: Exploring the association of Palaeolithic visual motifs and acoustic response', *Journal of the Acoustical Society of America*, 142 (3) (September 2017), 1345.

18 Ìegor Reznikoff, 'Prehistoric paintings, sound and rocks', op. cit.

19 From an *Anthology of Persian Poetry*, fifteenth century, Metropolitan Museum of Art (New York), Accession No. 13.228.19.

20 Amir Hosein Pourjavady, *Music Making in Iran from the Fifteenth to the Early Twentieth Century* (Edinburgh: University of Edinburgh Press, 2023), 11–13.

21 Ibid., 65.

22 James Hillson, 'Imagining Invention: The Character of the "Gothic Architect" and England, 1200–1400', in *British Art Studies*, Issue 6 (June 2017), https://doi.org/10.17658/issn.2058-5462/issue-06/jillson.

23 F. Woodman, 'John Wastell: Architect, Genius, and All-Round Mr Fix-It', in F. Woodman, Helen Lunnon and Gabriel Byng (eds.), *Medieval Art, Architecture and Archaeology in Cambridge* (London and New York: Routledge, 2022), 188–208.

24 Paul Binski, *Gothic Wonder: Art, Artifice, and the Decorated Style* (London and New Haven, CT: Yale University Press for the Paul Mellon Center for Studies in British Art, 2014).

25 Jill DeVonyar and Richard Kendall, *Degas and the Art of Japan* (New Haven, CT: Yale University Press, 2007). See also Hannah Wier, 'Edgar Degas in the era of *Japonisme*', on Saint Louis Art Museum website, 24th May 2022, https://www.slam.org/blog/edgar-degas-in-the-era-of-japonisme.

26 Jane R. Becker, catalogue entry for Object No. 29.100.554 (2023), Metropolitan Museum of Art online catalogue.

27 Nobuo Nakatani, 'The Friendship of Degas and Tadamasa Hayashi' (ドガと林 忠正 - 交友についての覚書), in *Edgar Degas* (Tokyo: Isetan Museum of Art, 1988), 244–245.

28 Kimberley A. Jones, 'The Allure of the Fan', in Henri Loyrette (ed.), *Degas at the Opera* (London & New York: Thames & Hudson, 2020), 243–252.
29 Jill DeVonyar and Richard Kendall, *Degas and the Art of Japan*, op. cit., 30–32.
30 Hélène Guyot and Rupert J.M. Medd, 'Eyewitness Accounts during the Putumayo Rubber Boom', in *Journeys* 20:2 (2019), 58–94; Margarita Serje, 'The Peruvian Amazon Co.: Credit and Debt in the Putumayo "Wild Rubber" Business', in *Enterprise & Society*, 22:2 (2021), 475–501.
31 Drew Reed, 'Manaus's Opulent Amazon Theatre – A history of Cities in 50 Buildings, Day 15', in the *Guardian*, 14th April 2015.
32 Benjamin Ramm, 'The Beautiful Theatre in the Heart of the Amazon Rainforest', *BBC News*, 16th March 2017, https://www.bbc.com/culture/article/20170316-the-beautiful-theatre-in-the-heart-of-the-amazon-rainforest (accessed 4th May 2024).
33 'Teatro Amazonas, Home of the Amazonas Opera Festival', Opera Latinoamerica website, https://www.operala.org/en/teatro-del-mes-teatro-amazonas-hogar-del-festival-amazonas-de-opera/ (accessed 4th May 2024).
34 Sjeng Scheijen, 'The Queer World of Sergei Diaghilev', in *Experiment: Journal of Russian Culture*, 17:1 (January 2011), 65–75; Luke Jennings, 'Sergei Diaghilev: First Lord of the Dance', in the *Observer*, 12th September 2010.
35 Natalia Sidlina and Matthew Gale (eds.), *Natalia Goncharova* (London: Tate, 2019), 14.
36 Davinia Caddy, *The Ballets Russes and Beyond: Music and Dance in Belle-Epoque Paris* (Cambridge: Cambridge University Press, 2012); Jane Pritchard, *Diaghilev and the Golden Age of the Ballet Russes 1909–1929*, (London: V&A Publishing, 2010).
37 'Rowena Cade: Our Master Builder', https://www.minack.com/our-story/rowena-cade (accessed 2nd July 2024).
38 Kate Desforges, *Burdekin's Utopian Visions: A Study of Four Interwar Texts* (University of Hull: unpublished PhD dissertation, January 2015).
39 1781 Collective website, https://www.1781collective.com/ (accessed 17th January 2024).
40 Stephanie Taralson, 'Bringing sexy Bach: How the 1781 Collective is changing the way we experience classical music', *Exberliner*, 19th September 2023.

Chapter 2: Feather on the Breath of God

1 Kerry McCarthy, 'Josquin in England: An unexpected sighting', *Early Music*, 53 (2014), 449–454.
2 There's been some speculation that they might have been the painter Arnold Dericksen, or George Gower; I personally think there's quite a resemblance between the way that the artist renders certain features and the way that the Flemish Anthonis Mor did. Eleanor Chan, '{Not}ation:

'The In/Visible Visual Cultures of Musical Legibility in the English Renaissance', in *Arts*, 12:75 (April 2023); Edward Town, 'A Portrait of the Miniaturist as a Young Man: Nicholas Hilliard and the Painters of 1560s London', in *British Art Studies* 17 (2020), 1–27.

3   Howard Ho, 'How Elsa Found Herself (Musically) & Why It's Amazing', YouTube (12th October 2020) (accessed 30th August 2023).

4   Sophus Helle, *Enheduana: The Complete Poems of the World's First Author* (New Haven, CT: Yale University Press, 2023).

5   Sidney Babcock and Erhan Tamur, *She Who Wrote: Enheduanna and Women of Mesopotamia ca. 3400–2000 BC* (New York: The Morgan Library & Museum 2022).

6   Colin Renfrew, *Prehistory: The Making of the Human Mind* (New York: Weidenfeld and Nicholson, 2012).

7   Bathja Bayer, 'The Mesopotamian Theory of Music and the Ugarit Notation: A Reexamination', reproduced in Joan Goodnick Westenholz et al., *Music in Antiquity: The Near East and the Mediterranean*, (DeGruyter, 2014), 18; J. Rahn, 'The Hurrian Pieces, ca. 1350 BCE: Part One – Notation and Analysis', in *Analytical Approaches to World Music Journal*, 1:1 (2011).

8   Armand D'Angour, 'The Song of Seikilos', in *Antigone Journal* (7th December 2021).

9   John Landels, *Music in Ancient Greece and Rome* (London & New York: Routledge, 1999), 252; Robert A. Rohland, *Carpe Diem: The Politics of Presence in Greek and Latin Literature* (Cambridge: Cambridge University Press, 2022), 1–2.

10 Robert A. Rohland (2022), op. cit., 5–6.

11 Armand D'Angour, 'The Song of Seikilos', op. cit.

12 Barbara Stühlmeyer, *Die Gesänge der Hildegard von Bingen: Eine musikologische, theologische und kulturhistorische Untersuchung* (Olms: Hildesheim, 2003); Franziska Hanel, 'Lieder und Bilder: Hildegard von Bingen als zentraler Punkt im Leben zweier Frauen: Barbara Stühlmeyer und Sabine Böhm', in *Frankenpost*, Hof, 18th September 2004.

13 Hildegard Bingen, *Riesencodex*, fol. 464v; Sarah L. Higley, *Hildegard of Bingen's Unknown Language: An Edition, Translation and Discussion* (Basingstoke: Palgrave Macmillan, 2007).

14 Bell Yung, 'Choreographic and Kinaesthetic Elements in Performance on the Seven-String Zither', in *Ethnomusicology*, 28:3 (1984), 505–517, at 506.

15 John Thompson, 'John Thompson and the Silk String Guqin', https://silkqin.com/01mywk/themes/women.htm (accessed 5th May 2023); https://silkqin.com/02qnpu/38sztq.htm#f1 (accessed 5th May 2023).

16 Madame Zhong, 思齊堂琴譜, *Sizhaitang Qinpu* (Handbook of the Hall for Contemplating the Various), 1620; Qinqu Jicheng (QQJC), Vol. 9, 70.

17 Zeyuan Wu, *Becoming Sages: Qin Song and Self-Cultivation in Late Imperial China* (Ohio State University, unpublished PhD dissertation, 2020), 157.

Notes

18 Stephen Addiss, Kenneth J. Dewoskin, Mitchell Clark, *The Resonance of the Qin in East Asian Art* (New York: China Institute Gallery, 1999), 53.
19 Susan Rankin, *Writing Sounds in Carolingian Europe: The Invention of Musical Notation* (Cambridge: Cambridge University Press, 2018).
20 Kay Kaufman Shelemay, Peter Jeffrey and Ingrid Monson, 'Oral and Written Transmission in Ethiopian Christian Chant', in *Early Music History*, 12 (1993), 55–117.
21 Getatchew Haile, 'Manuscript production in Ethiopia: On Ongoing Practice', in John Haines (ed.), *The Calligraphy of Medieval Music* (Turnhout: Brepols, 2007).
22 Kay Kaufman Shelemay, 'The Musician and Transmission of Religious Tradition: the Multiple Roles of the Ethiopian Dabtara', in *Journal of Religion in Africa*, 22:3 (January 1992), 244–246.
23 Kay Kaufman Shelemay, 'Zema: A Concept of Sacred Music in Ethiopia', in *The World of Music*, 24:3 (1982), 52–67.
24 Quoted in David Conway, *Jewry in Music: Entry to the Profession from the Enlightenment to Richard Wagner* (Cambridge: Cambridge University Press, 2012), 171.
25 Letter sent 16th July 1820, in Sebastian Hensel (ed.), *The Mendelssohn Family 1729–1847 From Letters and Journals*, trans. Carl Klingemann (London: Sampson Low & Co., 1884), Vol. I, 82.
26 Stephen Rogers, *The Songs of Fanny Hensel* (Oxford: Oxford University Press, 2021); Larry R. Todd, *Fanny Hensel: The Other Mendelssohn* (Oxford: Oxford University Press, 2009); Françoise Tillard, *Fanny Mendelssohn* (Portland: Amadeus Press, 1996).
27 Sebastian Hensel (ed.), op. cit., Vol. II, 203.
28 William M. Voelkle, *Holy Hoaxes: A Beautiful Deception* (London: Paul Holberton Publishing, 2023), 90–95.
29 Ibid.
30 Athanasius Kircher, *Oedipus Aegyptiacus* (Rome: Vitale Mascardi, 1652-4).
31 Eleanor Dobson and Nichola Tonks, *Ancient Egypt in the Modern Imagination: Art, Literature and Culture* (London: Bloomsbury, 2020). This revival is also stylistically responsible for the ideas behind Art Deco: see Bridget Elliot, 'Art Deco Worlds in a Tomb: Reanimating Egypt in Modern(ist) Visual Culture', in *South Central Review*, 25:1 (April 2008), 114–135, and James Curl Stevens, *The Egyptian revival: Ancient Egypt as the Inspiration for Design Motifs in the West* (Oxford: Routledge, 2005).
32 Juliet Bellow, 'Fashioning Cléopâtre: Sonia Delaunay's New Woman', in *Art Journal*, 68:2 (January 2009), 7–25; Felicia Rappe, 'L'oeil danse: décors et costumes de Robert et Sonia Delaunay pour Cléopâtre', in *Histoire de l'art*, 58:1 (2006), 105–114.
33 Chae-Lin Kim, 'The Deaf Body Beyond Music: Music Notation by Christine Sun Kim', in Floris Schuiling and Emily Payne (eds.), *Material Cultures of Music Notation* (London and New York: Routledge, 2022), 67–78.

34 Christine Sun Kim, 'The Enchanting Music of Sign Language', Ted Talk filmed in August 2015, https://www.ted.com/talks/christine_sun_kim_the_enchanting_music_of_sign_language/transcript.
35 Paulette Beete, 'Art Talk with Sound Artist Christine Sun Kim', in *National Endowment for the Arts*, 27 March 2017, https://www.arts.gov/art-works/2017/art-talk-sound-artist-christine-sun-kim (accessed 3rd December 2023).
36 Jessica A. Holmes, 'Expert Listening beyond the Limits of Hearing: Music and Deafness', in *Journal of the American Musicological Society*, 70:1 (2017), 171–220.
37 Ivan Hewett, 'The thought police want to destroy the arts, but classical music is unimpeachable', in the *Daily Telegraph*, 3rd November 2023.

Chapter 3: The Hand of Guido

1 Lydia Kee, 'Medieval Methods: Guido D'Arezzo's Innovative Approaches to Music Education', in *Musical Offerings*, 13:2 (November 2022), 59–71; Constant J. Mews and Carol J. Williams, 'Ancients and Moderns in Medieval Music Theory: From Guido of Arezzo to Jacobus', in *Intellectual History Review*, 27:3 (July 2017), 299–315.
2 Stefano Mengozzi, *The Renaissance Reform of Medieval Music Theory: Guido of Arezzo between Myth and History* (Cambridge: Cambridge University Press, 2010).
3 The common translation is the one to be found on the Eastman School of Music website: https://www.esm.rochester.edu/musicus/medieval-sights-sounds/ut-queant-laxis/#:~:text=So%20that%20your%20servants%20may,stained%20lips%2C%20Saint%20John.&text=the%20promise%20of%20thy%20greatness,name%20and%20his%20future%20story.
4 Thomas Christensen, 'Music Theory and Pedagogy', in Iain Fenlon and Richard Wistreich (eds.), *The Cambridge History of Sixteenth Century Music* (Cambridge: Cambridge University Press, 2019), 414–438. For a very thorough discussion of the afterlives of Guido's hand, see Cristle Collins Judd (ed.), *Tonal Structures in Early Music* (London & New York: Routledge, 1998) and Rebecca Herissone, *Music Theory in Seventeenth Century England* (Oxford: Oxford University Press, 2000).
5 Nicholas Baragwanath, *The Solfeggio Tradition: The Forgotten Art of Melody in the Long Eighteenth Century* (Oxford: Oxford University Press, 2020).
6 Alexander Rehding, 'Fine-Tuning a Global History of Music Theory: Divergences, Zhu Zaiyu, and Music-Theoretical Instruments', *Music Theory Spectrum*, 44:2 (Fall 2022), 260–275.
7 Joseph S.C. Lam, 'Zhu Zaiyu', in *Grove Music Online* (2001).
8 Ross Duffin, *How Equal Temperament Ruined Harmony, and Why You Should Care* (New York: W.W. Norton, 2007), 40.
9 Zhu Zaiyu, *A New Explanation of Musical Temperament* (1584), fol. 5a.
10 Alexander Rehding, 'Fine-Tuning a Global History of Music Theory', op. cit., 270.

11 Simon Stevin, 'Vande Spiegheling der Singconst', in R.J. Forbes, A.D. Fokker and A. Romein (eds.), *The Principal Works of Simon Stevin: Engineering, Music and Civil Life* (Amsterdam: C.V. Swets & Zeitlinger, 1966), 426–429.
12 Ross Duffin, *How Equal Temperament Ruined Harmony*, op. cit.
13 He was, perhaps, a bit too much of a Renaissance man and evades categorisation. Scholars suspect this is why he is not better known today. Rienk Vermij, 'Simon Stevin through the lens of his dedications', in *Centaurus* 63:3 (August 2021), 532–545.
14 Simon Stevin, 'Vande Spiegheling der Singconst', op. cit., 428.
15 Alexander Rehding, 'Fine-Tuning a Global History of Music Theory', op. cit., 260–275.
16 Joseph Needham and Kenneth Robinson, 'Sound (Acoustics)', in Joseph Needham (ed.), *Science and Civilisation in China: Vol. IV. Physics and Physical Technology Part 1. Physics* (Cambridge: Cambridge University Press, 1962), 126–228, at 224.
17 Bei Peng traces the documentary evidence of when Zhu's theories travelled; see Bei Peng, 'On the Western Reception of Prince Zhu Zaiyu's Music Theory from the Eighteenth to the Twentieth Century', in *International Communication of Chinese Culture*, 10:2–4 (December 2023), 133–149.
18 James Fujitani, 'The Ming Rejection of the Portuguese Embassy of 1517: A Reassessment', in *Journal of World History*, 27:1 (2016), 87–102.
19 Djoeke van Netten, 'The Richest Country in the World: Dutch Knowledge of China and Cathay and How to Get There in the 1590s', in Thijs Westeijn (ed.), *Foreign Devils and Philosophers: Cultural Encounters between the Chinese, the Dutch, and Other Europeans 1590–1800* (Leiden: Brill, 2020), 24–56.
20 For more on this fascinating story see Matthew Dimmock, *Elizabethan Globalism: England, China and the Rainbow Portrait* (London and New Haven, CT: Yale University Press for the Paul Mellon Center for Studies in British Art, 2019).
21 Gene Cho, *The Discovery of Musical Equal Temperament in China and Europe in the Sixteenth Century* (Lewiston, NY: Edwin Mellen Press, 2003).
22 Kees Zandvliet, *Mapping for Money: Maps, Plans and Topographic Paintings and Their Role in Dutch Overseas Expansion during the 16th and 17th Centuries* (Amsterdam: Batavian Lion International, 1998), 139.
23 Enormous thanks are due to my dear friend the scent historian Christine Griffiths, who has spent many years answering my questions on Piesse and random speculations about the relationship between scent and music.
24 William Tullett, 'Smell Organ', *Encyclopedia of Smell History and Heritage*, https://encyclopedia.odeuropa.eu/items/show/18, accessed 5th August 2024.
25 Charles Piesse, *Olfactics and the Physical Senses* (London: Piesse & Lubin, 1887).

26 G.W. Septimus Piesse, *The Art of Perfumery and Method of Obtaining the Odours of Plants* (London: Longman, Brown, Green & Longmans, 1855), 25.
27 These ideas, in fact, continue to interest experimental psychologists. See Anne-Sylvie Crisinel and Charles Spence, 'Fruity Note: Crossmodal Associations Between Odors and Musical Notes', in *Chemical Senses* 37:2 (February 2012), 151–158; Ophelia Deroy, Anne-Sylvie Crisinel and Charles Spence, 'Crossmodal correspondences between odors and contingent features: odors, musical notes, and geometrical shapes', in *Psychonomic Bulletin & Review*, 20:5 (October 2013), 878–896; and D.W. Wesson and D.A. Wilson, 'Smelling sounds: olfactory-auditory sensory convergence in the olfactory tubercle', *The Journal of Neuroscience*, 30:8 (2010).
28 William Sloane Kennedy, *In Portia's Garden* (Boston, MA: Bradlee Whidden, 1897), 15.
29 G.W. Septimus Piesse, *The Art of Perfumery*, op. cit., 27.
30 'Bibliographical Notice', *Journal of the Franklin Institute*, 83:6 (June 1867), 423–424, at 424.
31 Alexander Wallace Rimington, *Colour-Music: The Art of Mobile Colour* (London: Hutchinson, 1912), 57–60.
32 J. Ward, B. Huckstep, E. Tsakanikos, 'Sound-colour synaesthesia: to what extent does it use cross-modal mechanisms common to us all?', *Cortex: A Journal Devoted to the Study of the Nervous System and Behavior*, 42(2), (2006), 264–80.
33 Caroline Curwen, 'The role of synaesthesia in reading written musical key signatures', *Journal of Experimental Psychology: General*, Vol. 151, 10 (2022): 2284–2299; Caroline Curwen, 'Music-Colour Synaesthesia: Concept, Context and Qualia', in *Consciousness and Cognition*, 61 (May 2018), 94–106; Charles Spence and Nicola Di Stefano, 'Coloured hearing, colour music, colour organs, and the search for perceptually meaningful correspondences between colour and sound', in *i-Perception*, 13:3 (May 2022).
34 J. Ward, B. Huckstep, E. Tsakanikos, 'Sound-colour synaesthesia', op. cit.
35 K. Peacock, 'Synesthetic Perception: Alexander Scriabin's Colour Hearing', in *Music Perception*, 2:4 (1985), 483–506, at 495. And yet others saw it as violet: Amy Ione, Christopher Tyler, 'Neuroscience, history and the arts. Synesthesia: Is F-sharp colored violet?', *Journal of the History of the Neurosciences*, 13:1 (2004), 58–65.
36 Amy Ione, Christopher Tyler, 'Neuroscience, history and the arts', op. cit., 58.
37 Mary Gartside, 'An Essay on Light and Shade' (1805), 26.
38 George Fields, *Chromatics, or, the analogy, harmony and philosophy of colour* (1845), 18–19.
39 Alexander Wallace Rimington, *Colour-Music*, op. cit., 111–112.
40 Ibid., 31–32.
41 The *Merthyr Express* describes the problem as 'Mrs Hughes' indifferent health'; see the *Merthyr Express*, 9th April 2010. In 1919, Henry Holbrook

Curtis suggested Watts Hughes' Eidophone as a rehabilitation treatment for injured vocal cords, which to me implies that her ill health may very well have been of a nodule-adjacent nature. Henry Holbrook Curtis, *Voice Building and Tone Placing: Showing a New Method of Relieving Injured Vocal Cords by Tone Exercises* (London: Appleton & Co., 1919).

42 Rob Mullender, 'Divine Agency: Bringing to Light the Voice Figures of Margaret Watts Hughes', in *Sound Effects*, 8:1 (2019), 123–139; Ferran Lega Llados, 'Margaret Watts Hughes: The Forgotten Pioneer of Sound Art', in *Barcelona Research Art Creation*, 10:3 (October 2022), 116–136.

43 Megan Watts Hughes, 'Visible Sound', in *The Century Illustrated Monthly Magazine* (Toronto: University of Toronto, and New York: Scribner, 1891), 37–44.

44 Megan Watts Hughes, *The Eidophone Voice Figures: Natural and Geometrical Forms Produced by Vibrations of the Human Voice* (London: Christian Herald Company Ltd, 1904).

45 Teal Marz, 'Women of the Conversazioni', *The Royal Society Blog*, 8th March 2013, https://royalsociety.org/blog/2013/03/women-of-the-conversazione/ (accessed 28th June 24).

46 Rob Mullender, 'Divine Agency', op. cit., 137.

47 Woo Shingkwan, 胡成筠, *The Ceremonial Music of Zhu Zaiyu*, 4–6.

48 Ibid., 5.

Chapter 4: Sheet Music Scrolled Across the Inside of My Lung

1 'Chewing Gum's Michaela Coel', the *Independent*, 9th June 2017, https://www.independent.co.uk/arts-entertainment/tv/features/chewing-gum-michaela-coel-interview-tracey-gordon-andover-estate-beyonce-a7517861.html#.

2 Kathryn King, *Tranquillity, Transcendence, and Retreat: The Transformative Practice of Listening at Evensong* (University of Oxford: unpublished DPhil thesis, 2022); Kathryn King, 'Choral Evensong: More than Just a Song at Twilight', The Association of English Cathedrals Online, 15th February 2019, https://www.englishcathedrals.co.uk/latest-news/evensong-song-twilight-audience-grows/; Madeleine Davis, 'From the choir stalls to the altar', *Church Times*, 17th November 2017.

3 Amanda Eubanks Winkler, *Music, Dance, and Drama in Early Modern English Schools* (Cambridge: Cambridge University Press, 2020); Hannibal Hamlin, *Psalm Culture and Early Modern English Literature* (Cambridge: Cambridge University Press, 2004); Christopher Marsh, *Music and Society in Early Modern England* (Cambridge: Cambridge University Press, 2010); Jonathan Willis, *Church Music and Protestantism in Post-Reformation England: Discourses, Sites and Identities* (Farnham: Ashgate, 2010).

4 *Ecclesiastical Appeals Act 1532* (passed 7th April 1533). It was incredibly influential, even at the moment of first being passed. Walter Ullman,

'This Realm of England is an Empire', in *Journal of Ecclesiastical History*, 30:2 (1979), 175–203.

5   Lewis Bayly, *The Practice of Pietie* (London: John Hodgets, 1613), 464–467.
6   Georgianna Ziegler, 'Portraits of a Lady: The Self-Presentation of Esther Inglis, Protestant Limner', in *Renaissance Quarterly*, 76 (2023), 542–588, at 542.
7   Susan Frye, *Pens and Needles: Women's Textualities in Early Modern England* (Philadelphia: University of Pennsylvania Press, 2010); 'Materialising Authorship in Esther Inglis' Books', in *Journal of Medieval and Early Modern Studies*, 32:3 (2002), 469–491.
8   Georgianna Ziegler, 'Portraits of a Lady', op. cit.
9   Jamie Reid Baxter, 'Esther Inglis: A Franco-Scottish Jacobean Writer and her *Octonaires Upon the Vanity and Inconstansie of the World*', in *Studies in Scottish Literature*, 48:2 (2022), 50–118.
10 Samantha Arten, 'The Origin of Fixed-Scale Solmization in *The Whole Booke of Psalmes*', in *Early Music*, 46:1 (February 2018), 149–165; 'Singing as English Protestants: *The Whole Booke of Psalmes*' Theology of Music', in *Yale Journal of Music and Religion*, 5:1 (2019), 1–34.
11 Lots of her textile work was in fact made by Bess herself. See Susan Frye, 'Bess of Hardwick: Materializing Autobiography', in James Fitzmaurice, Naomi Miller and Sara Jayne Steen (eds.), *Authorizing Early Modern European Women* (Amsterdam: Amsterdam University Press, 2021), 87–100.
12 The Eglantine Table is an incredibly rich object. For more detailed discussion see Katie Bank, '(Re)creating the Eglantine Table', in *Early Music*, 48:3 (2020); Eleanor Chan, 'What We Mean When We Talk About Style: The "Redolent" Eglantine Table (c. 1568)', in *Word & Image*, 36:3 (2020), 248–260; John Milsom, 'The Music in Staff Notation', in Michael Fleming and Christopher Page (eds.), *Music and Instruments of the Elizabethan Age: The Eglantine Table* (Woodbridge: Boydell & Brewer, 2021), 69–100.
13 Katie Bank, '(Re)creating the Eglantine Table', op. cit.
14 For example, subjects from this study rated performances without a visible music stand more highly than those where the music stand was present: Aaron Williamon, 'The Value of Performing from Memory', in *Psychology of Music*, 27:1 (April 1999), 84–95. Performers themselves report preferring how memorising music primes them for performance but still note the vital role that the 'visual layout of the score' played in memorising the piece. Vera Fonte, Luis Pipa, Aaron Williamon and Tania Lisboa, 'Memorising Contemporary Piano Music as Described by Professional Pianists', in *Music & Science*, 5 (2022), 1–15, at 13.
15 Noémie Ndiaye, *Scripts of Blackness: Early Modern Performance Culture and the Making of Race* (Philadelphia: University of Pennsylvania Press, 2022), 24.

Notes

16 Abu'l-Fazl ibn Mubarak, *The History of Akbar*, trans. Wheeler M. Thackston (Cambridge, MA: Harvard University Press, 2015).

17 For more information on blackletter, see Patricia Fumerton, *The Broadside Ballad in Early Modern England: Moving Media, Tactical Publics* (Philadelphia: University of Pennsylvania Press, 2020); Juliet Fleming, *Cultural Graphology: Writing After Derrida* (Chicago: University of Chicago Press, 2016); Jonathan Sawday, *Blanks, Print, Space and Void in English Literature: An Archaeology of Absence* (Oxford: Oxford University Press, 2023).

18 Tara Hamling and Catherine Richardson, *A Day at Home in Early Modern England* (London and New Haven, CT: Paul Mellon Center for Studies in British Art, 2017), 205–206.

19 Freya Gowrley, *Fragmentary Forms: A New History of Collage* (Princeton: Princeton University Press, 2024).

20 Frances Spalding, *John Piper, Myfanwy Piper: Lives in Art* (Oxford: Oxford University Press, 2009).

21 Alexandra Harris, *Romantic Moderns: English Writers, Artists and the Imagination from Virginia Woolf to John Piper* (London: Thames & Hudson, 2010).

22 Nicole Phelps, 'Valentino Spring 2014 Couture', in *Vogue*, 21st January 2014, https://www.vogue.com/fashion-shows/spring-2014-couture/valentino (accessed 14th November 2022); Josh Duboff, 'Katy Perry Wears Music Notes-Emblazoned Dress to Grammys', in *Vanity Fair*, 26th January 2014, https://www.vanityfair.com/hollywood/2014/01/katy-perry-grammys-dress-2014 (accessed 14th November 2022).

23 Lauren Smith, 'Model marries in Katy Perry's Valentino Grammys dress', in *Glamour*, 23rd June 2014, https://www.glamourmagazine.co.uk/article/katy-perry-valentino-couture-music-note-dress-at-2014-grammy-awards (accessed 14th November 2022).

24 Metropolitan Museum of Art online catalogue, Object Nos. 2009.300.1226, 2009.300.1388a, b and 2009.300.1165a, b.

25 The Office for National Statistics, Census 2021: 'Religion: England and Wales', https://www.ons.gov.uk/peoplepopulationandcommunity/culturalidentity/religion/bulletins/religionenglandandwales/census2021 (accessed 1st November 2024).

26 Lucía Martínez Valdivia, 'Audiation: Listening to Writing', in *Modern Philology*, 119:4 (May 2022), 555–579, at 557.

27 Joan Acocella, 'Louise Bourgeois and her art', in *The New Yorker*, 27th January 2002; 'Louise Bourgeois: Insomnia Drawings from the Daros Collection', exhibition at the Fondation Beyeler, Zurich, 8th June–29th September 2019, https://www.fondationbeyeler.ch/en/exhibitions/past-exhibitions/insomnia-drawings (accessed 27th February 2023); Nancy Spector, 'Sutures of Night', on Hauser & Wirth, 27th September 2021, https://www.hauserwirth.com/ursula/34936-night-sutures-nancy-spector-louise-bourgeois/.

28 Siegmar Holsten (ed.), *Moritz von Schwind: Meister der Spätromantik* (Ostfildern-Ruit: G. Hatje for Staatliche Kunsthalle Karlsruhe, 1996).
29 For more on Joachim, see Katharina Uhde, *The Music of Joseph Joachim* (Woodbridge: Boydell & Brewer, 2018), 1–14.
30 *Briefwechsel zwischen Moritz von Schwind und Eduard Mörike (Correspondence between Moritz von Schwind and Eduard Mörike)* (Leipzig: A. Seeman, 1890); letter sent from Schwind to Mörike on 19th January 1869.

Chapter 5: One Sweet Liquorice Stick

1 Nicholas J. Conrad, Maria Malina and Susanne C. Münzel, 'New flutes document the earliest musical tradition in southwestern Germany', in *Nature*, 460 (2009), 737–740; Daniel S. Adler, 'The earliest musical tradition', in *Nature*, 460 (2009), 695–696; Christine Desdemaines-Hugon, *Stepping-Stones* (New Haven, CT and London: Yale University Press, 2010), 193.
2 Jonathan De Souza, 'Voice and Instrument at the Origins of Music', in *Current Musicology*, 97 (March 2014), 21–36; Lana Neal, *The Earliest Instrument: Ritual Power and Fertility Magic of the Flute in Upper Paleolithic Culture* (Hillsdale: Pendragon Press, 2015).
3 Anne Gerritsen, *The City of Blue and White: Chinese Porcelain and the Early Modern World* (Cambridge: Cambridge University Press, 2020).
4 Catalogue entry, Asian Civilisations Museum (Singapore), Accession No. 2002-00078.
5 Catalogue entry, Metropolitan Museum of Art Online Collection, Accession No. 2008.71.
6 Tao Tao Liu, *The Chinese Myths: A Guide to the Gods and Legends* (London: Thames & Hudson, 2022).
7 Timothy Peters, 'King George III (1738–1820): Re-Evaluation of his Mental Health Issues', in *British Journal of Psychiatry*, 203:2 (August 2013), 83; Timothy Peters, 'King George III, Bipolar disorder, Porphyria and Lessons for Historians', in *Clinical Medicine*, 11:3 (June 2011), 261–264; T.J. Peters and A. Beveridge, 'The Blindness, Deafness and Madness of King George III: Psychiatric Interactions', in *The Journal of the Royal College of Physicians of Edinburgh*, 40:1 (March 2010), 81–85.
8 Metropolitan Museum of Art, Accession No. 1991.17.89.
9 Heather J. Sharkey, 'A Famous Queen Mother from Benin', in *Expedition*, 61:2 (October 2019), 82; Alexandar Ives Bortolot, 'Women Leaders in African History: Idia, First Queen Mother of Benin', in the Heilbrunn Timeline of Art History, Metropolitan Museum of Art Online Collection, October 2003.
10 Alisa LaGamma, 'The Legacy of Benin Court Art: From Tragedy to Resilience', Metropolitan Museum of Art Perspectives, 4th March 2021, https://www.metmuseum.org/perspectives/benin-court-art-legacy.
11 Kathryn Wysocki Gunsch, *The Benin Plaques: A 16th Century Imperial Monument* (London and New York: Routledge, 2017).

12 Sean Kingsley, 'What Shipwrecks Reveal about the Origins of the Benin Bronzes', in *Smithsonian Magazine*, 5th April 2023; Tobias B. Skowronek et al., 'German brass for Benin Bronzes: Geochemical analysis insights into the early Atlantic trade', in *PLOS One*, 18:4 (5th April 2023).
13 Dan Hicks, *The Brutish Museums: The Benin Bronzes, Colonial Violence and Cultural Restitution* (London: Pluto Press, 2020).
14 Ibid., 5.
15 Laurence Danson, 'The Sultan's organ: presents and self-presentation in Thomas Dallam's Diary', *Renaissance Studies*, 23:4 (2009), 639–658; Jennifer Wood Linhart, 'An Organ's Metamorphosis: Thomas Dallam's Sonic Transformations in the Ottoman Empire', in the *Journal for Early Modern Cultural Studies*, 15:4 (October 2015), 81–105; Scott A. Trudell, 'An Organ for the Seraglio: Thomas Dallam's Artificial Life', in *Renaissance Studies*, 34:5 (November 2020), 766–783.
16 Jennifer Wood Linhart, 'An Organ's Metamorphosis', op. cit.
17 British Library Add MS 17480, 55v.
18 Jennifer Wood Linhart, 'An Organ's Metamorphosis', op. cit.
19 'The Delftware Collection of John F. Loudon', Aronson Delftware, https://www.aronson.com/collector-19th-century/ (accessed 10th December 2023); Henry Harvard, *Catalogue Raisonné des Objets d'Art et de Curiosité Composant La Collection de W.G.F. Van Romondt d'Utrecht* (Madrid: HardPress Publishing, 2020).
20 Caroline A. Drieënhuizen, *Koloniale Collecties, Nederlands Aanzien: De Europese Elite van Nederlands-Indië Belicht Door Haar Verzamelingen, 1811–1957* (University of Amsterdam: unpublished PhD thesis, 2012).
21 Rijksmuseum Collections Database, http://hdl.handle.net/10934/RM0001.COLLECT.14267.
22 'The Delftware Collection of John F. Loudon', op. cit.
23 Andrea Feeser, *Red, White and Black Make Blue: Indigo in the Fabric of Colonial South Georgia Life* (Athens, GA: University of Georgia Press, 2013); see also Blair Kling, *The Blue Mutiny: The Indigo Disturbances in Bengal, 1859–1862* (Philadelphia: University of Pennsylvania Press, 2016).
24 The bones of soldiers killed at the Battle of Waterloo were almost certainly used to create bone char to refine sugar; see Jack Blackburn, 'Bones from Battle of Waterloo used to make Sugar and Fertiliser', in *The Times*, 17th December 2023; and Sammy Gecsoyler, 'Archaeologists to dig in search of skeletons at Waterloo battlefield', in the *Guardian*, 20th August 2024.
25 See, for example, Rose Marie San Juan's exploration of the skull in still life: Rosie Marie San Juan, 'The Turn of the Skull: Andreas Vesalius and the Early Modern Memento Mori', in *Art History*, 35:5 (November 2011), 958–975; and Julie Hochstrasser Berger, 'Stil-Stende Dingen: Picturing Objects in the Dutch Golden Age', in Paula Findlen (ed.), *Early Modern Things* (New York and London: Routledge, 2021), 103–123.

26 Pieter Verstraete, 'Cathy Berberian's *Stripsody*: An Excess of Vocal Personas in Score and Performance', in Pamela Karantonis, Francesca Placanica and Pieter Verstraete (eds.), *Cathy Berberian: Pioneer of Contemporary Vocality* (New York and London: Routledge, 2014), 69–71.
27 Cathy Berberian, 'Preface' to *Stripsody* (New York: Edition Peeters, 1966).
28 Ellen Hooper, *Singers, Scores and Sounds: Making New Connections and Transforming Voices* (New York and London: Routledge, 2022), 111–147.
29 Kailan R. Rubinoff, 'The Early Music Vocality of Cathy Berberian', in Rebecca Cypess, Esteli Gomez and Rachael Lansang (eds.), *Historical Performance and New Music: Aesthetics and Practices* (New York and London: Routledge, 2024).
30 Cathy Berberian, quoted on http://cathyberberian.com.
31 Jim Malec, 'Taylor Swift: The Garden in the Machine', in *American Songwriter*, 10th May 2011.
32 Ali Shutler, 'Taylor Swift organises her lyrics into three "dorky" pen-named categories', in *NME*, 9th October 2022.
33 Nick Catucci, 'Taylor Swift Reaches for New Heights of Personal and Musical Liberation on *Lover*', in *Rolling Stone*, 23rd August 2019.

Chapter 6: Watching Paint Sing

1 Jeremy Summerly, 'The English cadence', *Leading Notes*, vi/1 (1996), 7–9, at 7.
2 If you'd like to know more about this most beloved, most peculiar, most mercurial of tropes, see my work on it: Eleanor Chan, 'The "English" Cadence: reading an Early Modern Musical Trope', in *Early Music*, 49:2 (February 2021), 17–34; Eleanor Chan, 'The Etymology of the "English" Cadence', in *Music & Letters*, 104:3 (August 2023), 347–373.
3 Catherine Padmore, 'Portrait of an Unknown Woman: Fictional Representations of Levina Teerlinc, Tudor Paintrix. Levina Teerlinc 1510/20–1576', in James Fitzmaurice, Sara Jayne Steen and Naomi Miller (eds.), *Authorizing Early Modern European Women* (Amsterdam: Amsterdam University Press, 2021), 33–48, at 35–6; Margaret Aston, *The King's Bedpost: Reformation and Iconography in a Tudor Group Portrait* (Cambridge: Cambridge University Press, 1993), 103–104.
4 Susan Frye, *Pens and Needles: Women's Textualities in Early Modern England* (Philadelphia: University of Pennsylvania Press, 2011), 75–115.
5 Polly Saltmarsh, '*Portrait of an Unknown Lady*: Technical Analysis of an Early Tudor Miniature', in *British Art Studies*, Issue 17, 3 (September 2020); Roy Strong, *Artists of the Tudor Court: The Portrait Miniature Rediscovered 1520–1620* (London: Victoria & Albert Museum, 1983), 53.
6 Caroline McManus, 'Queen Elizabeth, Dol Common, and the Performance of the Royal Maundy', in *English Literary Renaissance*, Vol. 32, Issue 2 (Spring 2002), 189–213.

Notes

7   Catherine Padmore, 'Portrait of an Unknown Woman', op. cit., 35–36.
8   Marianne Vedeler, *Silk for the Vikings* (Oxford: Oxbow Books, 2014); Mary Beth Griggs, 'The Vikings Had a Taste for Fine Persian Silk', in *Smithsonian Magazine*, 4th November 2013.
9   Lena Boëthius (translated by Alexia Grosjean), 'Anna Charlotta Sofia Casparsson', *Svenskt kvinnobiografiskt lexicon*, 8th March 2018, www.skbl.se/sv/artikel/AnnaCasparsson (accessed 1st March 2024); Fredrik von Feilitzen, 'Anna Casparsson', in *Den Otroliga Verkligheten* (Stockholm: Carlsson, 1994).
10 Letter from Ivy Priaulx Rainier to Barbara Hepworth, 26th June 1950, Tate Gallery Archive, TGA, 20132.1.164.19. Hepworth had a considerable archive of musical scores, all of which are also retained in the Tate archives. See Clare Nadal, *The Personal Library of Barbara Hepworth: A Case Study in the Interpretation and Curation of Artists' Libraries* (University of Huddersfield: unpublished PhD thesis, 2020), 105.
11 Eleanor Clayton, *Barbara Hepworth: Art & Life* (London and New York: Thames & Hudson, 2021), 24–25. See also Oliver Soden, 'Priaulx Rainier: Fearless and Pioneering Composer', on Engelsberg Ideas, 17th August 2021, https://engelsbergideas.com/portraits/priaulx-rainier-fearless-and-pioneering-composer/ (accessed 3rd June 2024).
12 Letter from Hepworth to Margaret Gardiner, 19th July 1950, Tate Gallery Archive, TGA 202016.
13 Eleanor Clayton, *Barbara Hepworth: Art & Life*, op. cit., 172–173.
14 Ibid., 173.
15 Ibid., 178. For more on *The Midsummer Marriage* see David Clarke, *The Music and Thought of Michael Tippett* (Cambridge: Cambridge University Press, 2001), 36–95.
16 Eleanor Clayton, *Barbara Hepworth: Art & Life*, op. cit., 174.
17 Letter from Hepworth to Priaulx-Rainier, 4th February 1951, Royal Academy of Music Archive, IPR 3/36/2/12.
18 Barbara Hepworth, *Carvings and Drawings: Barbara Hepworth* (London: Lund Humphries, 1952), Section 6.
19 Eleanor Clayton, *Barbara Hepworth: Art & Life*, op. cit., 197.
20 Robert M. Abramson, *Rhythm Games for Perception and Cognition* (New York: Music and Movement Press, 1973); Virginia Mead Hoge, 'More than Mere Movement: Dalcroze Eurythmics', in *Music Educators Journal*, 76:6 (1986), 42–46.
21 Barbara Hepworth, 'The Sculptor Speaks', in Sophie Bowness (ed.), *Barbara Hepworth: Writings and Conversations* (London: Tate Publishing, 2015), 161.
22 There's no record of whether the sculpture did end up in the gymnasium; it stood in the library of the school from 1961 until 13th June 2016, when the school sold it to finance bursaries for the students. See the Sotheby's Auction Catalogue, https://www.sothebys.com/en/auctions/ecatalogue/2016/modern-post-war-british-art-l16141/lot.11.html.

23. Charles Darwent, 'How Barbara Hepworth Got into a New Groove', in *Apollo*, 27th February 2023, https://www.apollo-magazine.com/barbara-hepworth-palais-de-danse-st-ives/ (accessed 30th March 2024).
24. Rasheed Araeen, 'Conversation with Aubrey Williams', in *Third Text*, 1:2 (1987), 25–52, at 25.
25. Reyahn King (ed.), *Aubrey Williams: Atlantic Fire* (Liverpool: National Museums Liverpool and October Gallery, 2010).
26. Kobena Mercer, 'Aubrey Williams: Abstraction in Diaspora', *British Art Studies*, Issue 8 (June 2018).
27. Rasheed Araeen, 'Conversation with Aubrey Williams', op. cit.
28. Wassily Kandinsky, *On the Spiritual in Art* (first published 1910, this edition New York: The Solomon Guggenheim Foundation, 1946), 39–49.
29. Rasheed Araeen, 'Conversation with Aubrey Williams', op. cit.
30. Philip Barco, 'How Toko Shinoda Made Gems of Abstract Expressionism', in *IdeelArt Magazine*, 10th March 2021, https://www.ideelart.com/magazine/toko-shinoda.
31. Iwaseki Tomoko, 'Snapshot of a Great, World-Class Female Artist Today: An Interview with Shinoda Toko', Gallery Sakuranoki website, 20th February 2012, https://www.sakuranoki.co.jp/en/interviews/toko-shinoda.
32. 'Listening to Toko Shinoda: Resonance / Toko Shinoda: Lyrical', exhibition at the Gifu Collection of Modern Arts, 4th April–23rd July 2014, https://www.gi-co-ma.or.jp/en/exhibitions/140404/.
33. Kimihiko Nakamura, 'Shinoda Tōkō: Ink, Abstraction and Radical Individualism', in *Women's Art Journal*, 43:1 (Spring/Summer 2022), 21–29.
34. Caroline Moore, 'The Artistic Evolution of Toko Shinoda', on The Koller Collection of Asian Art website (2020), https://www.asianartscollection.com/id/The-Artistic-Evolution-of-Toko-Shinoda/35.
35. Philip Barco, 'How Toko Shinoda Made Gems of Abstract Expressionism', op. cit.
36. Áine Mangaoang, '"I See Music": Beyoncé, YouTube, and the Question of Signed Songs', in Martin Iddon and Melanie Marshall (eds.), *Beyoncé: At Work, On Screen, and Online* (Bloomington, IN: Indiana University Press, 2020).
37. Nicholas R. Jones, 'Beyoncé's *Lemonade* Folklore: Feminine reverberations of *odú* and Afro-Cuban *orisha* iconography', in Kinitra D. Brooks and Kameelah L. Martin (eds.), *The Lemonade Reader* (London and New York: Routledge, 2019), 88–97. See also Helen Morales, *Antigone Rising: The Subversive Power of Ancient Myths* (London: Headline, 2020).
38. Martin A. Tsang, 'The Magnetic and Poetic Magic of Oshún as reflected in Beyoncé's *Lemonade*', in Kinitra D. Brooks and Kameelah L. Martin (eds.), *The Lemonade Reader*, op. cit., 123–132; see also Helen Morales, *Antigone Rising*, op. cit.
39. For discussion of Beyoncé's Afrofuturism, see Christin Smith and Loren Saxton Coleman, 'Ancestor is King: The Role of Afrofuturism in Beyoncé's

Black is King', in *Critical Studies in Media Communication*, 39:4 (August 2022), 247–259. For a general guide to Afrofuturism, see Eva Ulrike Pirker and Judith Rahn (eds.), *Afrofuturism's Transcultural Trajectories: Resistant Imaginaries Between Margins and Mainstreams* (London and New York: Routledge, 2023); Ytasha L. Womack, *Afrofuturism: The World of Black Sci-Fi and Fantasy Culture* (Chicago: Laurence Hill Books, 2013); Jean-Perre Bekolo, 'Afrofuturism', in *The Comparatist*, 47 (October 2023), 379–388.

Selected Bibliography

Rasheed Araeen, 'Conversation with Aubrey Williams', in *Third Text*, 1:2 (1987).

Samantha Arten, 'The Origin of Fixed-Scale Solmization in *The Whole Booke of Psalmes*', in *Early Music*, 46:1 (February 2018), 149–165.

Samantha Arten, 'Singing as English Protestants: *The Whole Booke of Psalmes*' Theology of Music', in *Yale Journal of Music and Religion*, 5:1 (2019), 1–34.

Margaret Aston, *The King's Bedpost: Reformation and Iconography in a Tudor Group Portrait* (Cambridge: Cambridge University Press, 1993), 103–104.

Katie Bank, '(Re)creating the Eglantine Table', in *Early Music*, 48:3 (2020).

Nicholas Baragwanath, *The Solfeggio Tradition: The Forgotten Art of Melody in the Long Eighteenth Century* (Oxford: Oxford University Press, 2020).

Juliet Bellow, *Modernism on Stage: The Ballets Russes and the Parisian Avant-Garde* (Farnham: Ashgate, 2013).

Juliet Bellow, 'Fashioning Cléopâtre: Sonia Delaunay's New Woman', in *Art Journal*, 68:2 (January 2009), 7–25.

Debra Benita Shaw, '*Swastika Night*: Katherine Burdekin and the Psychology of Scapegoating', in *Women, Science and Fiction: The Frankenstein Inheritance* (Basingstoke: Palgrave, 2000), 42–64.

Paul Binski, *Gothic Wonder: Art, Artifice, and the Decorated Style* (London and New Haven, CT: Yale University Press for the Paul Mellon Center for Studies in British Art, 2014).

Per-Arne Bodin and Franziska Bork Petersen, 'The Life of a Non-existent Ballet: Mjasin and Goncharova's *Liturgie*', in *Slovo: Journal of Slavic Languages, Literatures and Cultures*, 26 (2021), 8–24.

Lena Boëthius (translated by Alexia Grosjean), 'Anna Charlotta Sofia Casparsson', *Svenskt kvinnobiografiskt lexicon*, 8th March 2018, www.skbl.se/sv/artikel/AnnaCasparsson.

David Brett, 'The Aesthetical Science: George Field and the "Science of Beauty"', *Art History*, 9:3, September 1986.

Thomas Christensen, 'Music Theory and Pedagogy', in Iain Fenlon and Richard Wistreich (eds.), *The Cambridge History of Sixteenth Century Music* (Cambridge: Cambridge University Press, 2019), 414–438.

Gene Cho, *The Discovery of Musical Equal Temperament in China and Europe in the Sixteenth Century* (Lewiston, NY: Edwin Mellen Press, 2003).

Eleanor Clayton, *Barbara Hepworth: Art & Life* (London and New York: Thames & Hudson, 2021).

Daniel E. Commins, Yves Coppens and Takayuki Hidaka, 'Acoustics of the Lascaux Cave and its Facsimile Lascaux IV', in *Journal of the Acoustical Society of America*, 148 (2020), 918–924.

Nicholas J. Conrad, Maria Malina and Susanne C. Münzel, 'New flutes document the earliest musical tradition in southwestern Germany', in *Nature*, 460 (2009), 737–740.

Caroline Curwen, 'The role of synaesthesia in reading written musical key signatures', *Journal of Experimental Psychology: General*, Vol. 151, 10 (2022): 2284–2299.

Laurence Danson, 'The Sultan's organ: presents and self-presentation in Thomas Dallam's Diary', *Renaissance Studies*, 23:4 (2009), 639–658.

Charles Darwent, 'How Barbara Hepworth Got into a New Groove', in *Apollo*, 27th February 2023, https://www.apollo-magazine.com/barbara-hepworth-palais-de-danse-st-ives/.

Christine Desdemaines-Hugon, *Stepping Stones: A Journey through the Ice Age Caves of the Dordogne* (New Haven, CT and London: Yale University Press, 2010).

Kate Desforges, *Burdekin's Utopian Visions: A Study of Four Interwar Texts* (University of Hull: unpublished PhD dissertation, January 2015).

Jill DeVonyar and Richard Kendall, *Degas and the Art of Japan* (New Haven, CT: Yale University Press, 2007).

Eleanor Dobson and Nichola Tonks, *Ancient Egypt in the Modern Imagination: Art, Literature and Culture* (London: Bloomsbury, 2020).

John Levack Drever and Andrew Hugill (eds.), *Aural Diversity* (London and New York: Routledge, 2023).

Caroline A. Drieënhuizen, *Koloniale Collecties, Nederlands Aanzien: De Europese Elite van Nederlands-Indië Belicht Door Haar Verzamelingen, 1811–1957* (University of Amsterdam: unpublished PhD thesis, 2012).

Ross Duffin, *How Equal Temperament Ruined Harmony, and Why You Should Care* (New York: W.W. Norton, 2007).

Bridget Elliot, 'Art Deco Worlds in a Tomb: Reanimating Egypt in Modern(ist) Visual Culture', in *South Central Review*, 25:1 (April 2008), 114–135.

Farshid Emami, *Isfahan: Architecture and Urban Experience in Early Modern Iran* (Philadelphia: Penn State University Press, 2024).

Selected Bibliography

Bruno Fazenda et al., 'Cave acoustics in prehistory: Exploring the association of Palaeolithic visual motifs and acoustic response', *Journal of the Acoustical Society of America*, 142 (3), September 2017.

Andrea Feeser, *Red, White and Black Make Blue: Indigo in the Fabric of Colonial South Georgia Life* (Athens, GA: University of Georgia Press, 2013).

Fredrik von Feilitzen, 'Anna Casparsson', in *Den Otroliga Verkligheten* (Stockholm: Carlsson, 1994).

Seth Feman and Jonathan Frederick Waz (eds.), *Alma W. Thomas: Everything is Beautiful* (New Haven, CT and London: Yale University Press, 2021).

Emine Fetvacı, 'Paper as Artistic Medium at the Ottoman Court', in *Art History* (September 2024).

Emine Fetvacı, 'Music, Light and Flowers: The Changing Aesthetics of Ottoman Architecture', *Journal of Turkish Studies*, 32/I (Fall 2008), 221–240.

George Fields, *Chromatics, or, the analogy, harmony and philosophy of colour* (1845).

Carole Fritz et al., 'First Record of the Sound Produced by the Oldest Upper Palaeolithic Seashell Horn', in *Science Advances*, 7:7 (10th February 2021).

Carole Fritz, Mark D. Willis and Gilles Tosello, 'Reconstructing Palaeolithic Cave Art: The Example of Marsoulas Cave (France)', in *Journal of Archaeological Science*, 10 (December 2016), 910–916.

Susan Frye, *Pens and Needles: Women's Textualities in Early Modern England* (Philadelphia: University of Pennsylvania Press, 2011).

Susan Frye, 'Bess of Hardwick: Materializing Autobiography', in James Fitzmaurice, Naomi Miller and Sara Jayne Steen (eds.), *Authorizing Early Modern European Women* (Amsterdam: Amsterdam University Press, 2021), 87–100.

Anne Gerritsen, *The City of Blue and White: Chinese Porcelain and the Early Modern World* (Cambridge: Cambridge University Press, 2020).

Hélène Guyot and Rupert J.M. Medd, 'Eyewitness Accounts during the Putumayo Rubber Boom', in *Journeys*, 20:2 (2019), 58–4.

Getatchew Haile, 'Manuscript production in Ethiopia: On Ongoing Practice', in John Haines (ed.), *The Calligraphy of Medieval Music* (Turnhout: Brepols, 2007).

Alexandra Harris, *Romantic Moderns: English Writers, Artists and the Imagination from Virginia Woolf to John Piper* (London: Thames & Hudson, 2010).

Henry Harvard, *Catalogue Raisonné des Objets d'Art et de Curiosité Composant La Collection de W.G.F. Van Romondt d'Utrecht* (Madrid: HardPress Publishing, 2020).

Sophus Helle, *Enheduanna: The Complete Poems of the World's First Author* (New Haven, CT: Yale University Press, 2023).

Barbara Hepworth, 'The Sculptor Speaks', in Sophie Bowness (ed.), *Barbara Hepworth: Writings and Conversations* (London: Tate Publishing, 2015).

Dan Hicks, *The Brutish Museums: The Benin Bronzes, Colonial Violence and Cultural Restitution* (London: Pluto Press, 2020).

Sarah L. Higley, *Hildegard of Bingen's Unknown Language: An Edition, Translation and Discussion* (Basingstoke: Palgrave Macmillan, 2007).

James Hillson, 'Imagining Invention: The Character of the "Gothic Architect" and England, 1200–1400', in *British Art Studies*, Issue 6 (June 2017), https://doi.org/10.17658/issn.2058-5462/issue-06/jillson.

Howard Ho, 'How Elsa Found Herself (Musically) & Why It's Amazing', YouTube (12th October 2020).

Jessica A. Holmes, 'Expert Listening beyond the Limits of Hearing: Music and Deafness', in *Journal of the American Musicological Society*, 70:1 (2017), 171–220.

Henkan Honing, *The Origins of Musicality* (Cambridge MA: Massachusetts Institute of Technology, 2019).

Amir Hosein Pourjavady, *Music Making in Iran from the Fifteenth to the Early Twentieth Century* (Edinburgh: University of Edinburgh Press, 2023).

Stephen D. Houston, David Stuart and Karl Taube, *The Memory of Bones: Body, Being and Experience among the Classic Maya* (Austin, TX: University of Texas Press, 2006).

Amy Ione and Christopher Tyler, 'Neuroscience, history and the arts. Synesthesia: Is F-sharp colored violet?', *Journal of the History of the Neurosciences*, 13:1 (2004), 58–65.

Kimberley A. Jones, 'The Allure of the Fan', in Henri Loyrette (ed.), *Degas at the Opera* (London & New York: Thames & Hudson, 2020), 243–252.

Nicholas R. Jones, 'Beyoncé's *Lemonade* Folklore: Feminine reverberations of *odú* and Afro-Cuban *orisha* iconography', in Kinitra D. Brooks and Kameelah L. Martin (eds.), *The Lemonade Reader* (London and New York: Routledge, 2019), 88–97.

Lydia Kee, 'Medieval Methods: Guido D'Arezzo's Innovative Approaches to Music Education', in *Musical Offerings*, 13:2 (November 2022), 59–71.

Andrew Kettler, 'Making the Synthetic Epic: Septimus Piesse, the Manufacturing of Mercutio Frangipani, and Olfactory Renaissance in Victorian England', *The Senses and Society*, 10:1 (2015), 5–25.

Chae-Lin Kim, 'The Deaf Body Beyond Music: Music Notation by Christine Sun Kim', in Floris Schuiling and Emily Payne (eds.), *Material Cultures of Music Notation* (London and New York: Routledge, 2022), 67–78.

Kathryn King, *Tranquillity, Transcendence, and Retreat: The Transformative Practice of Listening at Evensong* (University of Oxford: unpublished DPhil thesis, 2022).

Reyahn King (ed.), *Aubrey Williams: Atlantic Fire* (Liverpool: National Museums Liverpool and October Gallery, 2010).

Miriam A. Kolar, 'Acoustics in Music Archaeology: Re-Sounding the Marsoulas Conch and Its Cave', in *Acoustics Today*, 18:2 (2022), 52–61.

Selected Bibliography

Ferran Lega Llados, 'Margaret Watts Hughes: The Forgotten Pioneer of Sound Art', in *Barcelona Research Art Creation*, 10:3 (October 2022), 116–136.

Andreas Maier, *The Central European Magdalenian: Regional Diversity and Internal Variability* (Dordrecht: Springer, 2015).
Áine Mangaoang, '"I See Music": Beyoncé, YouTube, and the Question of Signed Songs', in Martin Iddon and Melanie Marshall (eds.), *Beyoncé: At Work, On Screen, and Online* (Bloomington, IN: Indiana University Press, 2020).
Stefano Mengozzi, *The Renaissance Reform of Medieval Music Theory: Guido of Arezzo between Myth and History* (Cambridge: Cambridge University Press, 2010).
Kobena Mercer, 'Aubrey Williams: Abstraction in Diaspora', in *British Art Studies*, 8 (June 2018).
Abu'l-Fazl ibn Mubarak, *The History of Akbar*, trans. Wheeler M. Thackston (Cambridge, MA: Harvard University Press, 2015).
Rob Mullender, 'Divine Agency: Bringing to Light the Voice Figures of Margaret Watts-Hughes', in *Sound Effects*, 8:1 (2019), 123–139.

Clare Nadal, *The Personal Library of Barbara Hepworth: A Case Study in the Interpretation and Curation of Artists' Libraries* (University of Huddersfield: unpublished PhD thesis, 2020).
Kimihiko Nakamura, 'Shinoda Tōkō: Ink, Abstraction and Radical Individualism', in *Women's Art Journal*, 43:1 (Spring/Summer 2022), 21–29.
Noémie Ndiaye, *Scripts of Blackness: Early Modern Performance Culture and the Making of Race* (Philadelphia: University of Pennsylvania Press, 2022).
Lynda Nead, *The Female Nude: Art, Obscenity and Sexuality* (London: Routledge, 1992).
Gülru Necipoğlu, 'The Scrutinizing Gaze in the Aesthetics of Islamic Visual Cultures: Sight, Insight and Desire', in Olga Bush and Avinoam Shalem (eds.), *Gazing Otherwise: Modalities of Seeing In and Beyond the Lands of Islam (Muqarnas 32)* (Brill, 2015), 23–62.
Andy Needham, Izzy Wisher, Andrew Landley, Matthew Amy, Aimée Little, 'Art by Firelight? Using Experimental and Digital Techniques to Explore Magdalenian Engraved Plaquette Use at Montastruc', in *PloS One*, 17:4 (April 2022).

Catherine Padmore, 'Portrait of an Unknown Woman: Fictional Representations of Levina Teerlinc, Tudor Paintrix. Levina Teerlinc 1510/20–1576', in James Fitzmaurice, Sara Jayne Steen and Naomi Miller (eds.), *Authorizing Early Modern European Women* (Amsterdam: Amsterdam University Press, 2021), 33–48.
Timothy Peters, 'King George III (1738–1820): Re-Evaluation of his Mental Health Issues', in *British Journal of Psychiatry*, 203:2 (August 2013).

K. Peacock, 'Synesthetic Perception: Alexander Scriabin's Colour Hearing', in *Music Perception*, 2:4 (1985), 483–506.

Denis Peyrony, *Denis Peyrony: Journal d'un Préhistorien 1912–1948* (Les Eyzies: Musée du Préhistoire, 2017).

G.W. Septimus Piesse, *The Art of Perfumery and Method of Obtaining the Odours of Plants* (London: Longman, Brown, Green and Longmans, 1855).

Jakob Pietschnig, Martin Voracek and Anton K. Formann, 'Mozart Effect–Shmozart Effect: A Meta-Analysis', *Intelligence (Norwood)*, 38 (3) (2010), 314–323.

Susan Rankin, *Writing Sounds in Carolingian Europe: The Invention of Musical Notation* (Cambridge: Cambridge University Press, 2018).

Felicia Rappe, 'L'oeil danse: décors et costumes de Robert et Sonia Delaunay pour Cléopâtre', in Histoire de l'art, 58:1 (2006), 105–114.

Alexander Rehding, 'Fine-Tuning a Global History of Music Theory: Divergences, Zhu Zaiyu, and Music-Theoretical Instruments', *Music Theory Spectrum*, 44:2 (Fall 2022), 260–275.

Alexander Rehding, 'Music-Historical Egyptomania, 1650–1950', in *Journal of the History of Ideas*, 75:4 (2014), 545–580.

Ìegor Reznikoff, 'Prehistoric paintings, sound and rocks', in *Studien zur Musikarchäologie III. The Archaeology of Sound: Origin and Organisation*, edited by A.D. Kilmer and R. Eichmann, Papers from the 2nd Symposium of the International Study Group on Music Archaeology at Monastery Michaelstein (17th–23rd September) (Verlag Marie Leidorf GmbH, Rahden/Westf., 2002).

Alexander Wallace Rimington, *Colour-Music: The Art of Mobile Colour* (London: Hutchinson, 1912).

Benjamin Roberts, *Sex, Drugs and Rock 'n' Roll in the Dutch Golden Age* (Amsterdam: Amsterdam University Press, 2017).

Stephen Rogers, *The Songs of Fanny Hensel* (Oxford: Oxford University Press, 2021).

Robert A. Rohland, *Carpe Diem: The Politics of Presence in Greek and Latin Literature* (Cambridge: Cambridge University Press, 2022),

Kailan R. Rubinoff, 'The Early Music Vocality of Cathy Berberian', in Rebecca Cypess, Esteli Gomez and Rachael Lansang (eds.), *Historical Performance and New Music: Aesthetics and Practices* (New York and London: Routledge, 2024).

Polly Saltmarsh, '*Portrait of an Unknown Lady*: Technical Analysis of an Early Tudor Miniature', in *British Art Studies*, Issue 17, 3 (September 2020).

George Sawa, 'Al-Farabi's *polychord*: A re-exposition of Ptolemy's *kanon* as a didactic instrument for the tone system', in *Festschrift in Honour of Prof. Owen Wright* (Oxford University Press, 2015).

Sjeng Scheijen, 'The Queer World of Sergei Diaghilev', in *Experiment: Journal of Russian Culture*, 17:1 (January 2011), 65–75.

Margarita Serje, 'The Peruvian Amazon Co.: Credit and Debt in the Putumayo "Wild Rubber" Business', in *Enterprise & Society*, 22:2 (2021), 475–501.

Heather J. Sharkey, 'A Famous Queen Mother from Benin', in *Expedition*, 61:2 (October 2019).

Kay Kaufman Shelemay, Peter Jeffrey and Ingrid Monson, 'Oral and Written Transmission in Ethiopian Christian Chant', in *Early Music History*, 12 (1993), 55–117.

Larry Sherman and Dennis Plies, *Every Brain Needs Music: The Neuroscience of Making and Listening to Music* (New York: Columbia University Press, 2023).

Ali Shutler, 'Taylor Swift organises her lyrics into three "dorky" pen-named categories', in *NME*, 9th October 2022.

Natalia Sidlina and Matthew Gale (eds.), *Natalia Goncharova* (London: Tate, 2019).

Christin Smith and Loren Saxton Coleman, 'Ancestor is King: The Role of Afrofuturism in Beyoncé's Black is King', in *Critical Studies in Media Communication*, 39:4 (August 2022), 247–259.

Oliver Soden, 'Priaulx Rainier: Fearless and Pioneering Composer', on Engelsberg Ideas, 17th August 2021, https://engelsbergideas.com/portraits/priaulx-rainier-fearless-and-pioneering-composer/.

Frances Spalding, *John Piper, Myfanwy Piper: Lives in Art* (Oxford: Oxford University Press, 2009).

James Curl Stevens, *The Egyptian Revival: Ancient Egypt as the Inspiration for Design Motifs in the West* (Oxford: Routledge, 2005).

Barbara Stühlmeyer, *Die Gesänge der Hildegard von Bingen: Eine musikologische, theologische und kulturhistorische Untersuchung* (Olms: Hildesheim, 2003).

Barbara Swanson, 'Futurist Constructions of the Sacred: The Ballets Russes, *Liturgie*, and the Problem of a Musical Score', in Eftychia Papanikolaou and Markus Rathey (eds.), *Sacred and Secular Intersections in Music of the Long Nineteenth Century: Church, Stage and Concert Hall* (Lanham, MD: Rowman & Littlefield, 2022).

Stephanie Taralson, 'Bringing sexy Bach: How the 1781 Collective is changing the way we experience classical music', *Exberliner*, 19th September 2023.

Iwaseki Tomoko, 'Snapshot of a Great, World-Class Female Artist Today: An Interview with Shinoda Toko', Gallery Sakuranoki website, 20th February 2012, https://www.sakuranoki.co.jp/en/interviews/toko-shinoda.

Martin A. Tsang, 'The Magnetic and Poetic Magic of Oshún as reflected in Beyoncé's *Lemonade*', in Kinitra D. Brooks and Kameelah L. Martin (eds.), *The Lemonade Reader* (London and New York: Routledge, 2019), 123–132.

William Tullett, 'Smell Organ', *Encyclopedia of Smell History and Heritage*, https://encyclopedia.odeuropa.eu/items/show/18, accessed 5th August 2024.

Lucía Martínez Valdivia, 'Audiation: Listening to Writing', in *Modern Philology*, 119:4 (May 2022), 555–579.

Marianne Vedeler, *Silk for the Vikings* (Oxford: Oxbow Books, 2014).

Pieter Verstraete, 'Cathy Berberian's *Stripsody*: An Excess of Vocal Personas in Score and Performance', in Pamela Karantonis, Francesca Placanica and Pieter Verstraete (eds.), *Cathy Berberian: Pioneer of Contemporary Vocality* (New York and London: Routledge, 2014), 69–71.

William M. Voelkle, *Holy Hoaxes: A Beautiful Deception* (London: Paul Holberton Publishing, 2023), 90–95.

Megan Watts Hughes, *The Eidophone Voice Figures: Natural and Geometrical Forms Produced by Vibrations of the Human Voice* (London: Christian Herald Company Ltd, 1904).

Aaron Williamon, 'The Value of Performing from Memory', in *Psychology of Music*, 27:1 (April 1999), 84–95.

Jennifer Wood Linhart, 'An Organ's Metamorphosis: Thomas Dallam's Sonic Transformations in the Ottoman Empire', in the *Journal for Early Modern Cultural Studies*, 15:4 (October 2015), 81–105.

F. Woodman, 'John Wastell: Architect, Genius, and All-Round Mr Fix-It', in F. Woodman, Helen Lunnon and Gabriel Byng (eds.), *Medieval Art, Architecture and Archaeology in Cambridge* (London and New York: Routledge, 2022), 188–208.

Zeyuan Wu, *Becoming Sages: Qin Song and Self-Cultivation in Late Imperial China* (Ohio State University, unpublished PhD dissertation, 2020).

Serinity Young, *Women Who Fly: Goddesses, Witches, Mystics, and other Airborne Females* (Oxford: Oxford University Press, 2017).

Muriel T. Zaatar, Kenda Alhakim, Mohammed Enayeh and Ribal Tamer, 'The Transformative Power of Music: Insights into Neuroplasticity, Health, and Disease', in *Brain, Behaviour, & Immunity – Health*, 35 (February 2024), 1–11.

Acknowledgements

Thank you.

To my agent Emma Bal, untangler of yarns.

To everyone at Duckworth, but especially my editor Clare Bullock, for shaping this story and making it sing.

To Phoebe Fawcett, Daniela Ferrante, Duncan Heath, Claire Maxwell, Ben Murphy, Katie Read and Robert Sharman, for guiding this little book into the world, and to Mark Swan, for giving it such a beautiful little 'outfit'.

To the Thame Museum, Frances Spalding, Nancy Elder, Matthew Hollow, Heather Matthew and Dr Sophie Bowness for their kind assistance with the images; this book would not have been possible without them.

To my research community, including, but not limited to, Katie Bank, Richard Wistreich, Jane Grogan, Tim Shephard, Rachel Willie, Hannah Murphy, Fabrizio Nevola, Mark Williams, Kevin Killeen and Jenny Richards, for cultivating a space in which these kinds of thoughts and ideas have value, and for so passionately believing in, and fighting for, history as an experimental discipline.

To my first readers, Jenna, Povey, Rich and Alice W., for braving the depths of my unedited brain.

To the village that raised me. There are far, *far* too many of you to name, so I'll limit myself to a much-missed trio who never met each other, and never got to see or hear any of the ideas they helped create, but who would have each loved this book in their own ways: Bar Spurr, Philip Oliver, Graham Buche.

To Rich (again); I can't quite believe what the past sixteen years has thrown at us, but there truly is no one I would rather have been through it with.

And finally, a thank you, in the form of songs, good taste and bad, to a cross-section of the people who have gone into the making of this musical life:

'I Only Want to Be With You' by Dusty Springfield and 'Everlasting Love' by Gloria Estefan, for Rabz.

'Tragedy' by Steps, for Anna.

'Five Years Time' by Noah and the Whale, for Alice, Gavin and Andy.

'Strong Enough' by Cher, 'C'est La Vie' by B*witched and 'Murder on the Dancefloor' by Sophie Ellis-Bextor, for Alice, Heather, Emily, Emma, Sarah, Charlotte.

'Sir Duke' by Stevie Wonder/covered by Oomph, 'Fairytale of New York' (Felix's version) and most of *The Rocky Horror Picture Show*, for the whole team.

'Glamorous Indie Rock and Roll' by the Killers, for Alice (with a 3 a.m. mint chocolate Magnum, wandering home with the sun slowly rising behind us).

'Baba O'Riley' by the Who, 'Don't Look Back into the Sun' by the Libertines, 'Drops of Jupiter' by Train, 'Chocolate' by Snow Patrol and everything Kate Bush, for Ellie.

'The Only Exception' by Paramore (but *our* version), for Charlotte.

'Bohemian Rhapsody' by Queen, for Prash.

'Golden Brown' by the Stranglers, 'Champagne Supernova' by Oasis, 'Come on Eileen' by Dexys Midnight Runners, 'A Boy Named Sue' by Johnny Cash, 'The JCB Song' by Nizlopi and finally 'Captain Vegetable' from Sesame Street, for Jack, Alex, Bell, Hannah, Matthew, Eve, Ben, Silas, Finn, Megan and Timmy.

'Call Me Maybe' by Carly Rae Jepsen, for Emma.

Acknowledgements

'Lola' by the Kinks and 'Forever Young' by Bob Dylan, for Alishah.

'Let it Go' from *Frozen*, for Becky – and I suppose Pete, too, although you looked less than willing after the third rendition.

'This Ain't a Love Song' by Scouting for Girls and 'Fuck You' by Cee Lo Green, accidentally four times, for Jenna, Ellen and Alice.

'A Kiss from a Rose' by Seal, for Matt and Georgia.

'Take on Me' by Aha, for Rich and Alice, with a bed for a trampoline.

'Schaffe in Mir Gott' by Johannes Brahms, for Eli.

'Defying Gravity' from *Wicked*, by Stephen Schwarz, for Mary, Marcus, Oli and Jo, the various Elphabas to my Glindas and Glindas to my Elphabas.

'TiK ToK' by Ke$ha, for Lulu.

'You Belong with Me' by Taylor Swift and 'Some Nights' by Fun., for Snorlax.

'Believe' by Cher, for Grog.

'I Still Believe' by Frank Turner, for Jack, in loving memory of your doomed political career.

'Abendlied' by Joseph Rheinburger, 'What Hurts the Most' by Cascada, 'Sea, Sex and Sun' by Serge Gainsbourg, 'Africa' by Toto, 'Stabat Mater' by John Browne, 'Greater Love Hath No Man' by John Ireland, 'Alma Redemptoris Mater' by Roxanna Panufnik, 'Strengthen Ye the Weak Hands' by William Henry Harris, 'Such Seems Your Beauty Still' and 'Be Not Afeard' by Dominic de Grande and 'Nunc Dimitis' by Gustav/Imogen Holst, for the Choir.

'I'm an Albatraoz' by AronChupa and Little Sis Nora and 'Good Time' by Carly Rae Jepsen and Owl City for Marcus, in your terrible convertible.

'With One Look', performed by Patti LuPone and by Andrew Lloyd Webber, for my grandad. I suspect I'll never get to the bottom of what you told me about *Sunset Boulevard* or whether you were actually in the 1950s film version, but this song will always remind me of you.

'Dancing in the Dark' by Bruce Springsteen, for all inhabitants of Catz Bar 2009–11.

'Angels' by Robbie Williams, 'Don't Stop Believin'' by Journey, 'We Are Young' by F.U.N., and 'Here Comes the Hotstepper' by Ini Kamoze, for the Class of 2009.

'Complete History of the Soviet Union, to the Melody of Tetris' by Pig With the Face of a Boy, for Catz Englings, Easter Term 2011. Even now it still haunts me.

'Every Breath You Take' by Sting and the Police, played about 4,583,761 times, for my parents.

'Do, Re, Mi' by Rodgers and Hammerstein, for my granny and the minibus driver in Beijing.

'California Love', 'Changes' and 'Ghetto Gospel' by 2Pac, for all of my cousins, but especially for Hanni, Henrik, William, Melody and Diana, and especially especially for Xander.

'A Little Respect' by Erasure, for Topher.

'Three Lions '98' by Baddiel and Skinner and the Lightning Seeds, with improved lyrics, for Julia.

'Nobody to Love' by Sigma, for Dr Sir Uncle Gandalf-Magneto.

'Singet den Herrn' by Bach, for Marie-Louise Coleiro Preca, sometime President of Malta.

'Shut Up and Dance' by Walk the Moon, for Dave, sometime 'The Fellow' Waddilove.

'The Water' by Johnny Flynn and Laura Marling, for Ben and Alice.

'Barbra Streisand' by Duck Sauce, 'Crocodile Rock' by Elton John and 'These Boots Were Made for Walking' by Nancy Sinatra, for Nico.

'Ave Maria' by Robert Parsons and 'Surrexit Pastor Bonus' by Jean l'Héritier for Katie.

'Jumpin' Jumpin'' by Destiny's Child, for Christine.

Acknowledgements

'Teenage Dirtbag' by Wheatus, for Rich, Jack, Caleb and Joey, as you drunkenly cradle each other in the disco light.

'Out There' from *The Hunchback of Notre Dame*, for myself as I sobbed over my PhD in August 2016, with the PhD in the role of Judge Frollo and me in the role of Quasimodo.

The entire opening and closing scene of Kenneth Branagh's *Much Ado About Nothing* (1993), for Emma.

'When the Earth Stands Still' by Don Macdonald and performed by Lyyra, for Clare (just because it's beautiful).

'Little Lies' by Fleetwood Mac, 'Dreamer' by Supertramp, 'Head over Heels' by Tears for Fears, 'Bad Guy' by Billie Eilish, 'Juno' by Sabrina Carpenter and the entirety of Taylor Swift's *Folklore* and *Evermore* albums, for Ivy and Juno.

'Money for Nothing' by Dire Straits (remixed with our own spoken word Christmas Dinner 2024 edition), 'Overture' to 'The Wasps' by Ralph Vaughan Williams, 'Protocoligorically Correct' from *The Slipper and the Rose* and the *Ski Sunday* theme tune, for my siblings.

Also, 'Far Longer than Forever' from *The Swan Princess*, 'Queen of Hollywood' by the Corrs, 'Heaven' by DJ Sammy and 'Solo' by Clean Bandit, complete with seagull noises, for Mini.

'Closing Time' by Semisonic and 'A Spaceman Came Travelling' by Chris de Burgh, for Sarah.

'My Evaline' (your own, cursed version), for Wob, Dougie and Cherub (ad infinitum, performed at unsuspecting tourists in Venice).

'Oops I Did it Again' by Britney Spears, for Emma and Elly (you can both be Britney this time).

'That Don't Impress Me Much' by Shania Twain, 'Angelica' by Wet Leg, 'Get Shaky' by the Ian Carey Project, 'Disco 2000' by Pulp, 'Duel of the Fates' from *Star Wars* and the entire *Black Parade* album by My Chemical Romance, for Rich.

'I Was Glad' by Charles Hubert Hastings Parry and/or 'Wonderwall' by Oasis, for everyone I have ever sung with. Maybe even both at the same time. Let's give it a try.

Index

Page references in *italics* indicate images.

Abri de la Madeleine, France 3
abstract art 48, 209–50
   abstract expressionism 221, 233, 240
   Beyoncé and 243–50
   Casparsson and 217–21, *218*, *219*, 229, 248, 249
   Hepworth and 223–9, *226*, *228*, *230*
   Howells and 209–11
   Rainier and 223–5, 237
   Shinoda and 236–42, *238*, *240*, 248–9
   Sobel and 221–2, 229
   Teerlinc and 212–17, *213*, 222, 249
   Thomas and 221–2
   Williams and 229–35
Abu'l-Fazl: *A'in-I Akbari* 153
agbadza (form of dance) 98
ahianmwen-oro (bird of prophecy) 185–6, *187*, 188
Ahmed I, Sultan of the Ottoman empire 192
Akbar, Mughal Emperor 10–11, 153–4
Alexander the Great 12–13
Amaral, Crispim do 27
Amazon rainforest 25, 26, 43
American Music Awards (AMAs) (2019) 207–8
American Sign Language (ASL) 82–3

Amhara, Ethiopia, illuminated gospels from 70, *70*, 71, *71*
Anaphorae (Eucharistic Prayers) 69
Andrade, Simão de 102
Anglicanism 162
Angove, Charles 39, 40
Anonymous Bellermanni (musical manuscript) 56
Aphex Twin 124
Arezzo, Italy 89
Aristotle 114
Armenia 76–9, *80*, 200–201
   Armenian Apostolic Church 79
   Armenian genocide (1915–17) 79
arsis 56–7, 58
art for art's sake 85, 196
Art Nouveau 112
Arts and Crafts movement 112
Arundel Cathedral xxxi
audiation 165
AURORA 49
Australian Aborigines 6
Australian Ballet 34

Batavia 104
Behzād, Kamāl ud-Dīn 10
Benin-Igala or Idah War (1515–16) 187, 188
Bakst, Léon 32, 33
ballet xxv–xxvi, 22–4, 31, *32*, 33–7, *35*, 41, 42, 98, 117, 158

Ballets Russes 29, 31, *32*, 33–7, 35, 41, 42, 117, 158
bamboo flute 180
baroque pitch 104–5
Barrington, Emilie 124
Batman (TV series) 202, 203
Bay Psalm Book 135
Bayly, Lewis: *The Practice of Pietie* 139–40
Bāyqarā, Solṭān-Hosayn 13
Beatles 203, 204
Benin, kingdom of 185–90, 241
Bening, Simon 212
Berberian, Cathy 200–206
    Beatles Arias for Special Fans 204
    Stripsody 201–6, *201*
Bess of Hardwick Hall 147–55
Big Machine Records 207–8
Bingham, Judith: 'The Spirit of Truth' xxx, xxxiv
Björk 124
blackbird clockwork organ, Dallam's 190–93, *193*, 199, 208
blackletter typeface 136
Blanke, John 144
blue seventh, contemporary jazz 210
books, music 127–72
    audiation 165
    beauty of Western classical notation 168–9
    Bourgeois' music paper works 166–8
    'Cat Symphony', von Schwind 168–70, *170*
    collage 157–60
    dress, Sheet Music Notation 161
    Eglantine Table 148–50, *148*, 163
    Hardwick Hall 147–51, *148*, 156
    hymn books *see* hymn books
    Keaton Music Typewriter 164
    marginalia 169–71
    Musique textile panel 150–51

    'Notes on Copies' X account 169–70
    online market for sheet music art/vintage sheet music 163–4
    reading music as creative act 157
    Thame, wall painting from 154–6, *154*
    visual afterlife of sheet music 160–61
Borovansky Jubilee Ballet Company 33–4
Bourgeois, Louise 166–8, 172
Braque, Georges 32, 36
Brazil 25, 27, 28, 245–6
Bresee, Becky 48
Breuil, Abbé Henri 4
British Museum 188; Prints and Drawings Room 235
Brook, Peter xviii
bullroarer whistle 6, 8
Byrd, William 139, 226–7

Cade, Katharine 40
Cade, Rowena 38, *39*, 40
Cage, John: *Aria* 201
calligraphy 12, 63, 65, 125, 133, 141, 142, 155, 236, 239, 248–9
Cambridge Central Mosque 21
Cambridge University
    Great St Mary's 15–16
    King's College Chapel 14–16, *16*, *18*, 19, *19*, 20–21, 192
    Peterhouse College 14
    Trinity College 15
Camus, Albert 232–3
canticles 59, 61, 209
Capa, Benedetta 35
Carré, John le 210
Carter, Howard 78
Casparsson, Anna 217–21, 222, 229, 248, 249; *Life Saga from Blue Fairy Tales by Laboulaye* *218*, *219*, 221

Index

Cassatt, Mary 24; *Woman in a Loge* 24
Castel, Louis Bertrand 114
Catholic Church 4, 69, 78, 103, 139
Caverns, The, Tennessee 9
caves/cave paintings xxxvi, 3–10, *6*, 13, 15–16, 20, 176–7, 250
Cecchetti, Enrico 33
Century magazine 121
ceramics 27, 52, 177–9, 183–5, *184*, 194–200, *197*, 208
Chan, Eleanor: *Fields of Gold 252*, 253–4
Chanel, Coco 31–2
chant notation, medieval 58–61, *60*
Charles II, King of England 183
Chavín de Huántar, Peru 7
Chez Kiki, Montparnasse xxi
Chichester Cathedral xxxi
Chikanobu, Yōshū: *Concert of European Music 132*, 134
China
    Cultural Revolution 248
    East Asian lacquerware and 23
    Eleanor Chan and xxxi, 86–8, 125, 248
    equal temperament/Zhu Zaiyu and 95–9, *97*, *99*, 101–104, 125–6
    flute and 177, 179–80, 183
    pentatonic scale, ancient Chinese 180
    porcelain production 177, 183
    qin notation 64–8, *66*, *67*
    writing, invention of and 52
Chiuri, Maria Grazia 160
Chladni, Ernst 124
Cho, Gene 103
choir
    competition to get into xxxi
    defined xxxii
    Gloucester Cathedral Choir 209–10

    Hildegard and 61
    King's College Chapel, Cambridge and 20–21
    St Catharine's College Chapel Choir xxx–xxxi, 253
    St John's College Chapel Choir xxx–xxxi, 21, 21*n*
choral music xxx–xxxiii, 129–30, 134, 139, 140
Christianity 16, 69, 72–3, 76, 78, 80, 156, 157, 186, 246
Christmas xxvii, xxxi, 1–3, 20, 127
chromaesthesia 113–14
Church of England 130, 137, 138, 139
circle of fifths 101, 101*n*
clappers 185–90, *187*
Clark, Kenneth xxi
Cocteau, Jean 31, 32
Coel, Michaela 130
collage 152, 157–60, 167
Colloredo, Archbishop of Salzburg, Count Hieronymus 41
colour organ 110–19
colour wheel 114
Columbus, Christopher 25, 105
Commins, Daniel E. 7
community, music and xix, xxxvi, xxxvii, 85, 134, 137, 140, 141, 151, 177, 190, 215, 249, 250
communicative power of music xxxv–xxxvi
composer, earliest surviving compositions by a named 52–4, *54*
conch shell horn 5, 6, *6*, 8
copyright and music ownership 206–8
Cranmer, Archbishop Thomas 129
Cromwell, Oliver 21
Cromwell, Thomas 134, 140
crotchet 50–51, *50*, 50*n*, 135

C6 (note) 49
Curwen, Caroline 113
cymatics 124

d'Aveiro, John Alfonso 186
D'Angour, Armand 58
Dalcroze method 225–6
Dallam, Thomas 191–3, 199, 208;
    A Brefe Relation of my Travell from the Royall Cittie of London towards The Straite of Mariemediterranum and what happened by the waye 191
Daman, William 137
dance 13
    ballet xxv–xxvi, 22–4, 29–37, *32*, *35*, 41, 42, 98, 117, 158
    Ballets Russes 29–37, *32*, *35*, 41, 42, 117, 158
    Degas and xxv–xxvi, 22–4
    dervishes and 10, 11, 181–2
    etymology xxxii
    galliard 225, 226–7
    as visualisation of music 98
Darwent, Charles 229
Das, Manohar: *The Youth of Rum is Entertained in a Garden by a Fairy and her Maidens* 11, 12, *12*
däbtära (cantor who leads the service) 69, 72
David, King 136, 138
Day, John 136
deaf and hearing-impaired xviii, 81–3, 234
Debussy, Claude 37, 117
Degas, Edgar xxv–xxvi, 21–5
    Dancers, Pink and Green xxv–xxvi, *22*
    Fan Mount image of ballet dancers from the wings 22–4
    Orchestra Musicians 22
deggua 69
Delaunay, Sonia and Robert 32
delftware ceramics 194–200, *197*

Descartes, René 103, 104
Destiny's Child: 'Survivor' 243–4, 246
Diaghilev, Serge 29–38, 42
Dihlavi, Amir Khusrau: *Khamsa* (Quintet) 10–11, *11*
dilruba (form of sitar) 11
DiSalvo, Lino 48
Divan of Hafiz *11*
Dóm Tér, Szeged, Hungary 1–2, 41
Dowlais, Wales 119–20
Du Fay, Guillaume 20
Dunstable, John 20
Dutch Golden Age xxviii, xxix, xxx

Eilish, Billie: 'Bad Guy' 37
Edward IV, King 15
Eglantine Table 148–50, *148*, 163
egogo (double bell) 186–7, *189*
Egypt 48, 52, 76–8, 79, 132
Eidophone 120–24, *122*
eikon (work of visual art) 57
Elgar, Edward 173*n*; 'Cello Concerto in E Minor' 252
Elizabeth I, Queen of England 103, 135–6, 140–42, 144, 153, 155, 190–92, 212–15, *213*
Elizabeth I dances with Leicester 144
Elizabethan Maundy 212–16, *213*
Ely, Reynold 14, 15, 16
Emperor's Old Clothes, The (Sheet Music Notation dress) 161
English cadence 210
English Civil War (1642–51) 21
English Reformation xxxii, 139
Enheduanna: 'Hymn to Inanna' 53–4
equal temperament 94–105, *97*, *99*, 125, 126
Erizku, Awol 246
Esigie, King (or Oba) 185–90

Index

Ethiopia 69, 78, 246, 256
   Amhara, illuminated gospels from 70, *70*, 71, *71*
   Catholic Church 69
   Tewahedo Church 69–71, 72, 78
Etsy 163, 165
Euterpe 56
Evans, Myfanwy 158
Evelyn, John: *Accounts of Architects and Architecture* 17–18
evensong 15, 17, 20, 130, 209

Fernandes Júnior, Antonio Jose 25
Fabriano, Gentile di: *Coronation of the Virgin 131*, 133, 165
fan vaulting 15–19, *16*, *18*, 21
fans 24
Farrant, Richard 216
Fayrfax, Robert 20
Feast Day of St James 14, 14n
Ferdowsi: *Shahnameh* or Book of Kings 12
Fields, George: *Chromatics, or, the Analogy, Harmony and Philosophy of Colour* 115
First World War (1914–18) 40, 77, 119
florichords 108
Fludd, Robert: 'temple of music' *93*, 94
flute 6, 13, 173–85, *176*, *179*, *180*, *181*, *184*, 191, 196, 198, 208
Font-de-Gaume, France 3, 5, 6, 7, 9, 11, 13, 20, 41, 43
Frangipani, Marquis de 105–106
Free Trade Hall, Manchester 116
Frozen (film) 46–9, 73
Frozen II (film) 48–9
Fuller, Thomas: *Church-history of Britain* 138, 141
Futurism 33, 34–5

Galilei, Galileo 124
galliard (dance) 225–7

Galway, James 174–5, 185
Gapon, Georgy 30
gardens 10–13, *12*, 38, 39, 41, 128, 190, *193*, 223, 224, *226*, 227
Gartside, Mary: 'An Essay on Light and Shade' 114–15
Ge'ez 69, 72
Gentleman of the Chapel Royal 139, 215–17
Gentlemen and Choristers of the Chapel Royal 214, 215
George III, King of Great Britain and Ireland 182, 184
Gerritszoon, Dirck 103
Gershwin, George: *Rhapsody in Blue* 211
Gilbert and Sullivan 116
Glass Onion (film) 178
Glitch Mob 124
Gloucester Cathedral 209
Gloucester Service, or Howells' *Gloucester* 209–11
Glyndebourne xxvii, 42
   Opera House xxiv
Goes, Hugo van der 212
Gomes, Carlos: *Il Guarany* 28
Goncharova, Natalia 32–3, *32*, 34, 35, 36
Gongche 90
Goodman, Benny 185
Goryeo dynasty 178, *179*, 185
   Goryeo celadon flute 178–9, *179*
Gothic architecture 8, 17, 20, 96
Grammy Awards
   (2015) 160
   (2017) 244
graphic scores 62–3, 200–206
Great St Mary's, Cambridge 15–16
Greek culture, ancient xxiii, 52, 56–7, 85, 94, 100, 239, 256
Grünewald, Isaac 220
Guido's hand 88–94, *88*, *91*, 96, 109, 118, 125, 126

Gulezyan, Aram 76–9
guqin, or qin 64–8, *66*, *67*, 68*n*, 90, 95, 97, 98, *99*. See also qin/qin notation

Hohle Fels Cave, Germany 176
Hall of Bulls, Lascaux 7
Hardwick Hall 147–52, *148*, 156
harmony xxxiv, 2, 20, 87, 92, 104, 109, 114–15, 117, 125, 241, 253
Harris, Alexandra 158
Helis (shaman) 3–4, 8
Henry V, King of England 14
Henry VI, King of England 14
Henry VII, King of England 15
Henry VIII, King of England xxxii, 136, 139, 140
Hensel, Wilhelm 74, 75
Hepworth, Barbara 223–30
   Apollo 224, *230*
   Contrapuntal Forms 224, *226*
   Forms in Movement (Galliard) 225, *227*, *228*
   Forms in Movement (Pavan) 225
   Memorial 227–8
   Motet 224–5
   Winged Figure 228
Herat 10, 13
Herod Agrippa I, King 14
hexachord 90, 94, 101, 104, 109
Hicks, Dan 190
Hildegard von Bingen 59–63, 68, 73, 79, 83, 84
   Dendermonde Codex 59, *60*, 61
   Scivias 61, *62*
   Symphonia Harmoniae Caelestium Revelationum 59
Hoby, Margaret 137
Hohokam pottery 182
Holst, Gustav: 'Planets Suite' 222
Hooke, Robert 124
Hopi tribe 182
Hopkins, John 136, 138–9, 153
Howells, Herbert 209–11

Hughes, Megan 'Margaret' Watts 119–25; *The Eidophone Voice Figures: Natural and Geometrical Forms Produced by Vibrations of the Human Voice* 121–2, *122*, *123*
Huguenot 142
Hungarian folk song 1–2
hymn books 127–57, 162, 169, 171–2
   New English Hymnal 129
   Whole Booke of Psalmes, Collected into English Metre see *Whole Booke of Psalmes, Collected into English Metre*

Iara, goddess 27
Idia, Queen 187–8
idiophones 185–8, *187*
Igala kingdom 185, 186, 187–8
   Benin-Igala or Idah War (1515–16) 187, 188
illuminated manuscripts 69, *70–71*, 129, 133, 156, 212–13
India 12, 63, 90, 98, 120, 130, 153, 195, 218, 241
Inglis, Esther *143*, 163; *Argumenta psalmorum David's dedicacion* 141–4, *141*
Ingres, Jean-Auguste-Dominique: *The Valpinçon Bather* xxiii
instruments 173–208
   ahianmwen-oro (bird of prophecy) 185–6, *187*, 188
   blackbird clockwork organ 190–93, *193*, 199, 208
   candyfloss grand piano and guitar, Taylor Swift 206–8
   clappers 185–90, *187*
   double bell, or egogo 186–7, *189*
   flute 173–85, *176*, *179*, *180*, *181*, *183*, *184*
   graphic scores 200–206, *201*
   idiophones 185–8, *187*
   Mellotron 203–4

Index

porcelain delftware mandolin 194–8, *197*
   as visual extensions of our musical tastes and identities 208
International Exhibition (1878) 23
'Into the Unknown' (song) 48–9
Islam 17, 181, 192, 193, 246

jade flute 178–80, *180*, 198
Jahānāra, garden of 13
Japan 23, 34, 63, 90, 133, 134, 236, 239, 241
Jaques-Dalcroze, Émile 225
Jenny, Hans 124
Jesuit missionaries 103, 153, 241
Jesus 14, 34, 139, 210
Ji Kang 65
Jingdezhen 177
Joachim, Joseph 168
Joseph of Arimathea 139
Josephson, Ernst 217, 220
Journal of the Franklin Institute 109

King's College Chapel, Cambridge 14–16, *16*, *18*, 19, *19*, 20–21, 192
Kandinsky, Wassily 114, 233–5; *Concerning the Spiritual in Art* 233–4
kanun (a kind of zither) 191
Kashmiri, Muhammad Husain: *The Youth of Rum is Entertained in a Garden by a Fairy and her Maidens* 12
kathak (dance from India) 98
Keaton Music Typewriter 164
Kells, Book of 69
keman (kind of violin) 191
khaz music notation 78–80, *80*
Kim, Christine Sun 81–4, *81*, *82*, 85
   All. Day. and All. Night 83
   Waiting in a Line at a Grocery Store 81, 82, *82*
   When My Voice Can't Shut Up 81

kinaesthesia 114
Klint, Hilma Af 220
Knight, Laura xxv, 32, 112
Knowles-Carter, Beyoncé 243–50
   Black is King 246
   Lemonade 244, 246
   'Run the World (Girls)' 246
Kokopelli (fertility deity) 182, *183*, 185
Korea 34, 63, 81, 178–9, *179*, 185, 241
koron 50
kulning vocal technique 48, 49

language
   capacity for music evolve alongside capacity for xix, xxxv
   visual xxxvii, 52, 68, 76, 82–3, 216, 232
La Liturgie (ballet) 34–6
LABYRINTH: The Cabinet of Curiosities festival 41
ladder-like scale 93–4, *93*
Lascaux caves, France 7, 8, 9, 10, 11, 20, 41
Le Chat Noir, Paris xxi
Les Combarelles cave, France 4–5
Les Eyzies cave, France 3–4, 20
'Let it Go' (song from animation *Frozen*) 46–9
Lichfield Cathedral 96
Lichtenstein, Roy 203
Liezu yu feng (qin score) 65
Lind, Jenny 120
Lindisfarne Gospels 69
Ling Lun 179–80
lingua ignota or unknown language 59–60
Lloyd, Chris 42
Longmen Caves, China 95
Lord of the Rings Suite 174
Lotharingian or Messine style of notation 63

lotus dance 98
Loudon, John F. 194, 195, 196, 199
Lubin, Wilhelm 105–6

Massine, Léonide 31
musique concrète (experimental composition style) 203
Macau, China 87, 103, 104, 126
Magdalenian culture 3–5, 9
Man Ray: *Le Violon d'Ingres* xx–xxiii, *xxii*, 204
Manhattan Opera House 36
marginalia 169–71
Marinetti, Filippo 35
Markova, Alicia 33
Marsoulas, France, cave at 5–6, 6, 8, 9, 10, 11, 13, 43
Mary I, Queen of England and Ireland 212–13, 215, 216
Master of the Countess of Warwick: *Four Children Making Music* 44–6, *45*
mathematics xxix, 94, 95, 97, 98, 99, 100, 101, 109, 114, 119, 150, 152
Matisse, Henri 32, 220
Maundy ceremony 212–17, *213*
Mehmed III, Sultan of Ottoman empire 190–92, 208
Meissen porcelain factory, Germany 183
Mēlakartā music 90
melekket signs 72–3, 79, 84
Mellotron 203–4
Mendelssohn, Fanny 73–6; *Das Jahr* 74–6
Mendelssohn, Felix 73
Mersenne, Marin 103–4
Methodism 96, 138–9
Metropolitan Museum of Art, New York 188
Mevlevi Sema ceremony 181–2
Minack Theatre, St Ives 38–41, *39*, 43

miniatures 10, 12, 13, 213–15, *213*, 249
Mir iskusstva (*Мир искусства* or World of Art) 29–30
Mitchell, David: *Cloud Atlas* 210
Miu Miu 160
Moderna Museet, Stockholm 220
Morley, Thomas: *Plaine and Easie Introduction to Practicall Musicke* 137
Mozart, Wolfgang Amadeus 41–2
Mundy, William 216
music halls xxi, 116
music of the spheres 9–10
Music Room, Brighton Pavilion xvii–xviii
music video 243–7
musica humana 10
musica mundi 10
Musique (textile panel) 150–51, 165

National Museum of American History 196
Ndiaye, Noémie 152
Nead, Lynda xxi
neumes 59, 68
neuroplasticity xxxv
New English Hymnal 129
New Model Army 21
Newton, Isaac 114
ney (Persian flute) 180–81, *181*, 191
Nicholas II, Tsar of Russia 30
nodules xxvi–xxvii, xxx, 92, 120
nostalgia xxxii, 210, 256
notation, music 44–85, 205, 224
 beauty of Western classical notation 167–9
 Christine Sun Kim and 81–3, *81*, *82*
 clothing/fashion and 160–61
 crotchet 50–51, *50*
 Das Jahr 74–6

Index

earliest surviving compositions by a named composer 52–7, *54*, *55*
Egypt, ancient and 76–8
Ge'ez language and 69, 72
Greek culture, ancient and 56–7
khaz and 78–80, *80*
koron 50
'Let it Go' (song from animation *Frozen*) and 48–9
Lotharingian or Messine style of notation 63
Master of the Countess of Warwick: *Four Children Making Music* 44–6, *45*
medieval chant notation/Hildegard 58–63, *59*, *61*
melekket 72–3, 79, 84
neumes 59, 68
note as a visual object 49–50
oldest complete song in the world 55–8, *54*, *55*
origins xxxvi, 46–7, 51–7, *50*, *54*, *55*
political/communal nature of music and 85
qin notation 64–8, *66*, *67*
sheet music/music books and 127–8, 129, 133, 137, 142, 143–7, 149–50, 151–2, 157, 160–62, *161*, 165, 166–70, 172
writing, invention of and 52
Yared, St and 69–71
'Now You See Us' exhibition, Tate Britain (2024) 163

Ochún *245*, 246
ocular harpsichord 114
odophone 106–7, *106*, *107*
ōllamaliztli 25
Olmec people 25
organ, Dallam's blackbird clockwork 190–93, *193*, 199, 208
orientalism xxxvii, 23–4, 34, 78
Oshún 244–9, *245*, *247*
Ottoman empire 77, 79, 190, 191, 192, 193
Ozolua, Oba 186
Oxum 245, *245*

Paris Opéra, France 21–2
pavan 225
Périgord, France 3–4
Palais Garnier, France 22
Parade (ballet) 31
Parsons, Robert 139, 216
Pellegrinelli, Marcia 160
Perry, Katy 160
Persepolis 12
Persia 10, 12, 13, 34, 50, 76, 111, 177, 180–82, *181*, 218
perspective, visual 10, 23, 24, 33, 152, 198, 214, 242
Peruvian Amazon Company 26
Peterhouse College, Cambridge 14
petroglyphic art 182, *183*
Peyrony, Denis 4–5
Philip II, Holy Roman Emperor 103
Phillips, John 138, 141
piano 46, 74, 75, 110, 166, 170, 175, 182, 217, 221, 233
  Taylor Swift's sugar-frosted candyfloss 206–8
Picasso, Pablo 31, 32, 220, 233
Piccioli, Pierpaolo 160
Piesse & Lubin 105
Piesse, Charles 107
Piesse, Dr George William Septimus: *The Art of Perfumery* 105–10, *106*, *108*
Piper, John 157–9, 165
  Dungeness 158, *159*
  Harbour Scene at Newhaven 158, *159*
Pires, Tomé 102
pitch, mapping musical 86–126
  'baroque' pitch 104–5
  circle of fifths 101, 101*n*

colour organ 110–19
cymatics 124
Eidophone 120–24, *122*
equal temperament/Zhu Zaiyu 94–105, *97*, *99*, 125, 126
Fludd's 'temple of music' 93, 94
Guido's hand 88–94, *88*, *91*, 96, 109, 118, 125, 126
ladder-like scale 93–4, *93*
musical scales inspire innovation 110
odophone 106–7, *106*, *107*
scale, origins of modern 64, 88–94
scale term 93–4
Septimus Piesse's perfume scale 105–10, *106*
Stevin 99–104, 125
synaesthesia 113–14
twelve-tone equal temperament or '12tet' 99–100
voice flower 119–25, *122*, *123*
pitz 25
plurality of music 85
political, music as 85
Pollock, Jackson 233, 241
polyphonic music, European 101
polyrhythms 226
porcelain xxix, 103
　delftware mandolin 194–7
　delftware violin 197–200, *197*
　flutes 177, 178, 183–5, *184*
Portugal/Portuguese empire 27, 102–103, 104, 186, 188, 195, 256
Poulenc, Francis 34, 37, 238
Prez, Josquin des 20
primitivism 234
Prin, Alice Ernestine (alias Kiki de Montparnasse) xxi–xxiii, *xxii*, 204
printing, music and 131–2, 136–7, 150–53, 156, 157, 164, 166, 168, 202

Prokofiev, Sergei 34, 37
Protestantism 137, 139–40, 142, 156
psalms 59, 61, 130, 132, 135–42, *141*, 145–9, *144*, *145*, *146*, 152–3, 155
Puccini, Giacomo: *La bohème* xxiv, xxvii
Purser, Edward 55–6, 55n
Putumayo genocide (1879–1930) 26

Qasr-e Tarabafza 13
qin/qin notation 64–8, *66*, *67*, 68n, 90, 95, 97, 98, *99*
Qiu Ming: 'Solitary Orchid in Jieshi (or Stone Tablet) Mode' 68

rosemåling (form of decorative painting) 48–9, 73
Rūmī, Jalāl Aaad-Dīn Muhammad 181–2
Rainier, Ivy Priaulx 223–5, 237
Rambert, Marie 33
Ramozzoti, Eros 160
Rankin, Susan 68
Rawlings, Billy 39–40
reading music. *See* books, music
Rehding, Alexander 101
Reznikoff, Ìegor 8
Rhine, River 58–9
Rhodes, Henry 191
Rimington, Alexander Wallace 111–19; *Colour–Music: The Art of Mobile Colour* 111–13, 114
Rimsky-Korsakov, Nikolai 29, 114, 119; *Le Coq D'Or* 32
Rohland, Robert 57–8
Romanov dynasty 30
romantic modernism 158
Romondt, W.G.F. van 194
Rou Cao 64
Royal Academic College for Musical Performance, Berlin 168

Index

Royal Academy of Music, London 120
Royal Albert Hall, London 28–9, 119n
Royal Collection 183
Royal Opera House, London 224
Royal Privy Garden, Topkapı Palace, Constantinople 190, 193, *193*
Royal Society, London 124
rubber production 25–6, 28, 120, 228
Rum 10–11, *12*
Russia 29, 30–31, 33, 34, 35, 114, 231
    Orthodox church 35
    Revolution (1917) 30–31
Rutman, Robert 196

Salon d'Automne exhibition, Paris 30
Sacardim, Celestial 26–7
Sadko (ballet) 34–6, *34*, *35*
Safavid Persia 10, 13, 133
Salle Le Peletier, France 21–2
Saltsjöbaden 217
sama ritual ceremony 10–11, *11*
Satie, Erik 31, 37
scale xix, xxxvi
    'baroque' pitch 104–5
    Chinese pentatonic, ancient 180
    circle of fifths 101, 101n
    colour organ 110–19
    cymatics 124
    Eidophone 120–24, *122*
    equal temperament/Zhu Zaiyu 94–105, *97*, *99*, 125, 126
    Fludd's 'temple of music' 93, 94
    Guido's hand 88–94, *88*, *91*, *96*, 109, 118, 125, 126
    innovation and 110
    ladder-like scale 93–4, *93*
    odophone 106–7, *106*, *107*
    origins of modern 63–4, 88–94
    term 93–4
    Septimus Piesse's perfume scale 105–10, *106*
    synaesthesia 113–14
    twelve-tone equal temperament or '12tet'/Stevin 99–104, 125
    voice flower 119–25, *122*, *123*
Schiaparelli, Elsa 161–2, 166
Schubert, Franz 168, 169
Schumann, Clara 73
Schwind, Moritz von 168–70, *170*, 172
Scriabin, Alexander 114; 'Prometheus: A Poem of Fire' 119
Seikilos epitaph 55–8, *55*, 83, 84
Sert, Misia 31
1781 Collective 40, 41, 42
Shakespeare, William
    The Merchant of Venice 9–10
    The Tempest 38–40
Shaolin monastery, Dengfeng 95, 125
sheet music 127–72
    audiation 165
    beauty of Western classical notation 168–9
    Bourgeois' music paper works 166–8
    'Cat Symphony', von Schwind 168–70, *170*
    collage 157–60
    dress, Sheet Music Notation 161
    Eglantine Table 148–50, *148*, 163
    Hardwick Hall 147–51, *148*, 156
    hymn books *see* hymn books
    Keaton Music Typewriter 164
    marginalia 169–71
    Musique textile panel 150–51
    'Notes on Copies' X account 169–70

online market for sheet music art/vintage sheet music 163–4
reading music as creative act 157
Thame, wall painting from 154–6, *154*
visual afterlife of sheet music 160–61
Sheppard, John 139; *Deus Misereatur Nostri* 216
Shinegobu, Katagawa: *Flower Matching Contest No. 4 133*, 134
Shinoda, Tōkō 236–42, 248–9
  Cadenza 237, 239, *240*
  Interval 237, *238*
  Legato 237, 239
  Nocturne 237–8
  Symphony 236, 237
Shiraz, Iran 12
'Shire' theme tune, *Lord of the Rings* films 174–5
Shire, Warsan 244
Shostakovich, Dmitri 37, 231–2, 234, 235
Shōtei, Watanabe 23
Shrewsbury, George Talbot, Earl of 149, 152
shuhari, process of 236
Simeon, Biblical story of 210
Smeed, Tony 48
Sobel, Janet 221–2, 229
song
  oldest complete 55–8, *55*
  power of 46–9
Sophocles: *Electra* 224
Sound of Music, The 48, 87–8, 90
St Ives, Cornwall 223, 227
  Palais de Danse 227–8
  St Ives Festival 227
St James's Hall, Piccadilly 116
St John's College Chapel Choir xxx–xxxi, 21, 21n
St Petersburg Imperial University 29

Staples Center, Los Angeles 244
Sternhold, Thomas 136, 138, 153
Stevin, Simon 99–104, 125
  De Havenvinding 104
  On the Theory of the Art of Singing 100–101
stilettos and slingbacks, Miu Miu music notation 160–61
Stillingfleet, Benjamin: *Principles and Powers of Harmony* 114
Sting: 'Fields of Gold' 254
strapwork 193, 195, 198, 207
Stratford, Elizabeth xxxi
Stravinsky, Igor 34, 37, 117
Stühlmeyer, Barbara 59
Sufi Islam 10, *11*, 181–2
Sumeria, Mesopotamia 52–4, 57, 63, 132
Swedish modernism 220
Swift, Taylor 206–8
Sydney Opera House 29
synaesthesia 113–14

Théâtre de Châtelet, Paris 31
Trompe l'oeil 198
Tablet with Temple Hymn in cuneiform (1800–1600 BCE) 54, *54*
Taiyu Yiyin 65
Tallis, Thomas xxiv, 139, 215–16, 226
  'If Ye Love Me' xxx
  Lamentations of Jeremiah I and II 216
  'O Lord in Thee is all my Trust' 148, 149
  Spem in Alium 224–5, 227
tanbur (a kind of lute) 191
Tate Gallery 233
Teatro Amazonas 25–9, *26*, *27*, 42–3
Tedald, Bishop of Arezzo 89, *91*
Teerlinc, Levina 212–17, 222, 249
  An Elizabethan Maundy 212–17, *213*

The Manual of Blessing of Cramp Rings and Touching for Evil 212–13
Thame, Oxfordshire, wall painting from 154–7, *154*, 165
Thomas, Alma 221–2
Timurid, gardens of 10, 13
Tippett, Michael: *The Midsummer Marriage* 224, 227
Tralles 55
Trinity College, Cambridge 15
Tudor dynasty 15, 134, 140, 154, 210, 212, 224, 227
Tutankhamun 78
twelve-tone equal temperament or '12tet' 94, 99–100

United Nations, New York 228
United Provinces of the Netherlands 102–4, 142
Ur, ziggurat in 53

Valdivia, Lucía Martínez 165
Valentino Spring/Summer fashion show, Paris (2014) 160
Valois, Ninette de 33
venues
    architectural failures 28–9
    caves as 8–10, 13–14, 20
    empty and unused 29
    ephemeral, planned to be 38
    equal temperament and 95–6
    escapism and 42–3
    King's College Chapel, Cambridge 13–21, *16, 18, 19*
    as living artworks 34
    '£30 under 30 scheme' 42
    violence part of creation 29
Vereenigde Oost-Indische Compagnie (Dutch East India Company) 104
Vermeer, Jan 242; *Girl Interrupted at her Music* xxix
Victoria & Albert Museum, London 192

Vienna State Opera 168
violin *xxi*, xxiii, 112, 162, 168, 174*n*, 191, 194–9, *197*, 200
voice/vocal technique
    development of xxxii–xxxiii
    loss of xxvi–xxvii, xxviii, xxx, 92, 120
    techniques *see individual technique name*
    visualising things that can be done with 200–206
voice flower 119–25, *122, 123*

Who, The: 'Baba O'Riley' 37
Wagner, Richard 36, 37, 112, 116, 117, 168, 169
Wakefield Girls' High School 227
Wanli emperor 103
Warrau Amerindians 230
Wastell, John 15–16, *16*, 21
water, music and 12–13
Wesley, John 138–9, 141
Wesley, Samuel Sebastian 96
Westminster Tournament Roll (1511) 144
Wet Leg 246–7
White, T.H.: *The Once and Future King* 210
Whole Booke of Psalmes, Collected into English Metre 130–32, 136–57
    Eglantine Table and 148–50, *148*, 163
    'To The Reader' *144, 145, 146*
    typeface 155
Williams, Aubrey 229–35; *Shostakovich Symphony No. 6* 234
Williams, Pharrell 113
Wilmot, Earl of Rochester, John 138
Wood, Henry 119
writing, invention of 51–3

Wylkynson, Robert 20

Yared, St 69–72, 83–4, 85
Yorùbá religion 244–5

Zamarin, Roberto 201, 203
Zelter, Carl Friedrich 73
Zeng of Suizhou, Marquis 67–8

Zhengde emperor 102
Zhong, Madame: *Sizhaitang Qinpu* 66–8, 67
Zhu Zaiyu 95–100, 125; *Comprehensive Treatise on Music and Music Theory* 96–100, 97, 99
Zuni tribe 182